THE STATE OF THE WORLD'S CHILDREN 2006

ISBN-13: 978-92-806-3916-2
ISBN-10: 92-806-3916-1

The Library of Congress has catalogued
this serial publication as follows:
The State of the World's Children 2006

UNICEF, UNICEF House, 3 UN Plaza,
New York, NY 10017, USA

E-mail: pubdoc@unicef.org
Website: www.unicef.org

Cover photo: © UNICEF/HQ94-1393/Shehzad Noorani

Acknowledgements

This report would not have been possible without the advice and contributions of many inside and outside of UNICEF who provided helpful comments and made other contributions. Significant contributions were received from the following UNICEF field offices: Albania, Armenia, Bolivia, Botswana, Brazil, Burkina Faso, Cambodia, Cameroon, China, Colombia, Dominican Republic, Ecuador, Egypt, Guinea-Bissau, Jordan, Kenya, Kyrgyzstan, Madagascar, Malaysia, Mexico, Myanmar, Nepal, Nigeria, Occupied Palestinian Territory, Pakistan, Papua New Guinea, Peru, Republic of Moldova, Serbia and Montenegro, Sierra Leone, Somalia, Sudan, The former Yugoslav Republic of Macedonia, Uganda, Ukraine, Uzbekistan, Venezuela and Viet Nam. Input was also received from Programme Division, Division of Policy and Planning and Division of Communication at Headquarters, UNICEF regional offices, the Innocenti Research Centre, the UK National Committee and the US Fund for UNICEF.

Sincere thanks to Hanna Polak, Elena Poniatowska and Bethany Stevens for their special contributions.

EDITORIAL
Patricia Moccia, *Editor-in-Chief*; David Anthony, *Editor*; Chris Brazier, *Principal Writer*; Hirut Gebre-Egziabher; Paulina Gruszczynski; Tamar Hahn; Annalisa Orlandi; Meredith Slopen.

POLICY GUIDANCE
Elizabeth Gibbons, *Chief,* Global Policy Section, Division of Policy and Planning; David Stewart, *Senior Policy Advisor*, Global Policy Section.

STATISTICAL TABLES
Trevor Croft, *Chief,* Statistical Information Section, Division of Policy and Planning; Nyein Nyein Lwin; Edilberto Loaiza; Mary Mahy; Tessa Wardlaw, Sandi Zinmaw.

PRODUCTION AND TRANSLATION
Jaclyn Tierney, *Production Editor*; Allyson Alert; Marc Chalamet; Emily Goodman; Amy Lai; Najwa Mekki; Lisa Mullenneaux; Carlos Perellón; Catherine Rutgers; Edward Ying, Jr.

PHOTO RESEARCH
Ellen Tolmie, *Photography Editor*; Nicole Toutounji.

COVER DESIGN
Michelle Siegel, *Design Manager*; Maggie Dich.

MAPS
National Geographic Society Mapping Services; Boris De Luca.

DESIGN AND PREPRESS PRODUCTION
Prographics, Inc.

PRINTING
Brodock Press

DISTRIBUTION
Aaron Nmungwun, *Distribution Manager*; Elias Salem; Chetana Hein.

THE STATE OF THE WORLD'S CHILDREN 2006

Contents

1
Our Commitments to Children

2
The Root Causes of Exclusion

Invisible Children

Including Children

Working Together

Excluded and Invisible

Message from the Secretary-General of the United Nations

Since its inception, the United Nations has sought to build a better, safer, more peaceful world for the world's children and to press governments to uphold their responsibilities for the freedom and well-being of their young citizens.

As we mark the UN's 60th anniversary by reaffirming our commitment to the Millennium Declaration and the Millennium Development Goals, we also reaffirm the centrality of children in our efforts. It is for future generations, even more than our own, that the United Nations exists.

The publication of this year's *State of the World's Children* coincides with the beginning of UNICEF's 60th year. The report sheds light on lives in a world that is often hidden or neglected – a world of vulnerability and exclusion. And it calls on all of us to speak up for the rights of children and to act on behalf of those who need our protection.

Five years into our work on the Millennium Development Goals, we can see the many ways in which the goals are about children. If we can get it right for children – if we can deliver on our commitments and enable every child to enjoy the right to a childhood, to health, education, equality and protection – we can get it right for people of all ages. I believe we can.

Kofi A. Annan
Secretary-General of the United Nations

Foreword

In the past, UNICEF's annual *State of the World's Children* report has focused on specific issues such as HIV/AIDS, girls' education, nutrition, child labour and early childhood development. The cumulative story is one of tremendous advances for children, but there are also areas where progress is still vitally needed.

This year's report highlights the millions of children who have not been the beneficiaries of past gains, the ones who are excluded or 'invisible'. These are children without adequate access to education, to life-saving vaccines, to protection. Despite enormous efforts to reach children with needed services, millions continue to die every year.

The world has agreed upon a road map to a better future in the form of the Millennium Development Goals (MDGs), which stem from the Millennium Declaration, adopted in 2000 by 189 countries. The goals set quantitative targets to address extreme poverty and hunger, child and maternal mortality and HIV/AIDS and other diseases, while promoting universal primary education, gender equality, environmental sustainability and a global partnership for development by 2015. The MDGs serve as a framework to make the Millennium Declaration's vision of a world of peace, security, solidarity and shared responsibility a reality.

We are at a critical juncture in international efforts to achieve this vision. The stakes are high: If the MDGs are met, an estimated 500 million people will escape poverty by 2015; 250 million will be spared from hunger; and 30 million children, who would not have lived past their fifth birthday, will survive.

Each of the MDGs is connected to the well-being of children – from eradicating extreme poverty and hunger to providing clean drinking water. Failure to achieve these goals would have devastating consequences for the children of this generation and for the adults they will become if they survive their childhoods.

At current rates of progress, for example, some 8.7 million children under five will die in 2015. However, if the goal to reduce child mortality is met, an additional 3.8 million of those lives would be saved. Meeting the goals is, therefore, a matter of life or death – of progress or a step backward – for millions of children. It will also be crucial to the development of children's countries and societies.

Our focus on meeting the MDGs, however, must not overlook the millions of children who, even if the goals are met, will be left out. These are the children most in need: the poorest, the most vulnerable, the exploited and the abused.

Reaching these children – many of whom are currently beyond the reach of laws, programmes, research and budgets – is a challenge. And yet, meeting our commitments to children will be possible only if we approach the challenge head-on.

The MDGs are a catalyst for improved access to essential services, protection and participation for children, but they are not an end in themselves. Children around the globe deserve our commitment and dedication to helping provide them with a better world in which to live.

Ann M. Veneman
Executive Director
United Nations Children's Fund

Our Commitments to Children

A Millennium agenda for children

Millions of children make their way through life impoverished, abandoned, uneducated, malnourished, discriminated against, neglected and vulnerable. For them, life is a daily struggle to survive. Whether they live in urban centres or rural outposts, they risk missing out on their childhood[1] – excluded from essential services such as hospitals and schools, lacking the protection of family and community, often at risk of exploitation and abuse. For these children, childhood as a time to grow, learn, play and feel safe is, in effect, meaningless.

It is hard to avoid the conclusion that we, the adults of the world, are failing in our responsibility to ensure that every child enjoys a childhood. Since 1924, when the League of Nations adopted the Geneva Declaration of the Rights of the Child, the international community has made a series of firm commitments to children to ensure that their rights – to survival, health, education, protection and participation, among others – are met.

The most far-reaching and comprehensive of these commitments is the Convention on the Rights of the Child, adopted by the UN General Assembly in 1989 and ratified by 192 countries. As the most widely endorsed human rights treaty in history, the Convention, together with its Optional Protocols, lays out in specific terms the legal duties of governments to children. Children's survival, development and protection are now no longer matters of charitable concern but of moral and legal obligation. Governments are held to account for their care of children by an international body, the Committee on the Rights of the Child, to which they have agreed to report regularly.

In recent years, world leaders have not only reaffirmed and expanded these commitments

SUMMARY

ISSUE: Meeting the Millennium Development Goals (MDGs) and the broader aims of the Millennium Declaration would transform the lives of millions of children, who would be spared illness and premature death, escape extreme poverty and malnutrition, gain access to safe water and decent sanitation facilities and complete primary schooling. Though some regions and countries have fallen behind on the goals, they can still be met.

The Member States of the United Nations are committed to meeting the MDGs and have coalesced around a set of key initiatives to accelerate progress (*see below*). Putting these initiatives into practice will demand renewed commitment to the Millennium agenda and additional resources. It will also require a much stronger focus on reaching those children currently excluded from essential services and denied protection and participation. Unless many more of these children are reached, several of the MDGs – particularly the goal on universal primary education – will simply not be met on time or in full.

The children who are hardest to reach include those living in the poorest countries and most deprived communities within countries and those facing discrimination on the basis of gender, ethnicity, disability or belonging to an indigenous group; children caught up in armed conflict or affected by HIV/AIDS; and children who lack a formal identity, who suffer child protection abuses or who are not treated as children. These children, the factors that exclude them and make them invisible, and the actions that those responsible for their well-being must take to safeguard and include them are the focus of *The State of the World's Children 2006*.

ACTION: To meet the Millennium Development Goals for children, including the excluded and the invisible, the following is required:
- A massive push is needed to boost access to essential services for those children and their families currently missing out. This includes immediate interventions – dubbed 'quick impact initiatives' – that can provide a vital kick-start to human development and poverty reduction.
- Longer-term initiatives that are rooted in a human rights-based approach to development – many of which are already under way – must be stepped up or launched at the same time as the immediate interventions, helping to ensure that the latter are as effective as possible. Building up national capacities, through strategies led by national governments and local communities, is the best way to ensure the sustainability of these initiatives over the longer term.
- Deeper approaches must be taken that give special attention to the most vulnerable. This requires the participation of governments – through legislation, budgets, research and programmes – along with donors, international agencies, civil society and the media to reach children who are most at risk of missing out on the Millennium agenda.

but have also set specific time-bound goals as a framework for meeting them. The latest such commitments were made at the Millennium Summit in September 2000, from which the Millennium Declaration and, subsequently, the Millennium Development Goals (MDGs) emerged, and at the UN General Assembly's Special Session on Children in May 2002, which resulted in the outcome document 'A World Fit for Children'. These two compacts complement each other and, taken together, form a strategy – a Millennium agenda – for protecting childhood in the opening years of the 21st century.

This year, *The State of the World's Children* will focus on the millions of children for

The Millennium Development Goals are the central development objectives of the Millennium agenda

GOALS	TARGETS, 2015
1. **Eradicate extreme hunger and poverty**	Reduce by half the proportion of people living on less than a dollar a day
	Reduce by half the proportion of people who suffer from hunger
2. **Achieve universal primary education**	Ensure that all boys and girls complete a full course of primary schooling
3. **Promote gender equality and empower women**	Eliminate gender disparity in primary and secondary education preferably by 2005, and at all levels by 2015
4. **Reduce child mortality**	Reduce by two thirds the mortality rate among children under five
5. **Improve maternal health**	Reduce by three quarters the maternal mortality ratio
6. **Combat HIV/AIDS, malaria and other diseases**	Halt and begin to reverse the spread of HIV/AIDS. Halt and begin to reverse the incidence of malaria and other major diseases
7. **Ensure environmental stability**	Reduce by half the proportion of people without sustainable access to safe drinking water
	Achieve a significant improvement in the lives of at least 100 million slum dwellers by 2020
	Integrate the principles of sustainable development into country policies and programmes; reverse loss of environmental resources
8. **Develop a global partnership for development**	Develop further an open trading and financial system that is rule-based, predictable and non-discriminatory and that includes a commitment to good governance, development and poverty reduction – nationally and internationally
	Address the least developed countries' special needs, and the special needs of landlocked and Small Island Developing States
	Deal comprehensively with developing countries' debt problems through national and international measures to make debt sustainable in the long term
	In cooperation with the developing countries, develop decent and productive work for youth
	In cooperation with pharmaceutical companies, provide access to affordable essential drugs in developing countries
	In cooperation with the private sector, make available the benefits of new technologies – especially information and communications technologies

Sources: Adapted from United Nations, Millennium Declaration, 2000 and other UN sources.

whom these pledges of a better world remain unfulfilled. The report assesses global efforts to realize the MDGs, the central development targets of the agenda, and demonstrates the marked impact that their achievement would have on children's lives and future generations. It also explains how, with the MDGs focused on national averages, children in marginalized communities risk missing out on essential services such as health care, education and protection. It argues that children denied their right to a formal identity, suffering child protection abuses or facing early marriage, armed combat and hazardous labour are among those most at risk of exclusion from the Millennium agenda.

Reaching the MDGs should benefit not only the better off, but also those children who are most in need, whose rights are most abused and undervalued and who are currently excluded from services, marginalized and unprotected by society and the state. This is a report about those children and ways to include them in the Millennium agenda.

The Millennium agenda and children

Seeking to promote human progress through achievable goals

The Millennium Declaration is both visionary and pragmatic. Its vision is a world of peace, equity, tolerance, security, freedom, solidarity, respect for the environment and shared responsibility in which special care and attention is given to the vulnerable, especially children.[2] Its pragmatism lies in its central premise: Human development and poverty reduction are prerequisites for such a world, but progress towards them, in practical terms, is best made through specific, time-bound objectives that do not permit governments simply to pass on responsibility to future administrations and generations. Central to the agenda is a series of concrete objectives for human development, the MDGs, with a deadline of 2015 for the accomplishment of several major development concerns: child survival, poverty, hunger, education, gender equality and empowerment, maternal health, safe water,

HIV/AIDS, malaria and other major diseases, among other objectives.

Many of these goals share similar objectives to those set at the 1990 World Summit for Children, and every one of the MDGs is connected to the well-being of children – from eradicating extreme poverty and hunger to protecting the environment for future generations. Furthermore, the MDGs have unified the international community around a set of common development goals, creating a rare opportunity to improve the lives of children, who now make up more than 40 per cent of the developing world's population and half the population in the least developed countries.[3]

'A World Fit for Children' endorses all the ambitions of the Millennium Declaration and the MDGs. It enriches the Millennium agenda by emphasizing the importance of taking actions in the best interests of children to ensure that children are put first, that every child is taken care of and that no child is left out.[4] The compact is based on four main axes. The first, second and fourth seek to promote healthy lives, provide quality education and combat HIV/AIDS, respectively. In effect, they articulate subtargets and courses of action that will help achieve the MDGs for children. The third axis addresses protection for children against conflict and all forms of abuse, exploitation and violence. As this report attests, the lack of these protections not only undermines a child's well-being, but also increases the risk of exclusion from essential services.[5]

Meeting the Millennium Development Goals

Reaching the MDGs will improve the lives and prospects of millions of children

Achievement of the MDGs, though not a panacea for childhood's ills, would certainly go a long way towards making the world a better place for children. Simply put, if the goals are met over the next 10 years, millions of children will be spared illness, premature death, extreme poverty or malnutrition and will enjoy good-quality schooling, as well as access to safe water and decent sanitation facilities *(see Figure 1.1)*.

The implications for children of missing the MDGs would be grave

Missing the MDGs would have devastating implications for the children of this generation, and for the adults they will become if they survive their childhoods. At current rates of progress, for example, 8.7 million

Figure 1.1: Meeting the MDGs would transform millions of children's lives in the next 10 years

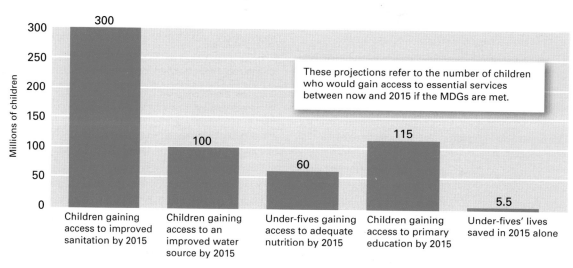

These projections refer to the number of children who would gain access to essential services between now and 2015 if the MDGs are met.

Source: UNICEF projections based on data in Statistical Tables 1-10, pp. 95-137 of this report. Notes on the methodology employed can be found in the References section, p. 89.

Figure 1.2: Global progress towards reducing under-five mortality by two thirds*

At current rates of progress the goal will be reached 30 years late

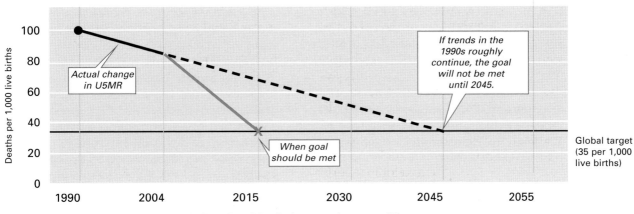

*Trends relate to developing countries only. For a list of developing countries, see p. 132.

Source: UNICEF projections based on under-five mortality data in Statistical Table 1, p. 101 of this report. Notes on methodology employed can be found in the References section, p. 89.

children under five will still die in 2015, whereas if the target were met 3.8 million of those lives would be saved in that year alone.[6] Similar calculations can be made for most of the other MDGs *(see Figure 1.3)*. Meeting the goals is, therefore, a matter of life or death, of development or regression, for millions of children. It will also be crucial to the progress of their countries and societies.

The generational implications of missing the targets would also be grave. Children in the early years are particularly vulnerable: Deprivation at this stage affects human beings throughout their whole life cycle. Those who are neglected or abused in the first years of life suffer damage from which they may never fully recover and that may prevent them from reaching their full potential as older children, adolescents and

Figure 1.3: At current rates of progress on the MDGs, millions of children who could have been reached will miss out

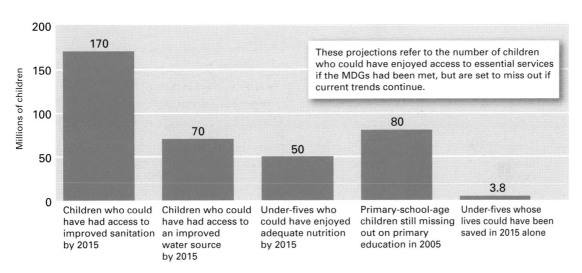

Source: UNICEF projections based on data in Statistical Tables 1-10, pp. 95-137 of this report. Notes on the methodology employed can be found in the References section, p. 89.

eventually as adults. Malnutrition not only weakens children physically, it also impairs their ability to learn. Those who do not complete primary school are less likely to have the literacy, numeracy and cognitive skills that improve their prospects of earning a decent income in adulthood. Children orphaned by HIV/AIDS are also at risk of missing out on school and the protection of a family that is an essential element of their development. Those subjected to violence, abuse or exploitation may endure psychosocial trauma that can affect them throughout their adult lives.

But it is not only these children who will suffer. Countries struggle to develop when their citizens grow up malnourished, poorly educated or ravaged by disease. These factors perpetuate poverty and low productivity and may lead to instability or even spill over into violence and armed conflict. The healthy development of children not only safeguards their own well-being, it is also the best guarantee of the future peace, prosperity and security that are central ambitions of the Millennium agenda.

The MDGs can be achieved – but urgent action is required

Though global progress towards the goals since 2000 has fallen below aspirations in some regions and countries, there is a broad consensus that they can still be achieved – in full and on time – provided that the necessary political will is demonstrated and the appropriate action taken.

Over the course of 2005, the Member States of the United Nations have coalesced around a set of key initiatives to accelerate progress towards the MDGs and to ensure that the gains made are sustainable and irreversible. These recommendations form a two-pronged strategy. First, a massive push must boost access to essential services for those children and families currently missing out. These immediate interventions – dubbed 'quick impact initiatives' – are outlined in detail in the 2005 report of the Millennium Project, recommended in the UN Secretary-General's report, and were endorsed by world leaders at the 2005 World Summit.[7] If implemented, they can

provide a vital kick-start to human development and poverty reduction.

But they are only an initial step. Longer-term initiatives that are rooted in a human rights-based approach to development, many of which are already under way, must be stepped up or launched at the same time as the immediate interventions. This will help ensure that the immediate interventions are as effective as possible. Experience has shown that top-down, supply-driven approaches to development, though often effective at increasing access to essential services and goods in the short to medium term, are not sustainable in the longer term. If national capacities are not built up and processes are not driven by national governments and local communities, even those interventions that are initially successful risk failure when international assistance diminishes or political priorities change.

The Millennium agenda: A beginning, not an end

The Millennium agenda is a key step towards meeting our commitments to children in the 21st century

Adopting the recommended immediate interventions and longer-term initiatives will increase the chances that the MDGs will be met by 2015. But in spite of the comprehensive nature of these strategies, there are millions of children who may not be reached by these initiatives alone. These are the children who are currently beyond the reach of laws, budgets, programmes, research and, often, the governments, organizations and individuals seeking to fulfil their rights. Not only do these children face exclusion from essential health-care services, education, safe drinking water and decent sanitation in the present, they are also likely to face exclusion from full participation in society as adults. Many of them suffer from protection violations that heighten the risk of their exclusion and make them, in effect, invisible. As this report will attest, only deeper approaches to child development, with special attention given to the most vulnerable children, will enable us to fulfil our commitments to children and ensure that the MDGs benefit the poorest.

The exclusion of these children, or any children, from the services, protection and opportunities that are theirs by right is unacceptable. The principles of universality and non-discrimination that underlie the Convention on the Rights of the Child, the Millennium Declaration and 'A World Fit for Children' must provide the framework for our actions concerning children and adolescents. Our commitments to children must not, under any circumstances, merely pay lip service to these principles while tacitly accepting that some children will remain hungry, in poor health and without education or protection from harm. Having ratified these binding international agreements, national governments – and the international institutions and civil society organizations that support them in their efforts – have obligations, both moral and legal, to do their utmost to ensure that no child is left out.

The Millennium agenda must, therefore, be seen as a driving force, with 2015 as a stepping stone, to providing universal access to essential services, protection and participation to children. To this end, those countries falling behind on the MDGs, the broader aims of the Millennium Declaration and the protection values championed by 'A World Fit for Children' must redouble their efforts to meet them, with ample support from donors and international agencies. Similarly, those countries deemed to be on course to meet specific goals, or the MDGs as a whole, should not rest on their laurels but strive to go beyond the headline targets of the goals to meet the challenge of eliminating disparities in children's health, education and access to essential services.

The remaining chapters of this *State of the World's Children* report will highlight the plight of the children in danger of being forgotten as the world focuses on achieving the MDGs. Ironically, these are the very children likely to be most in need of care and protection – the poorest and the most vulnerable, the exploited and the abused. As the world continues to press ahead with policies, programmes and funding to make the vision outlined in the Millennium Declaration a reality, it must not allow these children, who are excluded, marginalized and often invisible, to be forgotten.

Defining exclusion and invisibility of children

For the purposes of this report, children are considered as excluded relative to other children if they are deemed at risk of missing out on an environment that protects them from violence, abuse and exploitation, or if they are unable to access essential services and goods in a way that threatens their ability to participate fully in society in the future. Children may be excluded by their family, the community, government, civil society, the media, the private sector and other children.

The exclusion described in this report is closely related to the concept of social exclusion. Like poverty, there is no commonly agreed-upon definition of social exclusion, though it is a widely acknowledged phenomenon.[a] Governments, institutions, academics and international organizations all view exclusion differently, yielding a rich, but sometimes confusing, tapestry of perspectives. Yet amid the intellectual debates about the definition of exclusion, there is some degree of consensus about its main factors and aspects.

There is broad agreement that exclusion is multidimensional, including deprivations of economic, social, gender, cultural and political rights, making exclusion a much broader concept than material poverty. The concept of exclusion includes the reinforcing socio-political factors that are the basis of discrimination and disadvantage within society, requiring a strong focus on the processes and agents behind deprivation to guarantee inclusion and equality of opportunity.

Beyond these broad principles, there is considerably less agreement regarding the dimensions of exclusion. But there are three common elements – relativity, agency and dynamics – that are widely regarded as central:[b]

- **Relativity:** Exclusion can only be judged by comparing the circumstances of some individuals, groups and communities relative to others at a given place and time.
- **Agency:** People are excluded by the act of some agent. This focus on agency can help in the identification of the cause of exclusion and ways to remedy it.
- **Dynamics:** Exclusion may be based on bleak future prospects, not just current circumstances.

Exclusion from essential services and goods such as adequate food, health care and schooling clearly affects children's ability to participate in their communities and societies in both the present and the future. But there are also other rights violations – particularly child protection abuses and state neglect of children living outside the family environment – that restrict children's freedom and movement, limiting their representation or identification as a child who holds special rights. Like the dimensions of exclusion, these factors often overlap and intertwine, each exacerbating the next until, at the extremes, some excluded children are made invisible – denied their rights, physically unseen in their communities, unable to attend school and obscured from official view through absence from statistics, policies and programmes.

See References, page 89.

Equality in Education: The Universal Challenge

Millennium Development Goal 2, which calls for every boy and girl to complete primary schooling, is the only goal that is universal in its scope. As such, it reminds the world community of the need to focus explicitly on those children who might currently be excluded from the classroom.

Children living in the least developed countries, the poorest communities, and the most impoverished households are less likely to be enrolled in, or be able to regularly attend school, as are children in rural areas, children with disabilities and those living in areas affected by armed conflict. Children from ethnic and linguistic minorities face additional barriers as they struggle to learn the language of instruction. Getting children into school is only the beginning, however. Ensuring that they attend school regularly and complete their studies with the skills that will allow them to achieve future success are the ultimate objectives.

In many countries, girls are less likely to attend school than boys, particularly at higher levels of education. Gender parity for all levels of education, a key target of Millennium Development Goal 3, is an essential component of transforming gender relations and guaranteeing that boys and girls are provided with equal opportunities to reach their full potential. In 2005, 54 countries were found to require additional efforts to achieve this goal.[*] They must be supported to undertake the initiatives to achieve equality in education by 2015.

Ensuring that every child receives a primary education will require additional resources, but this goal cannot be seen as optional or unattainable. Putting every boy and girl in the world in a good-quality primary school would cost between $7 billion and $17 billion per year – a relatively small amount compared to other government expenditures.[**] The benefits of such an investment would be immeasurable in terms of the health, productivity and social well-being of children today and of future generations.

[*] UNICEF, *Progress For Children: A report card on gender parity and primary education (No. 2)*, UNICEF, New York, June 2005.
[**] UN Millennium Project, Task Force on Education and Gender Equality, *Toward universal primary education: investments, incentives, and institutions*, Earthscan, London, 2005, p. 9.

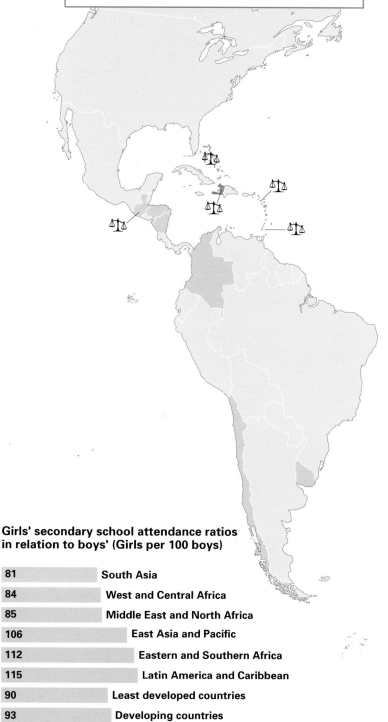

MDG 2 and MDG 3 call for governments and international donors and agencies to include all children currently excluded from education. The universal challenge of these goals embodies the spirit of the Millennium agenda, which seeks to reach out to the excluded, especially children.

Girls' secondary school attendance ratios in relation to boys' (Girls per 100 boys)

81	South Asia
84	West and Central Africa
85	Middle East and North Africa
106	East Asia and Pacific
112	Eastern and Southern Africa
115	Latin America and Caribbean
90	Least developed countries
93	Developing countries
93	World

Source: Derived from UNESCO Institute for Statistics data (1998-2002), including the Education for All 2000 Assessment, as reported in Statistical Table 5, pp. 114-117.

Education for All

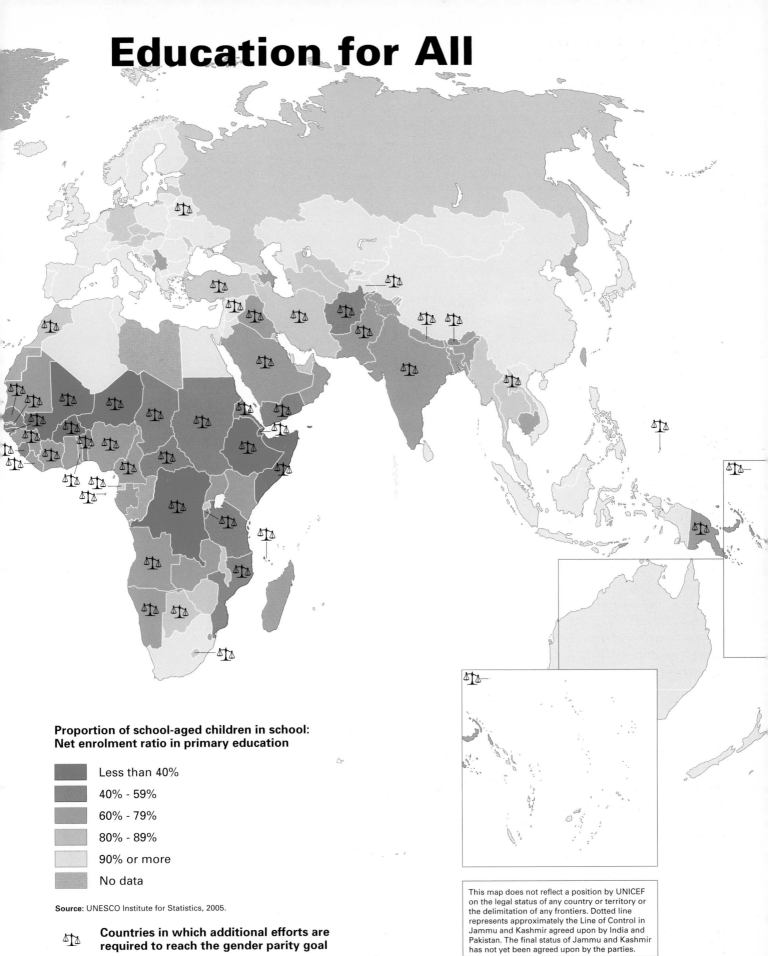

Proportion of school-aged children in school: Net enrolment ratio in primary education

- Less than 40%
- 40% - 59%
- 60% - 79%
- 80% - 89%
- 90% or more
- No data

Source: UNESCO Institute for Statistics, 2005.

Countries in which additional efforts are required to reach the gender parity goal

Source: UNICEF, *Progress for Children: A report card on gender parity and primary education (No. 2)*, UNICEF, New York, June 2005.

This map does not reflect a position by UNICEF on the legal status of any country or territory or the delimitation of any frontiers. Dotted line represents approximately the Line of Control in Jammu and Kashmir agreed upon by India and Pakistan. The final status of Jammu and Kashmir has not yet been agreed upon by the parties.

The Root Causes of Exclusion

The children most at risk of missing out on the Millennium agenda, and on their rights under the Convention on the Rights of the Child, live in all countries, societies and communities. An excluded child is one who lives in an urban slum in Venezuela and takes care of her four siblings; a Cambodian girl living alone with her brothers because her mother had to go elsewhere to find a job; a Jordanian teenager working to help his family and unable to play with his friends; an orphan in Botswana who lost his mother to AIDS; a child confined to a wheelchair and unable to attend school in Uzbekistan; or a young boy working as a domestic in Nepal.

At first glance, these children's lives may appear poles apart: Each of them faces a different set of circumstances and struggles to overcome distinct obstacles. Yet they all have something in common: They are almost certainly excluded from essential goods and services – vaccines, micronutrients, schools, health-care facilities, water and sanitation, among others – and denied the protection from exploitation, violence, abuse and neglect, and the ability to participate fully in society, which is their right.

Exclusion harms children on many levels

At the national level, the exclusion of children from their rights to essential services is often the product of macro factors, such as mass poverty, weak governance, the uncontained spread of major diseases such as HIV/AIDS, and armed conflict. At the subnational level, among vulnerable and marginalized groups, exclusion is also the result of disparities in access to services on the basis of income and geographic location, and through overt discrimination on the grounds of gender, ethnicity or disability.

Violations of protection rights – including the loss or lack of a formal identity, the

SUMMARY

ISSUE: Exclusion acts against children in all countries, societies and communities. At the national level, the root causes of exclusion are poverty, weak governance, armed conflict and HIV/AIDS. Statistical analyses of key MDG indicators related to child health and education show a widening gap between children growing up in countries with the lowest level of development, torn by strife, underserved by weak governments or ravaged by HIV/AIDS and their peers in the rest of the developing world. These factors not only jeopardize these children's chances of benefiting from the Millennium agenda, they also increase the risk that they will miss out on their childhood and face continued exclusion in adulthood.

Because the MDGs are based on national averages, inequalities among children within the same country that contribute to, and result in, their exclusion may be obscured. Disaggregated data from national statistics and household surveys indicate sharp disparities in health-care and education outcomes on the basis of household income and geographic location. Inequalities in children's health, rate of survival and school attendance and completion also fall along the lines of gender, ethnicity or disability. These inequities may occur because children and their caregivers are directly excluded from services, because they live in areas that are poorer and more poorly serviced, because of the high costs of access to essential services, or because of cultural barriers such as language, ethnic discrimination or stigmatization.

ACTION: Tackling these factors requires swift and decisive action in four key areas:

- **Poverty and inequality.** Adjusting poverty-reduction strategies and expanding budgets or reallocating resources to social investment will assist millions of children in the poorest countries and communities.
- **Armed conflict and 'fragile' States.** The international community must seek to prevent and resolve armed conflict and engage with countries with weak policy/institutional framework to protect children and women and provide essential services. Emergency responses for children caught up in conflict should include services for education, child protection and the prevention of HIV transmission.
- **HIV/AIDS and children.** Greater attention should be given to the impact of HIV/AIDS on children and adolescents and to ways of protecting them from both infection and exclusion. The Global Campaign on Children and HIV/AIDS will play a significant role in this regard.
- **Discrimination.** Governments and societies must openly confront discrimination, introduce and enforce legislation prohibiting it, and implement initiatives to address exclusion faced by women and girls, ethnic and indigenous groups and the disabled.

Figure 2.1: The least developed countries are the richest in children

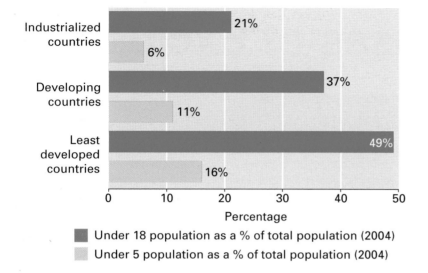

Industrialized countries — 21%, 6%
Developing countries — 37%, 11%
Least developed countries — 49%, 16%

Percentage (0 10 20 30 40 50)

■ Under 18 population as a % of total population (2004)
▨ Under 5 population as a % of total population (2004)

Source: UNICEF calculations based on data from United Nations Population Division.

absence of state protection for children deprived of family support, the exploitation of children and premature entry into adult roles – also leave individual children exposed to exclusion.

This chapter focuses on the factors that cause children to be excluded from essential services – mostly of health care and education – at the national and subnational levels. These impediments, often long-standing and deeply entrenched, are the product of economic, social, gender and cultural processes that can be addressed and must be altered. Even if they persist, our binding commitments to children compel us to take the necessary actions to mitigate their impact. (The many factors that deprive children of protection against violations of their rights at the individual level, which lessens their visibility in their societies and communities, will be examined in Chapter 3).

Macro-level causes of exclusion

Poverty, armed conflict and HIV/AIDS are among the greatest threats to childhood today.[1] They are also among the most significant obstacles to the achievement of the Millennium agenda for children at the regional and country levels. Statistical analyses of key MDG indicators related to child

health and education – under-five mortality, malnutrition, primary school enrolment, among others – show a widening gap in the health and education of children growing up in countries with the lowest level of development, torn by strife or ravaged by HIV/AIDS, compared with their peers in the rest of the world. Without a concerted effort, children in these countries will become even more excluded over the next decade.

Children in the least developed countries are most at risk of missing out

Children are disproportionately represented among the poor, since the least developed countries tend to have the youngest populations, and income-poor families tend to have more children than richer ones. Poor children are more likely to be engaged in labour, which could mean missing out on an education and, as a result, on the opportunity to generate a decent income that would allow them to escape poverty in the future.[2] Denied a decent standard of living and, often, education, information and vital life skills, they are vulnerable to abuse and exploitation.

Poverty reduction is a central objective of the Millennium agenda, targeted explicitly in two of the eight goals (MDG 1 and MDG 8), and a significant factor in the other six. In MDG 1, the primary aim is to reduce income poverty by cutting in half the proportion of people living on less than a dollar a day; in MDG 8, a key objective is to address the special needs of the least developed countries.

Raising incomes through economic growth is an essential component of poverty-reduction strategies and has been particularly successful in Asia since 1990.[3] But economic growth by itself is insufficient to address the ways in which children experience material poverty – i.e., as deprivation of essential services and goods. The extent of this deprivation is appalling: More than 1 billion children suffer from one or more extreme forms of deprivation in adequate nutrition, safe drinking water, decent sanitation facilities, health-care services, shelter, education and information.[4]

Children living in the least developed countries are the most likely to face severe

Why children in the least developed countries risk missing out

	Least developed countries	Developing countries	World
Survival			
Under-five mortality rate (per 1,000 live births, 2004)	155	87	79
Infant mortality rate (per 1,000 live births, 2004)	98	59	54
Nutrition			
Proportion of under-fives who are moderately or severely underweight (percentage, 1996-2004[a])	36	27	26
Proportion of under-fives suffering from moderate or severe stunting (percentage, 1996-2004[a])	42	31	31
Immunization			
Proportion of one-year-old children immunized against DPT3 (percentage, 2004)	75	76	78
Proportion of one-year-old children immunized against HepB3 (percentage, 2004)	28	46	49
Health care			
Proportion of under-fives with an acute respiratory infection taken to a health provider (percentage, 1998-2004[a])	38	54[b]	54[b]
Proportion of under-fives with diarrhoea receiving oral rehydration and continued feeding (1996-2004[a])	36	33[b]	33[b]
HIV/AIDS			
Adult prevalence rate (15-49 years, end-2003)	3.2	1.2	1.1
Adults and children living with HIV (0-49, thousands, 2003)	12,000	34,900	37,800
Education and gender parity			
Percentage of primary school entrants reaching grade 5 (administrative data, 2000-2004[a])	65	78	79
Net primary school attendance ratio, boys (1996-2004[a])	60	76	76
Net primary school attendance ratio, girls (1996-2004[a])	55	72	72
Net secondary school attendance ratio, boys (1996-2004[a])	21	40[b]	40[b]
Net secondary school attendance ratio, girls (1996-2004[a])	19	37[b]	37[b]
Demographics			
Life expectancy at birth (years, 2004)	52	65	67
Proportion of population urbanized (percentage, 2004)	27	43	49
Women			
Adult literacy parity rate (females as a percentage of males, 2000-2004[a])	71	84	86
Antenatal care coverage (percentage, 1996-2004[a])	59	71	71
Skilled attendant at delivery (percentage, 1996-2004[a])	35	59	63
Lifetime risk of maternal death, 2000 (1 in:)	17	61	74

[a] Data refer to the most recent year available during the period specified.
[b] Excludes China.
Sources: For a complete list of the sources used to compile this table, see Statistical Tables 1-10, pp. 95-137.

Figure 2.2: Children living in the poorest countries are most at risk of missing out on primary and secondary school

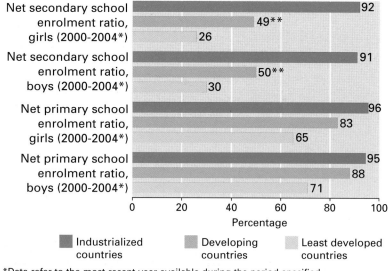

Net secondary school enrolment ratio, girls (2000-2004*)
92
49**
26

Net secondary school enrolment ratio, boys (2000-2004*)
91
50**
30

Net primary school enrolment ratio, girls (2000-2004*)
96
83
65

Net primary school enrolment ratio, boys (2000-2004*)
95
88
71

0   20   40   60   80   100
Percentage

- ■ Industrialized countries
- ■ Developing countries
- ■ Least developed countries

*Data refer to the most recent year available during the period specified.
** Excludes China.
Sources: Demographic and Health Surveys (DHS) and Multiple Indicator Cluster Surveys (MICS).

Figure 2.3: Most of the countries where 1 in 5 children die before five have experienced major armed conflict since 1999

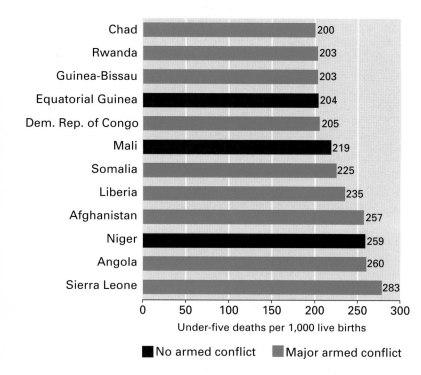

Country	Under-five deaths per 1,000 live births
Chad	200
Rwanda	203
Guinea-Bissau	203
Equatorial Guinea	204
Dem. Rep. of Congo	205
Mali	219
Somalia	225
Liberia	235
Afghanistan	257
Niger	259
Angola	260
Sierra Leone	283

0   50   100   150   200   250   300
Under-five deaths per 1,000 live births

- ■ No armed conflict
- ■ Major armed conflict

Sources: Data on child mortality: UNICEF, United Nations Population Division and United Nations Statistics Division; Data on major armed conflicts: Stockholm International Peace Research Institute, *SIPRI Yearbook 2005.*

deprivation and, consequently, are among those at greatest risk of missing out on the Millennium agenda. The statistical evidence of their impoverishment is alarming, particularly those indicators related to children and women's development and well-being *(see Panel: Why children in the least developed countries risk missing out, page 13).* In almost all cases, the least developed countries are lagging far behind the rest of the developing world.

Two MDG indicators – under-five mortality and completion of primary education – aptly illustrate the risks of exclusion faced by children living in the least developed countries. In 2004, 4.3 million children – one out of every six live births – died before the age of five in these countries alone.[5] Although under-fives in the least developed countries make up only 19 per cent of the world's under-fives, they account for over 40 per cent of all under-five deaths. Of those who live to reach primary school age, 40 per cent of boys and 45 per cent of girls will not attend school. Of those who enter primary school, over one third will not reach grade five; and around 80 per cent of all children of secondary school age will not attend secondary school.[6]

Armed conflict and poor governance escalate the risk of exclusion for children

Armed conflict causes children to miss out on their childhood in a multitude of ways. Children recruited as soldiers are denied education and protection, and are often unable to access essential health-care services. Those who are displaced, refugees or separated from their families face similar deprivations. Conflict heightens the risk of children being exposed to abuse, violence and exploitation – with sexual violence often employed as a weapon of war.[7] Even those children who are able to remain with their families, in their own homes, may face a greater risk of exclusion because of the destruction of physical infrastructure, strains on health-care and education systems, workers and supplies, and increasing personal insecurity caused by the conflict or its remnants – such as landmines and unexploded ordnance.

Firm evidence of the impact of armed conflict on children's exclusion is limited, in part because of gaps in research and data collection on the numbers of children caught up in conflict. Nevertheless, the available linkages are indicative of the extent of exclusion – and alarming. Of the 12 countries where 20 per cent or more of children die before the age of five, nine have suffered a major armed conflict in the past five years *(see Figure 2.3: Most of the countries where 1 in 5 children die before five have experienced major armed conflict since 1999, page 14)*, and 11 of the 20 countries with the most elevated rates of under-five mortality have experienced major armed conflict since 1990. Armed conflict also has devastating effects on primary school enrolment and attendance. For example, the nine conflict-affected countries where 1 in 5 children dies before the age of five have an average net primary school attendance ratio of 51 per cent for boys and 44 per cent for girls, well below the corresponding averages of 60 and 55, respectively, for the least developed countries as a whole.[8]

The breakdown in governance that often accompanies armed conflict and the destruction caused to public administration and infrastructure are key reasons for the high rates of under-five mortality and low rates of educational participation and attainment. But armed conflict is not the only form of state failure. 'Fragile' States are characterized by weak institutions with high levels of corruption, political instability and weak rule of law.[9] Such States often lack the resources to adequately support an efficient public administration.[10] As the government is often incapable of providing basic services to its citizens, the standard of living in these countries can degenerate both chronically and acutely.

Tragically, these governance failures result in children becoming more excluded from essential services. Children living in countries that are unable to implement national development strategies to meet the MDGs will be among those most at risk of missing out on whatever benefits are derived from the Millennium agenda. One such country is Haiti, already the poorest country in the Americas by most indicators and plagued by

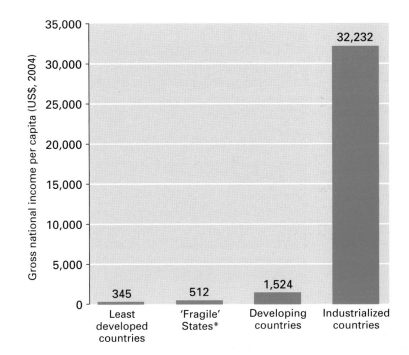

Figure 2.4: 'Fragile' States* are among the poorest

Gross national income per capita (US$, 2004)

- Least developed countries: 345
- 'Fragile' States*: 512
- Developing countries: 1,524
- Industrialized countries: 32,232

* Countries with weak policy/institutional frameworks. A list can be found in the References section, p. 91.

Sources: World Bank, *2004 Country Policy and Institutional Assessment* (CPIA), Overall Rating, Fourth and Fifth Quintiles; and *World Development Indicators 2005.*

political violence for most of its recent history. The country has seen a further deterioration in child well-being amid the political turmoil of the last two years. Access to education has been affected by hikes in school fees, and some 60 per cent of rural households still suffer from chronic food insecurity, with 20 per cent extremely vulnerable.

Another example of a fragile State is Somalia, a country that has long been among the least developed. Its progress on human development has been further constrained by the lack of a functioning national administration since 1991. Over this 14-year period, progress on human development has been scant, with rival warring factions claiming jurisdiction over specific territories. The result is starkly apparent in education: The net primary attendance ratio is lower than anywhere else in the world, at just 12 per cent for boys and 10 per cent for girls, according to the latest estimates.[11] The recent re-establishment of schooling by many

Figure 2.5: Children account for an increasing proportion of people living with HIV

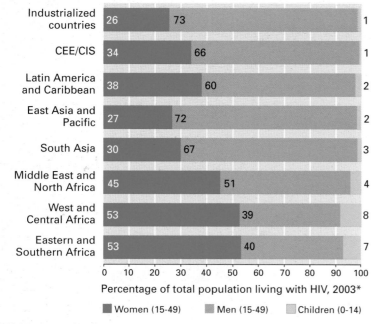

	Women (15-49)	Men (15-49)	Children (0-14)
Industrialized countries	26	73	1
CEE/CIS	34	66	1
Latin America and Caribbean	38	60	2
East Asia and Pacific	27	72	2
South Asia	30	67	3
Middle East and North Africa	45	51	4
West and Central Africa	53	39	8
Eastern and Southern Africa	53	40	7

Percentage of total population living with HIV, 2003*

*Figures may not add up to 100% due to rounding.

Source: UNICEF calculations based on data from Joint United Nations Programme on HIV/AIDS, *Report on the Global HIV/AIDS Epidemic*, 2004.

communities – with the support of international agencies – is a welcome development, but years of underinvestment have left Somalia lagging behind the rest of the developing world in education.

Strengthening governance in fragile States is considered by many, and with good justification, to be a prerequisite for meeting the goals of the Millennium agenda. Donors and international agencies may be wary of increasing non-humanitarian assistance to the government of a fragile State, but their commitments to children must compel them to engage with these States to ensure that children's rights are protected and their needs met. The simple truth is that children cannot wait until governance improves – long delays may result in them missing out on their childhood altogether.

HIV/AIDS is wreaking havoc with children's lives in the worst-affected countries

Combating HIV/AIDS is a central objective of the Millennium Development Goals, specifically addressed in MDG 6. Children

living with or affected by HIV/AIDS, or in countries with high prevalence rates, face an extremely high risk of exclusion from access to essential services, care and protection, as parents, teachers, health workers and other basic service providers fall sick and eventually die. The epidemic is tearing away at the social, cultural and economic fabric of families, the first line of protection and provision for children that safeguards against their exclusion from essential services and exposure to harm. Some 15 million children have already lost one or more parents to the disease, and millions more have been made vulnerable as the virus exacerbates other challenges to the health and development of families, communities, provinces and, in the worst-affected countries, whole nations.[12] Of those orphaned by AIDS, 12.1 million, or more than 80 per cent, are in sub-Saharan Africa, reflecting not only the region's disproportionate burden of HIV infection, but also the epidemic's relative maturity.[13]

The protracted illness and eventual death of parents and other caregivers exert enormous pressures on children, who often have to assume adult roles in treatment, care and support. Surviving siblings can suffer stigma and discrimination in their communities and societies, experience greater exposure to violence, abuse and exploitation and drop out of school for a variety of reasons.

In addition to orphaning and the loss of caregivers, lack of access to essential services and increased risk of missing out on an education, HIV/AIDS also threatens the very survival of children and young people. Every day, nearly 1,800 children under 15 are infected.[14] Children under 15 account for 13 per cent of new global HIV infections and 17 per cent of HIV/AIDS deaths annually.[15] The pandemic has reversed the gains in child survival made in many of the worst-affected countries and has dramatically reduced average life expectancy in those countries, particularly in southern Africa.[16]

With the pandemic spreading to more and more countries and population groups, the worst impact on children is still to come. It is estimated that in 2004, almost 5 million people became infected with HIV – the most in a single year since the pandemic began in the early 1980s. Young people aged between 15 and 24 years now account for nearly one third of people living with HIV/AIDS globally.[17] Given that it can take up to a decade for any decrease in HIV prevalence to be translated into lower death rates from AIDS – owing in large part to the slow roll-out of antiretroviral treatments – deaths from AIDS will continue and the number of orphans will rise. In those countries where HIV/AIDS is already at epidemic levels, tackling the disease is imperative not only to meet MDG 6, but also to reverse recent increases in under-five mortality rates – particularly in Eastern and Southern Africa – and to reduce the risk of exclusion from education and the protection of a family environment for orphans and other vulnerable children.

Subnational factors that can result in exclusion

National aggregates fail to capture the full picture of exclusion for children

Assessment of indicators related to children's well-being is most frequently undertaken at the national level. There are a number of reasons for this: The national level is the fundamental unit of statistical analysis for countries; estimates for national aggregates are generally more widely available than for any sub-country group; standardization of statistics often requires national-level and nationally funded survey programmes; and international agencies also compile national aggregates on key indicators related to the Millennium agenda. The national government is also the signatory to international commitments to children and the principal trustee for their implementation.

However, assessing child well-being on the basis of national aggregates alone has its limitations. National averages are, by nature, summary measures that most clearly depict the situation of the majority; as such, they do not provide a full picture. To gain a more complete understanding of the exclusion that some children face within a country, disaggregated indicators derived from national statistics or household surveys are required. Data that are disaggregated geo-

graphically – as well as by gender, ethnic group or other salient dimensions – are key to identifying the risk of exclusion and are immensely useful as a tool for programme design. Disaggregated data are particularly important for advocacy and policy purposes in countries where the national averages may indicate that, based on current trends, some or all of the MDGs will be met.

Disaggregated national statistics or household surveys on children's well-being are not available in all countries. But the existing evidence, based on the Demographic and Health Surveys (DHS) and Multiple Indicator Cluster Surveys (MICS), is fairly comprehensive and indicates a clear result: Within countries, there are usually significant disparities in child well-being and development across geographical and other axes.

These disparities reflect exclusion in relative terms, quantifying a child's well-being compared to that of his or her peers. A country with a high national average of primary school attendance or enrolment, for example, may still face wide internal variations owing to the marginalization of particular segments of the population. One such coun-

try is Venezuela, where survey data from DHS and MICS indicate that although net primary school attendance approaches 94 per cent, almost 15 per cent of children of primary school age living in the poorest 20 per cent of households miss out on primary education, compared with less than 2 per cent in the richest quintile.

One of the biggest risks for children is that, with the MDGs being based on national averages, such inequalities within countries may be obscured. The magnitude of these disparities can be great, and they risk being ignored when MDG-based strategies are being developed and implemented. This is particularly true in countries where the majority of children are afforded the minimum health-care and education thresholds set out in the Millennium agenda. In such settings, the sharp divide between the most privileged children and those denied access to essential services contributes to their further marginalization and may in itself be a root cause of discrimination.

Income inequalities threaten children's survival and development

In every developing country where disaggregated data by household income are avail-

able,[18] children living in the poorest 20 per cent of households are significantly more likely to die before the age of five than those living in the richest 20 per cent.

Latin America and the Caribbean is the region with the highest inequalities in household income in the developing world; countries in this region also have among the highest inequalities in child mortality. The country with the greatest inequality in under-five mortality is Peru, where children living in the poorest quintile are five times more likely to die before their fifth birthday than children from the wealthiest 20 per cent of the population.

Though disparities in under-five mortality rates are not as sharply pronounced in other regions, they can still be marked. On average, a child born into the poorest 20 per cent of households is three times more likely to die than a child born into the richest quintile in East Asia and the Pacific region, two and a half times more likely to die in the Middle East and North Africa and around twice as likely in the South Asia and CEE/CIS regions. Although several of the countries in these regions are either on track or making good progress towards MDG 4, the poorest children are still twice as likely to die before five as the richest children (see Panel: Income disparities and child survival, page 20).

Within countries, low income is a major deterrent to primary school participation. Children of primary school age from the poorest 20 per cent of households in developing countries are 3.2 times more likely to be out of primary school than those from the wealthiest 20 per cent. Moreover, 77 per cent of children out of primary school come from the poorest 60 per cent of households in developing countries; this disparity is even greater in Latin America and the Caribbean (84 per cent) and Eastern and Southern Africa (80 per cent).[19]

Children living in rural areas and among the urban poor often face a high risk of exclusion

Rural areas tend to be poorer and more difficult to reach with health-care services and education than urban areas. Accordingly, in nearly all countries where household data on child mortality rates are available, rural children are more likely to die before the age of five than their urban peers. Some 30 per cent of rural children in developing

countries are out of school, compared with 18 per cent of those living in urban areas, and over 80 per cent of all children out of primary school live in rural areas. Possible barriers to their attendance include distance, the likelihood that their parents are less educated or do not value formal education and the failure of governments to attract good teachers to the countryside.[20]

Geographic divides often overlap with income inequality within urban communities. In many of the world's cities, the most impoverished citizens live in slums, tenements and shanty towns, areas which are geographically separate from the most affluent. More than 900 million people live in slums; most lack access to safe drinking water, improved sanitation facilities, sufficient living space and decent quality housing with secure tenure.[21] The exclusion of children living in these communities – which are often severely lacking in essential services and state protection – can sometimes approach levels experienced in rural areas.[22]

Inequalities in children's health, rate of survival and school attendance and completion also fall along the lines of gender, ethnicity

Figure 2.6: In several regions, girls are more likely to miss out on primary school than boys

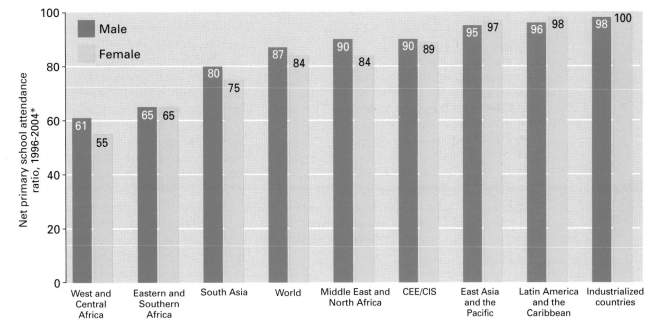

*Data refer to the most recent year available during the period specified.

Source: United Nations Children's Fund, *Levels, Trends and Determinants of Primary School Participation and Gender Parity*, Working Paper, 2005.

Income disparities and child survival

In 2004, an estimated 10.5 million children died before they reached age five,[a] most from preventable diseases. Combating these unnecessary deaths and meeting Millennium Development Goal 4 – reduce child mortality by two thirds between 1990 and 2015 – will be a central focus for all those working towards the fulfilment of the promises of the Millennium agenda for children.

Addressing the inequalities and disparities within countries must be an essential component of all programmes and policies that aim to reduce child mortality.

In countries where household data are available from surveys such as the Demographic and Health Surveys and the Multiple Indicator Cluster Surveys, it is clear that children living in the poorest 20 per cent of households are significantly more likely to die during childhood than those living in the richest 20 per cent of the population.[b]

The least developed countries tend to have lower inequalities in child survival between rich and poor, with mortality rates remaining high even in the richest families. Countries in sub-Saharan Africa, for example, have lower levels of disparity in child mortality rates than less impoverished developing regions.

Income disparities often translate into disparities in the nutritional status of children. Over 5.5 million children under five die every year from causes related to malnutrition.[c] Encompassing more than just hunger, malnutrition can lead to weakened immune systems when vitamin A is lacking and a child is neither hungry nor underweight. Even when it does not cause death, malnutrition can inflict lifelong damage on a child's health and development.

Vaccine-preventable diseases cause more than 2 million deaths every year, of which approximately 1.4 million occur in children under age five.[d] While huge strides have been made worldwide to increase vaccination coverage, there is still room for improvement. Tragically, the poorest children are also at a disadvantage when it comes to immunization. The richest children are more than twice as likely to have received the measles vaccination as the poorest 20 per cent of children in Azerbaijan, the Central African Republic, Chad, the Democratic Republic of the Congo, Niger and northern Sudan.

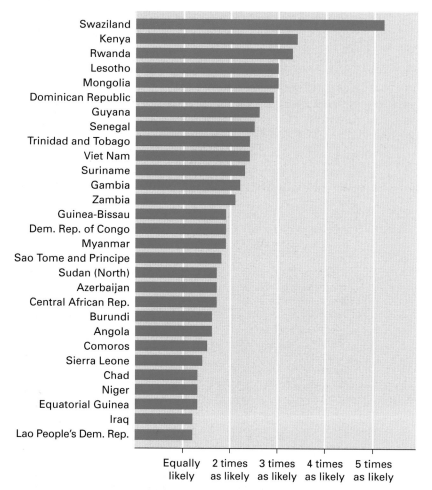

How likely is a poor child to be underweight compared to a rich child?

Swaziland
Kenya
Rwanda
Lesotho
Mongolia
Dominican Republic
Guyana
Senegal
Trinidad and Tobago
Viet Nam
Suriname
Gambia
Zambia
Guinea-Bissau
Dem. Rep. of Congo
Myanmar
Sao Tome and Principe
Sudan (North)
Azerbaijan
Central African Rep.
Burundi
Angola
Comoros
Sierra Leone
Chad
Niger
Equatorial Guinea
Iraq
Lao People's Dem. Rep.

| Equally likely | 2 times as likely | 3 times as likely | 4 times as likely | 5 times as likely |

In 13 countries where data are available, children from the poorest 20 per cent of the population are more than twice as likely to be underweight for their age, and in Swaziland they are five times as likely to be underweight.

Source: UNICEF calculations based on data from Demographic and Health Surveys (DHS) and Multiple Indicator Cluster Surveys (MICS).

How likely is a poor child to die before age 5, compared to a rich child?*

*Individual lines within the regional block each represent a country surveyed.

Source: UNICEF calculations based on data from Demographic and Health Surveys (DHS) and Multiple Indicator Cluster Surveys (MICS).

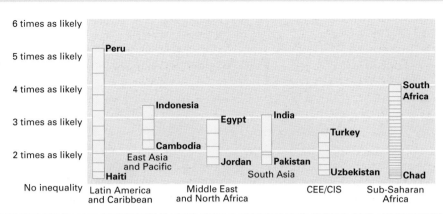

If income disparities are not addressed, it is likely that the poorest children will continue to make up a disproportionate share of the child mortality figures, even if national goals are met. Overall, in 23 of the 56 countries with household surveys allowing for disaggregation by income, poorer children are more than twice as likely to die before their fifth birthday, with some of these countries making progress towards the goals at the national level and others failing.

See References, pages 90-91.

How likely is a rich child to be vaccinated against measles compared to a poor child?

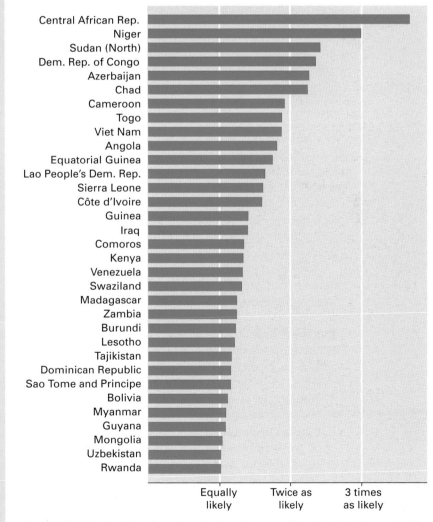

Source: UNICEF calculations based on data from Demographic and Health Surveys (DHS) and Multiple Indicator Cluster Surveys (MICS).

© UNICEF/HQ99-1146/Tomislav Peternek

or disability. These inequities occur when children and their caregivers are directly excluded from services because they live in areas that are poorer and more poorly serviced, or because cultural barriers such as language, ethnic discrimination or stigmatization prevent them from receiving needed services.

Discrimination against girls excludes them from education

Gender discrimination is specifically addressed by MDG 3, which promotes gender equality and the empowerment of women, with the attached target of eliminating gender disparity in education.

Education provides the opportunity for girls (and boys) to become more empowered and self-confident as they acquire the range of knowledge, skills, attitudes and values critical to negotiating an equal place in society. Gender inequality in education means that for every 100 boys out of primary school, there are 117 girls who also miss out on primary education.[23] While the gender gap in primary education has been closing

steadily since 1980, many countries have failed to meet the MDG 3 target of gender parity in primary education by 2005, and the regions with the highest gaps will have to make even greater gains if gender parity is to be achieved as part of universal primary school completion by 2015.

Gender gaps in secondary education are even more pronounced: of 75 developing countries surveyed by UNICEF, only 22 were on course to meet the MDG 3 target of gender parity at the secondary school level, while 25 were far from the goal.[24] Girls' exclusion from education in comparison to boys – especially in South Asia, sub-Saharan Africa and the Middle East and North Africa – is one of the clearest statistical indicators of gender discrimination.

But gender discrimination is both more subtle and all-pervasive than can be measured in the statistics about gender parity in schooling. Gender plays a major part in determining which children end up being excluded from essential services and are, therefore, most at risk of missing out on the Millennium agenda. Many of the groups of children considered in this report are not taken beyond the reach of international development efforts by their gender alone, but their gender clearly plays a major part in determining their vulnerability. Gender discrimination also results in limited access of women to basic health-care services, which increases the risk of maternal and child mortality.

Women's disempowerment results in exclusion for their children. Mothers are generally the first caregivers for children. In situations and settings where they are denied access to basic services, essential resources, or information, it is the children who suffer the greatest exclusion. Impediments to progress in the fight against gender discrimination include the continued lack of good quality data disaggregated by sex, the paucity of financial and technical resources for women's programmes at both international and national levels and the lack of representation in the political sphere.[25]

Discrimination on the basis of ethnicity is widespread

Ethnicity is a set of characteristics – cultural, social, religious and linguistic – that forms a distinctive identity shared by a community of people. It is a natural expression of human diversity and a source of strength, resilience and richness in the human family. But when a child faces discrimination because of ethnicity, the risk of exclusion from essential services and protection rises sharply.

There are some 5,000 ethnic groups in the world, and more than 200 countries have significant minority ethnic or religious groups. Most countries – around two thirds – have more than one religious or ethnic group that accounts for at least 10 per cent of the population.[26] Some ethnic groups are spread across national borders – for example, the Roma in Central and Eastern Europe or residents of Chinese descent in many countries in South-East Asia. Some are minorities, accounting for a small proportion of the national population, while others make up a significant share of the population but have little power in society as a result of their isolation and, very often, deep historical disadvantage.[27]

© UNICEF/HQ01-0675/Alejandro Belaguer

A common thread among ethnic groups is that they often face considerable marginalization and discrimination. Almost 900 million people belong to groups that experience disadvantage as a result of their identity, with 359 million facing restrictions on their religion. Around the world, some 334 million people face restrictions or discrimination related to their language. In over 30 sub-Saharan African countries (containing 80 per cent of the region's population), for instance, the official language is different from the one most commonly used, and only 13 per cent of children in these countries are taught in their mother tongue in primary school.[28]

Discrimination on the basis of ethnicity can erode self-worth and confidence in

The marginalization of Roma communities and their children

The Roma population constitutes Europe's largest and most vulnerable minority, estimated at between 7 and 9 million people. With no historical homeland, roughly 70 per cent of Roma live in Central and Eastern Europe (CEE), and in former Soviet Union countries. Nearly 80 per cent live in countries that joined the European Union (EU) in 2004 or are in the process of negotiating EU membership.[a]

Exclusion in all its dimensions – social, political, economic or geographic – has affected Roma for centuries and has taken the form of overt ethnic discrimination. Faced with prejudices and fears that they are an inferior and dangerous people, Roma tend to live in ghettos, segregated from the rest of society, and are even barred from restaurants and other public places.[b]

Roma are also among the most impoverished cultural groups in Central and Eastern Europe. Research shows that nearly 84 per cent of Roma in Bulgaria and 88 per cent of Roma in Romania live below the national poverty lines. Poverty among Roma is even higher in Hungary, with 91 per cent of the group living below the national poverty line.[c] Because of limited education, a low level of skills and discrimination in the labour market, in some Roma settlements not a single person is regularly engaged in formal employment.[d] Many Roma children attend separate schools or are segregated when attending mainstream schools. Roma children attending Roma-only schools find themselves in overcrowded classes as a result of geographic and socio-economic segregation.[e]

As many as 75 per cent of Roma children in Central and Eastern Europe are placed in special schools for the mentally disabled,[f] but not for genuine health reasons. This practice, which is common, is related to the economic benefits that come with special education. In some CEE countries, children who are sent to schools for the mentally challenged receive food subsidies, educational materials and transportation, as well as room and board. Roma parents often agree to place their children in special schools without fully understanding the long-term consequences of their action, and even if they do, some families think they have no other alternatives.[g]

A study conducted in 2001 by the Open Society Institute (Budapest), a private grant-making foundation, found that 64 per cent of Roma children in the second grade placed in special schools in Bulgaria, the Czech Republic, Hungary and Slovakia were considered 'mentally challenged'. Over a two-year period, the majority of these students, when placed in special-education pilot classes, were able to meet the requirements of the mainstream curriculum.[h]

As disturbing as it is, this picture of exclusion is by no means complete. For instance, in Serbia and Montenegro, national statistics on education do not always include the most-excluded children. Issues affecting Roma girls are still not addressed in Romania, where the greatest number of Roma people, between 1 and 2 million, live. Moreover, in Bosnia and Herzegovina, attendance of Roma children in schools is sporadic, and they are almost completely absent from the upper grades of primary and secondary schools.

The education system is not the only one that is failing Roma children. More than half of the children abandoned in medical institutions in Romania – 57 per cent – are of Roma ethnic origin. Often lacking the appropriate identity documents and birth certificates necessary for health insurance enrolment, Roma communities

children and deprive them of opportunities for growth and development, blunting the promise that is every child's birthright. Prejudice at community and institutional levels can restrict opportunities for members of an ethnic group. In terms of career choices and advancement, access to political office or community leadership, members of ethnic minorities may find their participation in society limited – even where there are laws prohibiting bias and exclusion. Exclusion based on ethnicity can lead to armed conflict and even ethnic violence – witness the atrocities along ethnic lines being committed in Darfur, Sudan, since 2003.

Indigenous children can face multiple barriers to full participation in society

Indigenous peoples have many characteristics and experiences in common with ethnic minorities, but they are distinct from them. Indigenous communities are more likely than ethnic minorities to insist on their right to a separate culture linked to a particular territory and their history. They have generally maintained their own language, culture and their children have very limited access to health-care services and are heavily dependent on state welfare and other transfer payments. In Romania, Roma men and women are less likely to have health insurance and to be enrolled in a family physician's practice than their Romanian counterparts.

Efforts are being made to address the situation. The Roma Education Initiative (REI), a project of the Open Society Institute, in cooperation with Children and Youth Programs in New York, is attempting to eliminate discrimination in the school systems in CEE countries – including reintegration of Roma children from special schools into formal education and enabling them to succeed in school on equal terms with their peers – through a three-year project launched in 2002.[i] The Slovak Government has recently designed a set of strategies that specifically recognize and address the issues of the Roma minority. Moreover, in 2004, UNICEF Romania, in partnership with the Romanian Federation of NGOs Active in Child Protection Issues, launched the "Leave No Child Out" campaign dedicated to combating discrimination against Roma children and enhancing their access to education. So far, the campaign has reached about 65 per cent of the country's Roma population.

See References, page 91.

and social organization distinct from the dominant trends of the societies in which they live. They are also likely to identify themselves as indigenous and be identified as such by other groups.[29] In certain countries, such as Bolivia, Denmark (Greenland) and Guatemala, they represent the majority of the population. There are some 300 million indigenous peoples in more than 70 countries, around half of whom live in Asia.[30]

Indigenous children can suffer cultural discrimination and economic and political mar-

ginalization. They are often less likely to be registered at birth and more prone to poor health, to low participation in education and to abuse, violence and exploitation.[31] The Committee on the Rights of the Child has expressed concern about the particular position of indigenous children in Australia, Bangladesh, Burundi, Chile, Ecuador, India, Japan and Venezuela.[32] Many of them are still denied their rights under the Convention on the Rights of the Child, especially with regard to birth registration, access to education and health-care services.

Information on the extent to which indigenous children are denied their rights to survival, health-care services and education relative to the national average is limited. Case studies in individual countries suggest that infant and child mortality rates are higher among indigenous groups than in the national population. In the hill province of Ratanakiri, Cambodia, for example, infant mortality rates are more than twice the national average, while in Australia the mortality rate for indigenous infants is three times the overall rate.[33] Many factors contribute to these disparities, including environmental conditions, discrimination and poverty. Health-care services – including vaccination against preventable diseases – are often lacking in areas inhabited by indigenous peoples. In Mexico, for instance, there are an estimated 96.3 doctors per 100,000 people nationally but only 13.8 per 100,000 in areas where indigenous people make up 40 per cent or more of the population.[34]

Indigenous children are less likely to be registered at birth, in part owing to the absence of information on the issue in their mother tongue. This can result in chronically low levels of registered children at birth: For example, in the Amazonian region of Ecuador only 21 per cent of under-fives have a birth certificate, compared with the national average of 89 per cent.[35] The distance to the nearest registration office and the cost of the certificate can also be severe deterrents. National legislation that prohibits indigenous peoples from registering their children with indigenous names can also prove a strong disincentive to obtaining a birth certificate; in Morocco, for example,

Living with disability *by Bethany Stevens*

I spent the first two weeks of my life in a neonatal intensive care unit in Bremerhaven, Germany, on a United States military base. Shortly after I took my first breath, a young captain told my father that I had a condition that would cause most people around the world to take me to the top of a mountain and leave me there.

The condition is a rare congenital bone disease called *osteogenesis imperfecta*, which affects only about 0.008 per cent of the world's population.[a] It causes brittle bones resulting in fractures and, in its most extreme form, death. I have a moderate type of *osteogenesis imperfecta* and have only had 55 fractures. I have undergone 12 surgeries to strengthen my legs through the insertion of metal rods into my bone marrow, as well as one attempt to prevent further curvature of my spine by fusing bone into the curves.

In addition to the physical pain of operations and fractures, I have been plagued with feelings of shame and self-contempt as a result of the social stigma of disability. This is an issue I continue to grapple with today as a 24-year-old law student. As a child, I did not realize how significant the social reality of being disabled was, as I felt that I was a normal child who simply had physical limitations. Still, the reality of fracturing on a random basis was frightening and stressful to both my mother and myself. When I was younger, my mother believed that I might fracture while playing so she isolated me from my peers. I calculated how much time I have spent alone, healing from various injuries, and came up with seven years of my life – a figure that does not include the years prior to my schooling.

My first educational experience was at the age of three when I began to attend a preschool in Colorado, USA, composed exclusively of disabled children. I thought it would be wonderful to get to interact with my peers, but our ability to socialize was limited by their significantly more extreme disabilities. A few years later we moved to California, where I began attending an elementary school as the only disabled child integrated with able-bodied students. I loved school because it gave me the much-needed opportunity to engage in human interaction. But there were still times when I felt socially isolated because of my disability, particularly when it came to socializing beyond the confines of my school.

When I was eight years old, I was sent to a school for disabled children to receive top-quality physical therapy following a re-rodding procedure on my legs. While I received excellent physical therapy, the education was remedial at best. What I learned in my first year of school was taught to me a second time. It was a nice mental hiatus, but I am glad and lucky that my time there lasted only one year.

I returned to my small elementary school in the mountains of California and was content to interact with people of similar intellectual calibre. I began to develop friendships, but had to leave school for about a year to receive a spinal fusion. While healing, I was taught by a home-schoolteacher for an hour a day. Again, I experienced a void in mental stimulation.

During the early 1990s, I enjoyed several years without experiencing any substantial medical issues and remained in school. But when I entered adolescence and – like all children my age – began to become aware of my changing body and to experience physical attraction to other people, things took a turn for the worse. I developed feelings of sexual attraction at the same rate as my peers, yet experienced a significant temporal gap between having these feelings and being able to express them. I felt lost, alone and angry at myself and the world.

I internalized feelings of hatred towards my body, which I now believe were garnered through images of normalized beauty standards perpetuated by the media and by social stigma. Nowhere did I find positive images expressing the humanity of disabled people – only those in which we were depicted as objects intended to provoke pity or sympathy. My self-esteem plummeted, and I felt like I would never escape from feelings of despair. These intense emotions were exacerbated by the fact that I had to leave all of my good friends behind and go to a school on the other side of town, as the school my friends were going to attend was inaccessible to disabled students.

These feelings did not magically disappear when I moved across the country to a small town in South Carolina. If anything, they grew. From the ages of 11 to 16 I hated myself; when I looked in the mirror I would cringe. This period of my life resonates with me today, as I can still feel the scars of those experiences.

My life's purpose became clear when I began attending the University of Florida. As a student, I developed a passion for disability activism. Through arguing points of equality, beauty and pride in disability, I internalized these ideas and developed the desire to catalyse positive change for disabled people. I have had the opportunity to represent the United States at two international conferences on disability rights in Norway, published reports through the United Nations and Rehabilitation International, and organized large campus events featuring various notable disabled individuals.

Through these experiences, I came to understand how the stigma related to disability leads to social and economic oppression all over the world. The reality is that the majority of people, around 80 per cent in the United States alone, will become disabled at some point in their lifetime.[b] It is my professional aspiration to initiate a national lobbying agency that would work not only within the established legal system, but also through direct action to encourage individuals, legislators and corporations to reconstruct the social identity of disability.

Positive social evolution for disabled persons can occur with education. Information about issues affecting the disabled could be added to public school curriculums, and training sessions to raise awareness about these issues could be mandated for large companies, similar to race and sexual harassment training. Governments need to include disability issues in educational requirements. People often harbour negative ideas about other groups of people because of lack of awareness and knowledge.

There is a duality in the need for a cognitive revolution, existing within able-bodied and disabled populations. All too often we internalize negative stigmas concerning our disability because we cannot see our beauty. For most of my life I was the only disabled person I knew, and I found it truly difficult to look into the mirror and see an aesthetically different person, and yet still see beauty. We need a sense of internal pride, as much as society needs to accept our abilities and assets. This realization has catalysed my desire to compile a book about the beauty in disability, featuring interviews and photographs of both notable and unknown disabled persons. The book will be dedicated to all disabled people who struggle to see their beauty, much as I did for so many years.

After years of struggling to overcome the feeling of inadequacy and shame that plagued my childhood and early adulthood, I now believe that being disabled is the best thing that has ever happened to me. Never would I have been afforded the wonderful opportunities I have experienced had it not been for my disability. These opportunities and the development of pride in my existence came with a pivotal move into my father's home when I was 16 years old. He recognized my humanity and encouraged it to flourish, teaching me how to drive and supporting my securing of a job. He allowed me freedom that my mother would have never condoned, and with it I forged an identity that I love. It is wonderful to finally love myself. It is crucial that other parents of children with disabilities allow their children to obtain a sense of independence because it is necessary for self-sufficiency. It is my hope that I can assist those living with disability in my community, as my father did me, so that young people like me no longer internalize feelings of shame about being disabled.

Bethany Stevens is a law student at the University of Florida (UF) and has been a disability activist for five years. Ms. Stevens directed a campaign and petition process that resulted in the opening of an accommodated testing centre for students with disabilities at UF. She is the president of the Union of Students with Disabilities, founder of Delta Sigma Omicron and recently directed the Building a DisAbility Movement conference hosted at UF.

See References, page 91.

Amazigh people must register their children with a recognized Arabic name[36] *(see Chapter 3: Invisible Children, for a fuller discussion on the risk of exclusion from birth registration).*

In most countries, indigenous children have low school enrolment rates. Scarce educational facilities, governments' failure to attract qualified teachers prepared to work in the remote areas where many indigenous people live and the perceived irrelevance of much of the school curriculum for the local

community – all act as disincentives to school participation. When they attend school, indigenous children often begin their formal education at a disadvantage to other children because they are unfamiliar with the language of instruction. Research indicates that it takes until the third grade before their comprehension begins to match that of children who speak the dominant language.[37]

Neglect and stigmatization can result in exclusion for children with disability

There are an estimated 150 million children with disabilities in the world, most of whom live with the reality of exclusion. The vast majority of children with disabilities in the developing world have no access to rehabilitative health-care or support services, and many are unable to acquire a formal education.[38] In many cases, disabled children are simply withdrawn from community life; even if they are not actively shunned or maltreated, they are often left without adequate care. Where special provision is made for children with disabilities, it often still involves segregating them in institutions – the proportion of disabled children living in public institutions has increased, for instance, in the countries of Central and Eastern Europe since the onset of political transition.[39]

Many disabilities in developing countries are directly attributable to deprivations of essential goods and services, especially in early childhood. Lack of prenatal care adds to the risk of disability, while malnutrition can result in stunting or poor resistance to disease. Disabilities resulting from poor nutrition or lack of vaccines can be addressed by concerted action and donor support. The worldwide assault on polio – a major cause of physical disability in the past – has resulted in a dramatic reduction in the disease, from 350,000 cases in 1988, when the Global Polio Eradication Initiative was launched, to 1,255 at the end of 2004.[40] The disease is now endemic in only six countries – Afghanistan, Egypt, India, Niger, Nigeria and Pakistan – although transmission has been re-established in several countries. But despite this remarkable progress, not every child has been reached, and the gains remain at risk of reversal until every child is immunized.

Between 250,000 and 500,000 children are still blinded each year by vitamin A deficiency, a syndrome easily prevented by oral supplementation costing just a few cents (given every 4-6 months).[41] Children involved in hazardous labour or who have been conscripted as soldiers face greatly heightened risks of disabling physical injury. Landmines and explosive remnants of war continue to maim or disable children even in countries that are no longer in conflict. Of the 65 countries that suffered mine casualties between 2002 and 2003, nearly two thirds had not experienced active conflict during the period.[42]

Regardless of the cause, or where they live, children with disabilities require special attention. Given the higher risk they face of being excluded from school and within their societies, communities and even households, children living with disabilities are liable to end up forgotten in campaigns for development that focus on statistical targets based on national aggregates.

Tackling the root causes of exclusion

The strategies to achieve the Millennium agenda advanced in the reports of the United Nations Millennium Project and of the Secretary General address many of the broad factors mentioned in this chapter and call on governments, donors and international agencies to tackle them. Less emphasis is given, however, to specific measures that would prevent exclusion for children facing extreme poverty, armed conflict, weak governance, HIV/AIDS, and discrimination in all its forms – particularly if, despite the increased efforts of the international community, these factors persist over the coming decade.

Children in the least developed countries require special attention

Addressing the special – and urgent – needs of the least developed countries has become a priority objective for the international community in recent years. In May 2001,

the Brussels Declaration and Programme of Action for the Least Developed Countries for the Decade 2001-2010 were endorsed by the United Nations General Assembly. But progress on the plan has not matched its ambition. Despite significant advances by some least developed countries towards the plan's individual goals, as a group they have made only limited inroads towards eradicating poverty and fostering sustainable development.

Reducing poverty in the least developed countries will require greater efforts in five major areas: national development strategies, official development assistance, full debt cancellation, fair trade and enhanced technical assistance from donors.[43] Measures agreed in 2005 at both the Group of Eight (G-8) Summit in July and the World Summit in September will go some way towards increasing official development assistance and reducing external debt burdens for the least developed countries. But for development strategies to be truly effective and sustainable, they require a stronger focus on children, who account for around half of the population in these countries. As Chapter 4 will attest, poverty-reduction processes, and budgets in particular, will need to be adjusted to expand or reallocate resources for the social development required to diminish the deprivations faced by millions of children living in the least developed countries. In addition, even bolder initiatives may well be required on official development assistance, debt reduction and fair trade to ensure that the Millennium agenda is met for the world's most impoverished nations.

Conflict resolution and prevention are required to safeguard children and women

Preventing and resolving armed conflict are central objectives of the peace and security aims of the Millennium agenda, outlined in detail in the Millennium Declaration. With children and women most at risk from armed conflict – accounting for around 80 per cent of all deaths among civilians due to armed conflict since 1990[44] – conflict prevention and resolution are vital to ensure their protection and access to essential services. Where conflict does occur, emergency

The Global Campaign on Children and AIDS

Every minute, a child under 15 dies of an AIDS-related illness.[a] Every minute, another child becomes HIV-positive. Every minute, four young people between the ages of 15 and 24 contract HIV.[b]

These stark facts underline the devastating impact that HIV/AIDS is having on children and young people. The children of sub-Saharan Africa are hardest hit, but unless the HIV pandemic is halted and sent into retreat, Asia is on course to have higher absolute numbers of HIV infections by 2010.[c] Millions of children, adolescents and young people orphaned, made vulnerable or living with HIV are in urgent need of care and protection. If rates of HIV infection and AIDS-related deaths continue to rise, the crisis will persist for decades, even as prevention and treatment programmes expand.

HIV/AIDS is denying millions of children their childhood. The disease exacerbates the factors that cause exclusion, including poverty, malnutrition, inadequate access to basic social services, discrimination and stigmatization, gender inequities and sexual exploitation of women and girls.

National governments committed themselves to addressing the impact of HIV/AIDS on children in the Declaration of Commitment endorsed at the United Nations General Assembly Special Session on HIV/AIDS in 2001. But progress has been slow. Children are often overlooked when strategies on HIV/AIDS are drafted, policies formulated and budgets allocated. At the 2005 World Summit, world leaders pledged to scale up responses to HIV/AIDS through prevention, care, treatment, support and mobilization of additional resources.

The Global Campaign on Children and AIDS – *Unite for Children. Unite against AIDS* – launched in October 2005, is a concerted push to ensure that children and adolescents are not only included in HIV/AIDS strategies, but become their central focus. An overarching aim of the campaign is to meet Millennium Development Goal 6, which aims to halt and reverse the spread of HIV/AIDS by 2015. Achievement of the campaign goals will also have positive implications for the other MDGs.

Although global in reach, the campaign will have a strong focus on the most-affected countries in sub-Saharan Africa, home to 24 of 25 countries with the world's highest levels of HIV prevalence.[d] The campaign seeks to provide a child-focused framework around country programmes in four main areas, dubbed the 'Four Ps':

Prevent infection among adolescents and young people

Reduce HIV/AIDS risks and vulnerability by increasing access to and use of youth-friendly and gender-sensitive prevention information, life skills and services.

Prevent mother-to-child HIV transmission

Increase provision of affordable and effective services that help HIV-positive pregnant girls and women avoid transmitting the virus to their children. Prioritize care, support and treatment programmes for HIV-infected children and pregnant women.

Provide paediatric treatment

Provide affordable paediatric HIV drugs, such as cotrimoxazole, to prevent opportunistic infections.

Protect and support children affected by HIV/AIDS

Make sure a higher proportion of the neediest children receive quality family, community and government support, including education, health care, birth registration, nutrition and psychosocial support.

The Global Campaign on Children and AIDS involves partners from every sector of the global community. It aims to unite as many people, organizations and agencies as possible under its call to action. From the outset, the campaign was positioned within harmonized approaches, especially the 'Three Ones' principles that were endorsed by a consensus of governments, international organizations, donors and civil society; the WHO and UNAIDS '3 by 5' Initiative, which aims to provide sustained treatment for 3 million people living with HIV/AIDS; and national poverty reduction strategies.

In partnership, governments and agencies, activists and scientists, corporations and community workers, and as many others as possible will work through the campaign to ensure that this is the last generation of children that bears the bitter burden of HIV/AIDS.

See References, page 91.

responses should consist not only of providing essential services and goods, but also preventing the separation of families and helping to reunite them, initiating the resumption of schooling, organizing child protection and preventing HIV/AIDS.[45]

Children living in 'fragile' States must not be forgotten

'Fragile' States require particular attention, since a dysfunctional government will complicate efforts to implement any policy or obtain any non-humanitarian development assistance. Nonetheless, continued engagement with governments of such States – and also non-state actors who may wield substantial power within these countries – is often vital to safeguard children living in these countries from exclusion. Children must not be forgotten by the international community because of their countries' failings.

A global campaign to mitigate the impact of HIV/AIDS on children is under way

The international community is stepping up its efforts to tackle HIV/AIDS through a series of initiatives. These efforts are crucial to check the spread of the disease and to make treatment widely available. Far greater attention must be given, however, to the impact of the pandemic on children and adolescents, especially girls, and to ways of protecting them from both infection and exclusion. To this end, UNICEF and its partners have launched a global campaign on children and AIDS (see Panel page 30).

Governments and societies must openly address discrimination

Tackling discrimination requires a multi-pronged approach. Many elements of discrimination are rooted in long-held societal attitudes, which often governments, civil society and the media are reluctant to confront. Yet confront them they must, if they are to fulfil their commitments to children. Targeted initiatives to address the exclusion faced by women and girls, ethnic and indigenous groups and the disabled are needed, along with legislation to prohibit discrimination, and greater research on these groups' needs and well-being. Taken by themselves, however, such measures may only serve to reduce discrimination, not tackle its root causes. For these initiatives to bring about lasting change, they must be accompanied by a courageous, open discussion – involving the media and civil society – on societal attitudes that foster or tolerate discrimination. The future of children at risk of exclusion as a result of discrimination depends on such courageous action.

Swift and decisive action is required

A childhood cannot wait for extreme poverty to be eradicated, armed conflict to abate, the HIV/AIDS pandemic to subside, or for governments and societies to openly challenge attitudes that entrench discrimination and inequalities. Once past, a childhood can never be regained. For millions of children, their childhood and their future depend on swift and decisive action being taken now to address these threats.

Extreme and Relative Poverty: Precursors to Exclusion

MDG 1 focuses on halving extreme poverty by 2015. While the most widely used measure of poverty is the proportion of people whose income is less than $1 a day, poverty has multiple definitions and numerous ways of affecting children. Children experience extreme poverty differently than adults: Child poverty cannot be understood only in terms of family income, and responses must take children's experiences into account. For them, poverty is experienced as both material and developmental deprivation.* The exclusion resulting from poverty can have lifelong impacts.

Children do not have to live in extreme poverty to feel excluded. Research suggests that when children do not consider themselves to be part of families whose material conditions are close to what is considered 'normal' for their community, the impact is greatly felt.** This relative deprivation is based on the idea that people decide how well off or deprived they are – what they should deserve or expect – by comparing themselves to others. Measuring the distribution of wealth within a country or territory by comparing the differences in resources available to the wealthiest and poorest sections of society is one simple way to gauge inequality.

Even if the goal to end the extreme poverty faced by millions is achieved, relative deprivation – the inequality and exclusion faced by children and their families – will continue unless specific measures to encourage equality and social mobility are pursued, including the allocation of resources for education, health care and other interventions to ensure that the rights of every child are fulfilled.

* UNICEF, *State of the World's Children 2005*, New York, 2004, p. 16.

** See, for example, Christian Children's Fund, *Children in Poverty: The Voices of Children*, 2003.

Proportion of the population living on less than $1 a day by region

55%	West and Central Africa
38%	Eastern and Southern Africa
33%	South Asia
14%	East Asia and Pacific
10%	Latin America and Caribbean
4%	Central and Eastern Europe
3%	Middle East and North Africa
22%	Developing countries
41%	Least developed countries
21%	World

Source: Derived from World Bank, 2005 World Development Indicators, as reported in Statistical Table 7, pp. 122-125.

A Decent Standard of Living

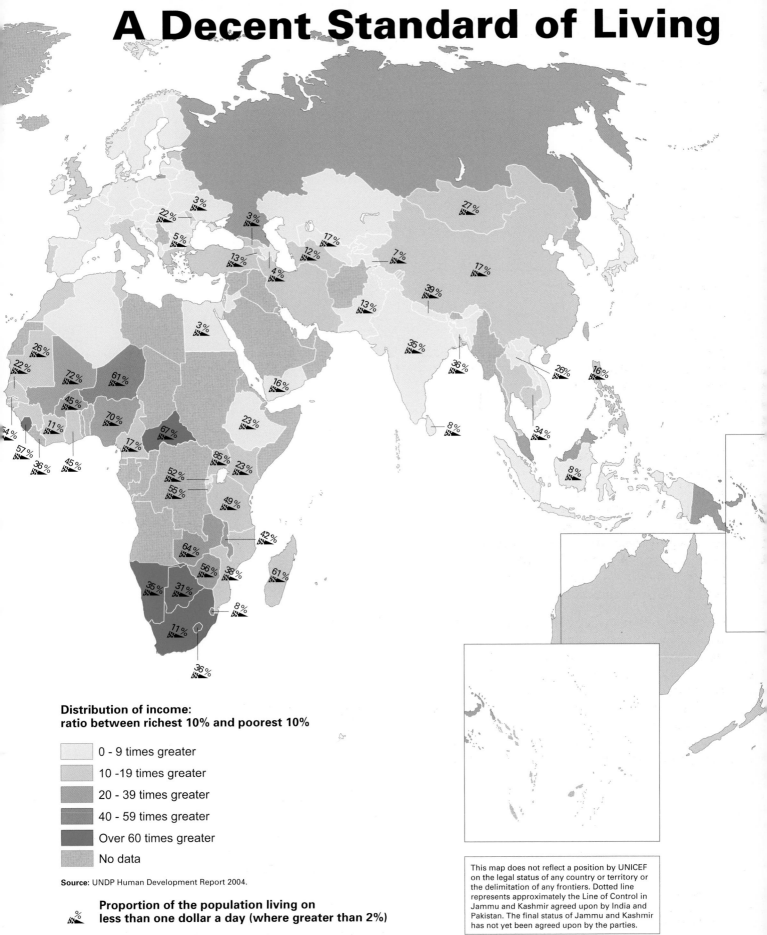

Distribution of income:
ratio between richest 10% and poorest 10%

- 0 - 9 times greater
- 10 -19 times greater
- 20 - 39 times greater
- 40 - 59 times greater
- Over 60 times greater
- No data

Source: UNDP Human Development Report 2004.

Proportion of the population living on
less than one dollar a day (where greater than 2%)

Source: World Bank, 2005 World Development Indicators.

This map does not reflect a position by UNICEF on the legal status of any country or territory or the delimitation of any frontiers. Dotted line represents approximately the Line of Control in Jammu and Kashmir agreed upon by India and Pakistan. The final status of Jammu and Kashmir has not yet been agreed upon by the parties.

Invisible Children

Children risk becoming 'invisible' if their right to protection is unmet

The root causes of exclusion – extreme poverty, poor governance, armed conflict, HIV/AIDS, inequalities and discrimination – have pernicious consequences beyond excluding children from essential services. They also foster conditions that heighten the risk of children being exploited, neglected, trafficked or abused. The breakdown in the rule of law that often accompanies armed conflict, for example, can leave children exposed to sexual violence or exploitation. Children orphaned or made vulnerable by HIV/AIDS are not only at greater risk of missing out on an education, they may also face stigmatization and neglect in their communities. Those who traffic children look not in the rich suburbs but in the slums and among the most destitute for their victims.

By ratifying the Convention on the Rights of the Child, governments pledged to safeguard children from harm, abuse, exploitation, violence and neglect. Yet for millions of children, the violation of this right to protection is the main cause of their exclusion. Many of them could claim membership in more than one of the groups considered in this chapter. For example, many children engaged in forced, hazardous and exploitative labour have been trafficked, while large proportions of all the children considered will not have been registered at birth. Marginalized and excluded, children suffering from violations of their right to protection have collided with the very worst elements of adult experience, from prostitution to hazardous labour, so that the only element of their childhood that remains is that which makes them more vulnerable, more exploitable.

Children are visible in their families, communities and societies when their rights are

SUMMARY

ISSUE: At the extremes, children can become invisible, in effect disappearing from view within their families, communities and societies and to governments, donors, civil society, the media and even other children. For millions of children, the main cause of their invisibility is violations of their right to protection. Firm evidence of the extent of these violations is hard to acquire, but several factors appear central to increasing the risk of children becoming invisible: the lack or loss of formal identification; inadequate State protection for children without parental care; the exploitation of children through trafficking and forced labour; and premature entry of children into adult roles such as marriage, hazardous labour and combat. Children affected by these factors include those not registered at birth, refugees and displaced children, orphans, street children, children in detention, children in early marriages, hazardous labour or combat, and trafficked and indentured children.

ACTION: Making children visible requires creating a protective environment for them. The key elements of a protective environment include:

- Strengthening the capacity of families and communities to care for and protect children.
- Government commitment to child protection by providing budgetary support and social welfare policies targeted at the most excluded and invisible children.
- Ratification and implementation of legislation, both national and international, concerning children's rights and protection.
- Prosecution of perpetrators of crimes against children, and avoidance of criminalizing child victims.
- An open discussion by civil society and the media of attitudes, prejudices, beliefs and practices that facilitate or lead to abuses.
- Ensuring that children know their rights, are encouraged to express them and are given vital life skills and information to protect themselves from abuse and exploitation.
- Availability of basic social services to all children without discrimination.
- Monitoring, transparent reporting and oversight of abuses and exploitation.

Key to building the protective environment is responsibility: All members of society can contribute to ensuring that children do not become invisible. While families and the State have the primary responsibility for protecting children, ongoing and sustained efforts by individuals and organizations at all levels are essential to break patterns of abuse.

fully met, and they are provided with essential services and protection from harm. Their visibility diminishes, however, when they are deprived of parental care or face violence or abuse within the home. They also risk becoming less visible within their communities and societies when they do not attend school, are locked away in a workplace or are otherwise exploited, suffer abuse or violence outside the family environment, or are simply not viewed or treated as children. Children may effectively disappear from official view if their very existence and identity is not legally or formally acknowledged and recorded by the state or if they are routinely omitted from statistical surveys, policies and programmes. But we can also be blind to children's plight even when they are right in front of our eyes, as is the case with children living and working on the streets. All of these children, without exception, require a level of protection that the world, until now, has manifestly failed to deliver.

At the extremes, these children in effect disappear from everybody's view – they become invisible in their communities and societies. Firm evidence on the extent of the protection violations that increase the risk of children becoming invisible is hard to acquire, but four factors appear central to many of them: the lack or loss of a formal identity; inadequate State protection for children without parental care; the exploitation of children through trafficking and forced labour; and children's premature entry into adult roles, such as marriage, hazardous labour and combat. While these factors are not the only ones that cause children to become invisible, they are certainly among the most significant, with consequences that often extend far beyond the years of childhood.

Loss or lack of a formal identity or documentation

Every child is entitled to a formal identity, including birth registration, the right to acquire a nationality and the right to know and be cared for by their parents. The Convention on the Rights of the Child makes it clear, in Articles 7 and 8, that it is the duty of governments to ensure that these rights are respected and enforced.

Without formal registration at birth or identification documents, children may find themselves excluded from access to vital services, such as education, health care and social security. Reuniting families separated from their children through natural disaster, displacement or exploitation, such as trafficking, is often complicated by a lack of formal documentation. Though many children may face exclusion because they do not possess identity documents, the two groups that appear most at risk are those unregistered at birth and those who have been displaced or separated from their families.

Without birth registration, children are invisible in official statistics

Exclusion operates from the very beginning of life for the estimated 48 million children in 2003 – 36 per cent of total births that year – whose birth went unregistered.[1] Having a child's identity officially acknowledged and registered is a fundamental human right, as stipulated by Article 7 of the Convention on the Rights of the Child. Registration enables a child to obtain a birth certificate, which is the most visible evidence of a government's legal recognition of the child as a member of society. A birth certificate is also proof of the child's fundamental relationship with parents and, generally, also determines nationality.

Birth registration may be needed for access to services later in life, from a place in school to treatment in a hospital. Cases of child marriage where the spouse is believed to be underage but the exact age cannot be firmly established are almost impossible to prosecute. Children who are unregistered at birth may also miss out on any protection that exists against premature conscription into the armed forces or, if they come into conflict with the law, against prosecution and punishment as adults. When they grow up, they may be unable to apply for a formal job or a passport, open a bank account, get a marriage license or vote. A birth certificate may also be needed to obtain social security, family allowances, credit and a pension.[2]

Although most countries have mechanisms for registering births, the number of births actually registered varies from country to

Figure 3.1: Birth registration* in the developing world

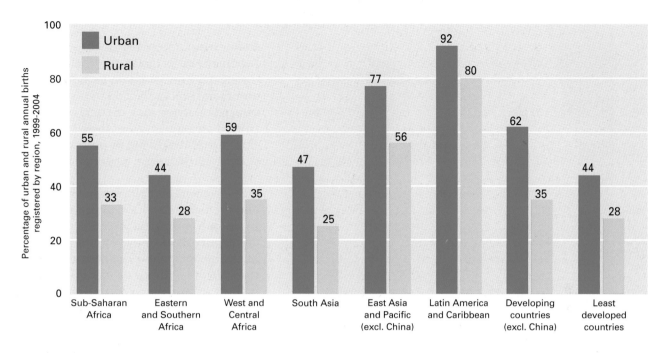

* **Birth registration:** Percentage of children under 5 years of age who were registered at the time of the survey. The numerator of this indicator includes children whose birth certificate was seen by the interviewer or whose mother or caretaker says the birth has been registered.

Regional averages: These aggregates do not include all countries in each region. However, sufficient data covering more than 50 per cent of the target population was available to generate the averages for the regions shown. Averages for East Asia and Pacific and the developing countries do not include China.

Data range: Data refer to the most recent year available during the period specified.

Source: Multiple Indicator Clusters Surveys (MICS), Demographic and Health Surveys (DHS) and other national surveys.

country based on infrastructure, administrative capacity, available funds, access to the population and technology for data management. The value of birth registration is often overlooked due to the continuing lack of awareness that registration is a critical measure to secure the recognition of every person before the law, to safeguard their rights and to ensure that any violation of these rights does not go unnoticed.[3]

Registration may not be seen as important by society at large, by a government facing severe economic difficulties, by a country at war or by families struggling with day-to-day survival. It is often considered to be no more than a legal formality, unrelated to child development, health, education or protection. Other factors that influence birth registration levels include the existence of an adequate legislative framework, enforcement of existing legislation on birth registration, sufficient infrastructure to support the logis-

tical aspects of registration and the barriers that families can encounter during registration, such as fees and distance to the nearest registration centre.[4]

According to the latest UNICEF estimates, on average over half – 55 percent – of births in the developing world (excluding China) each year go unregistered, a proportion that rises to 62 per cent in sub-Saharan Africa.[5] In South Asia, the share is higher still, at 70 per cent. Almost half the children in the world who are denied their right to a legal identity at birth live in this region: In Bangladesh, only 7 per cent of all children are registered at birth. There is wide variation in levels of birth registration, from the Occupied Palestinian Territory and the Democratic People's Republic of Korea, where virtually 100 per cent of births were registered in 2004, to Afghanistan, Uganda, and the United Republic of Tanzania, where the rate is less than 7 per cent.[6]

© UNICEF/HQ03-0121/Bill Lyons

During the same year, the total number of people displaced within their own countries by conflict or human rights violations amounted to roughly 25 million.[10]

Refugee and internally displaced children face many risks, given the violence and uncertainty surrounding both their flight and their lives in the country and/or place of asylum. They may become separated from their families, lose their homes and find themselves living in poor conditions that jeopardize their health and education.

Displacement complicates birth registration and the issuance of travel documents, thereby compromising displaced persons' right to an identity. Both refugees and internally displaced people may have been forced to leave their homes without proper documentation, making it difficult to establish their identities. They may, therefore, be unable to prove their right to receive basic social services, such as education or health care, or to work in a different part of the country.[11]

The loss of family protection, and inadequate resources to address the needs and challenges that refugee and internally displaced children face, can leave them at significant risk of military recruitment by armed groups and forces, abuse and sexual exploitation. Girls are especially at risk of abduction, trafficking and sexual violence, including rape used as a weapon of war.

Where the displacement is long term and the affected children have a different ethnic or linguistic background from people in the host locality, they may face discrimination and be deterred from school attendance as a result.[12] Upon return, both internally displaced people and refugees may find their homes and their land taken over by others, including local authorities, and may not be able to prove their ownership of their property. They may also be rejected by their own communities because they fled during the crisis or violence while others remained.[13]

Primary responsibility for both refugee and displaced children lies with national governments. However, the Office of the United Nations High Commissioner for Refugees (UNHCR) has a mandate to assist

Unregistered births can serve as an indicator of other forms of social marginalization and disparity within countries or territories. Unregistered children are more likely to be the children of the poor: According to household surveys from 2003, in the United Republic of Tanzania children born into families in the richest 20 per cent of the population are over 10 times more likely to be registered than those living in the poorest 20 per cent of households.[7] Location is also an important constraint on registration: Rural children are 1.7 times more likely to be unregistered than their urban peers. Other factors that contribute to disparities in birth registration include mothers' education, loss of parents, religion and ethnicity.[8]

Refugee and displaced children and women often lack visibility in their place of refuge

At the end of 2004, roughly 48 per cent of all refugees worldwide were children.[9]

and protect refugees, while the International Committee of the Red Cross (ICRC) has a mandate to assist internally displaced people if displacement is a result of armed conflict and internal violence. Unlike refugees, however, internally displaced persons are not protected by specific international conventions but only by a set of guiding principles that are morally, not legally, binding.

The international community and UNHCR have developed a wealth of international norms, policies and guidelines to improve the protection and care of refugee women and children. In practice, however, there is still a gap in their application and implementation, due to resource constraints (both financial and human) and to uneven priorities and accountability at the level of institutions, as well as within the international community.[14] When governments (both of donor countries and countries that have internally displaced people or host refugees) and the collaborative international response fail to allocate resources and implement effective interventions targeted at displaced women and children, these groups risk being excluded and becoming invisible within their place of refuge.

Inadequate state protection for children requiring special assistance

Families have the primary responsibility for caring for and protecting their children. But for numerous reasons – the loss of parents, separation related to displacement, domestic violence and abuse, extreme poverty, among others – many children are deprived of a loving, caring family environment. When, for whatever reason, family protection for children breaks down, States parties are obliged under Articles 20 and 22 of the Convention on the Rights of the Child to provide them with special protection and assistance.

State failure to protect children without parental care leaves them vulnerable and, often, invisible

For all too many children, this assistance is not forthcoming. Instead, they have to fend for themselves in the adult world. It is no surprise, then, that they often find themselves at risk of exclusion from essential services and of being exploited.

Children who lack family protection, on a temporary or permanent basis, are not the only groups of children that States parties have pledged to provide with special care and attention. States are also bound under Articles 20 and 40 of the Convention on the Rights of the Child to protect children who are already in their care, for example, in institutions or detention. In the latter case, it is the government's duty to preserve the dignity and worth of children who have infringed the law. Again, the evidence available suggests that children in detention risk being underserved by governments.

This section examines the risk of invisibility for three key groups of children who require special assistance from State parties and who often lack that protection: orphaned children, street children, and children in detention.

Loss of parents can leave children less visible and less protected

Increasing numbers of children are forced by the death of one or both parents to assume responsibility, not only for their own lives, but also for those of their younger siblings, often with tragic consequences for their rights and development.

At the end of 2003, there were an estimated 143 million orphans[15] under the age of 18 in 93 developing countries.[16] More than 16 million children were orphaned in 2003 alone. A major contributing factor to these alarming figures is the HIV/AIDS pandemic, without which the global number of orphans would be expected to decline.[17]

Education is often among the first casualties for an orphan. Children may drop out of school because the domestic burdens upon them become too great or because new caregivers within their community or extended family are unprepared to meet the costs attached to education. If that happens, they also become more exposed to exclusion from other services, including vital information about health, nutrition and life skills,

Figure 3.2: Orphaned children under age 18 in sub-Saharan Africa, Asia and Latin America and the Caribbean

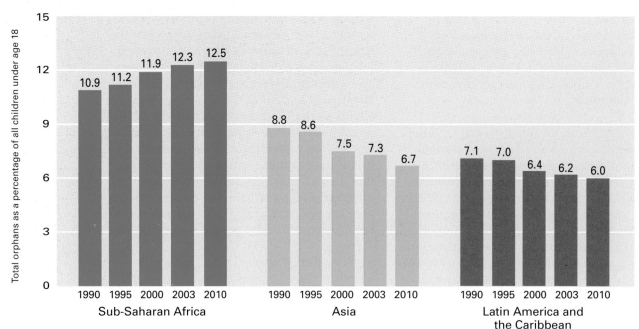

Note: Total orphans are children under age 18 whose mothers or fathers (or both) have died. The figures for 2010 are projections.

Source: Joint United Nations Programme on HIV/AIDS, United Nations Children's Fund, United States Agency for International Development, *Children on the Brink 2004: A joint report of new orphan estimates and a framework for action*, UNAIDS/UNICEF/USAID, New York, July 2004.

such as how to help protect themselves from violence and abuse.

Orphaned children are much more vulnerable to protection violations. The death of a parent, in situations where no adequate alternative care systems are in place, opens up a protection gap. Children living on their own are at much greater risk of abuse and exploitation. Assessments by the International Labour Organization (ILO) have found that orphaned children are much more likely than non-orphans to be working in commercial agriculture, as street vendors, in domestic service and in the sex trade. In the Ethiopian capital, Addis Ababa, for example, 28 per cent of the child domestic workers interviewed in one study were orphaned.[18] A study of children working – many in prostitution – in Zambia found that one third were single or double orphans.[19]

Though physically visible, street children are often ignored, shunned and excluded

Street children are among the most physically visible of all children, living and working on the roads and public squares of cities all over the world. Yet, paradoxically, they are also among the most invisible and, therefore, hardest children to reach with vital services, such as education and health care, and the most difficult to protect.

The term 'street children' is problematic as it can be employed as a stigmatizing label. One of the greatest problems such children face is their demonization by mainstream society as a threat and a source of criminal behaviour. Yet many children living or working on the streets have embraced the term, considering that it offers them a sense of identity and belonging. The umbrella description is convenient shorthand, but it should not obscure the fact that the many children who live and work on the street do so in multifarious ways and for a range of reasons – and each of them is unique, with their own, often strongly felt, points of view.[20]

The exact number of street children is impossible to quantify, but the figure almost certainly runs into tens of millions across the world.[21] It is likely that the numbers are increasing as the global population grows and as urbanization continues apace: 6 out of 10 urban dwellers are expected to be under 18 years of age in 2005.[22] Indeed, every city in the world has some street children, including the biggest and richest cities of the industrialized world.

Most street children are not orphans. Many are still in contact with their families and work on the streets to augment the household income. Many others have run away from home, often in response to psychological, physical or sexual abuse. The majority are male, as girls seem to endure abusive or exploitative situations at home longer (though once they do leave their home and family, they are generally less likely to return).[23]

Once on the street, children become vulnerable to all forms of exploitation and abuse, and their daily lives are likely to be far removed from the ideal childhood envisioned in the Convention on the Rights of the Child. In some cases, those who are entrusted to protect them become the perpetrators of crimes against them. Street children often find themselves in conflict with the police and other authorities and have been harassed or beaten by them. They have been rounded up, driven outside city limits and left there. And they have been murdered by vigilantes in the name of 'cleaning up the city', often with the complicity or disregard of local authorities.

Children in detention should be among those most visible to national authorities, but they are often not treated like children

Logic would suggest that children held within the criminal justice system should be among the most visible children of all, readily accessible to interventions that ensure their access to health care, education and protection. But often children in conflict with the law effectively cease to be regarded as children. Instead, their perceived transgression is considered to remove them from childhood protection, exposing them to treatment either in exactly the same way as adult offenders or, worse, to having their vulnerability as children abused.

© UNICEF/HQ01-0614/ Shehzad Noorani

Data on children in detention are scarce, but estimates indicate that more than 1 million children are living in detention as a result of being in conflict with the law.[24] Yet in this area there is no excuse for the lack of information. Unlike many of the other children considered in this report, children caught up in the criminal justice system in most countries have been processed and are available to official scrutiny.

Nevertheless, it is clear that violent abuse of children in detention is a widespread and serious problem. In its 37th session, the Committee on the Rights of the Child raised a number of concerns about the procedures for and protection of children caught up in the justice system in Brazil, among other countries, including reports of torture and extrajudicial killings in detainment facilities.[25]

Children are at risk of violence while in detention both before and after any trial they may undergo. This can include physical and sexual violence by adult detainees, guards, police or other juvenile inmates. The correctional regime is itself at times excessively violent, involving indefinite detention, long periods of isolation or, alternatively, co-mingling with adult prisoners in overcrowded and unsanitary conditions. In a small number of countries, the death penalty is still applied to juvenile offenders. The

Children of the streets *by Elena Poniatowska*

According to the 'Estudio de Niños Callejeros' – an official study of street children – there are 11,172 children living and working on the streets in Mexico City, the world's largest city. They wash cars and buses, run errands and carry soft drinks. Boys hate being loaders. Either they end up with spinal injuries or are run down by cars. Underlying it all is smog, heavy traffic and extreme poverty in addition to violence, social disintegration and environmental deterioration. Drugs and delinquency are commonplace.

In the street the children wash windshields and swallow fire. Almost all the passers-by are indifferent to the magic in their faces and hands. They wait for clients with their instruments in their hands, and in the darkness the studs on their *charro* outfits sparkle, their wide-brimmed hats glitter. They are guitars, violins, trumpets of Jericho, voices in search of a listener, jugglers, clowns, magicians. The red light never stops for them, and the show goes on until three or four in the morning, especially on Fridays and Saturdays, when couples feel romantic and give them a few more pesos.

All those who pass by see them, but they are invisible. They do not exist. The police look at them without seeing them. Everything isolates them, denounces them.

School can bring further anguish for these children, even the most innocent ones. It is hard for them to retain what they are taught: They have lost their capacity for concentration. Besides, they do not want to know anything about roofs or walls: What can compare to the street? The street is an addiction.

In the street, everything is raw: reality, food, eyes, solidarity. Nothing has to be elaborated. Everything is thrown in their faces: aggressive nicknames, ruthless laughter, plunder, sneering, ridicule, the scar that never heals, the manhandling, the crudeness.

Only the street is theirs. It compensates for loneliness, rejection, lack of love. It lures them. It gives them the money they never got at home. It gives them rhythm, tempo and immediate retribution. "I'm someone, I'm something, I just earned my dinner."

Time is different for these children. They do not care what day it is. The days of the week trap them. The hours are the hours of their disaster. They know only two seasons, dry and rainy. The rainy season (from June to September) is the bad one because afternoon paralyzes all street activities. It is also impossible to play ball, and that is one thing they love.

Elena Poniatowska is a writer, journalist and professor, who, though born in Paris, has lived in Mexico since she was a child. She has written several celebrated books and is the recipient of numerous awards and honours, including a Guggenheim Fellowship, an Emeritus Fellowship from Mexico's National Council of Culture and Arts, and the Mexican national award for journalism.

problem of violence against children in detention is being addressed in the United Nations Secretary-General's Study on Violence Against Children, the report of which is due to be released in 2006.

According to a group of international experts convened in April 2005 as part of the UN Secretary-General's study, the key factors that facilitate violence against children in the justice system are:

- Impunity and lack of accountability by law enforcement agents, institutions and staff that are responsible for violence against children.

- The overuse of detention, particularly pre-trial detention, including the detention of non-offenders.

- The lack of community-based alternatives to the formal justice system and of alternatives to detention, including care and protection systems.

- The lack of appropriate juvenile justice systems, including appropriate facilities and separation from adults.

- The lack of external controls on institutions, including effective independent complaints and investigation procedures, independent monitoring and access by non-governmental organizations.

- The 'acceptability' of violence in society, leading to tolerance of violence at all levels: family, school and community.

- The lack of training and sensitization of law enforcement and juvenile justice personnel.

- 'Tough on crime' policies, negative media and discriminatory images of street children and other socio-economically disadvantaged children.[26]

Governments have a clear responsibility to protect children in detention from abuse and harm. But they must also question whether a child should be in detention at all. Detention should always be a last resort: In many cases it is too readily adopted as an immediate response to antisocial or disruptive behaviour by children and adolescents, as if removing them out of sight and out of mind is a goal in itself, rather than an unintended consequence.

Premature entry into adult roles

Childhood should be a separate space from adulthood, a time when children can grow and play, rest and learn. This distinction embodies the spirit of the Convention on the Rights of the Child, which delineates rights that are particular to children as distinct from adults.

Children engaged in adult roles are often no longer viewed as children

In its Preamble, the Convention on the Rights of the Child recognizes that children's bodies and minds are less mature than those of adults;[27] consequently, roles appropriate for adults may not be suitable for children. Performing adult roles will inevitably result in children missing out on their childhood, and therefore facing a higher risk of exclusion and invisibility.

Children, especially girls, often take on adult roles by caring for family members, often siblings, or by working to contribute to the family income. Being orphaned and living in extreme poverty are two clear examples of circumstances where children may have little choice but to adopt these roles. These children risk exclusion from protection and essential services.

Adult roles often carry a high risk of injury to children's physical and mental well being. This is particularly true of three types of roles: combat, marriage and hazardous labour. Children engaged in these activities are not only prevented from having a childhood, but also often risk death or serious injuries that can have lifelong consequences.

Obstacles to the reintegration of former child soldiers can lead to their isolation

Hundreds of thousands of children are caught up in armed conflict as combatants, messengers, porters, cooks and sex slaves for armed forces and groups.[28] Some are abducted or forcibly recruited; others are driven to join by poverty, abuse and discrimination, or by the desire to seek revenge for violence enacted against them and their families.[29] While under the control of the armed groups, these children are excluded from essential services and protection.

Ending the recruitment of child soldiers and returning them to their families and communities is an obvious prerequisite for them to gain inclusion and prevent further violations of their rights. Disarmament, demobilization and reintegration (DDR) programmes use a variety of interventions, ranging from back-to-school initiatives to psychosocial support. Stigmatization can be reduced when reintegration support targets the community as a whole. But despite these initiatives, many obstacles to the full reintegration of child soldiers remain.

Girls, in particular, may benefit less from DDR initiatives. Save the Children reports that since it began working with children associated with armed groups in the Democratic Republic of the Congo, fewer than 2 per cent of children passing through their programmes and interim care centres have been girls, though they estimate that 40 per cent of all children involved with armed groups are female. Similarly, in Sierra Leone, less than 5 per cent of girls known to have been involved in militias benefited from DDR initiatives.[30]

Numbers of girl soldiers are routinely underestimated, and girls are often not considered real soldiers because they perform mainly non-combat functions. As a result, most of them return to their communities without any formal assistance or counselling, leaving them with a host of unresolved psychosocial and physical issues. Moreover, girls abducted or forcibly recruited who return with babies born in captivity may be rejected by their families and communities because of the stigma attached to rape and to giving birth to so-called 'war babies' or 'babies born of rape'. For these girls, being marginalized by DDR programmes represents an additional layer of invisibility to those imposed by their involvement in conflict and with militias.

Early marriage robs girls of their childhood

Every year, millions of girls disappear into early marriage – defined as formal marriages, or customary and statutory unions recognized as marriage, before the age of 18. On marrying, a girl is expected to set aside her childhood and assume the role of a woman, embarking immediately upon a life that includes sex, motherhood and all the household duties traditionally expected of a wife.

Although early marriage sometimes extends to boys as well, the number of girls involved is far greater. According to an analysis of household survey data for 49 developing countries conducted by UNICEF in 2005, 48 per cent of South Asian females aged 15 to 24 had married before age 18. (At 18, a girl is still considered a child under the

Children and young people in detention in Nigeria

Her eyes welled up as she struggled to hold back the flood of tears that threatened to ruin her neatly pressed coveralls. Soon the floodgates opened as she recounted the details of the past five and a half years spent in jail. Nkeiruka became pregnant while unmarried, which is considered a taboo among the Igbo community in Nigeria to which she belongs. In December 1999, the then 15-year-old Nkeiruka gave birth unassisted at home, and her child died as a result of complications. Her uncle accused her of killing her newborn, and Nkeiruka and her mother Monica were arrested and taken to prison in Anambra state. Now 21, Nkeiruka faces an uncertain future: Deprived of a formal education while in prison and possessing few skills, she is uncertain of the reception she and her mother will receive from the community and family when they return home.

A proper investigation was never conducted, no evidence of the alleged crime was found and the original case file disappeared. Nkeiruka and her mother slept in a cell with up to 37 women for around 1,971 days. "Much like the many other children and young people who are incarcerated in Nigeria, they were forgotten," says Nkolika Ebede of the International Federation of Women Lawyers in Anambra, who, in a UNICEF-supported project, helped secure their release.

Nkeiruka was one of over 6,000 children and teenagers in Nigeria who are in prison or juvenile detention centres.[a] About 70 per cent of them are first-time offenders,[b] usually arrested for misdemeanours such as vagrancy, petty stealing, truancy or simply wandering or hanging around the streets. Others are detained at the request of their parents or guardians, who say that they are out of control. Many of these children come from broken homes and large poor families, or are orphans. According to Uche Nwokocha of the Society for the Welfare of Women Prisoners in Enugu, children – some still quite young – have been held in custody by the police in the place of their parents.

Young people, especially girls, are also victims of criminal acts such as domestic violence, rape, sexual exploitation and trafficking. However, due to aberrations and delays in the administration of justice, especially during investigations leading to trial, these child victims can find themselves in jail. Their parents are denied access to them and they are deprived of due process, detained under deplorable conditions, put in contact with adult criminals, at risk of physical and sexual abuse, and often denied their right to bail. Many children are forced to admit to being older than they are or the police change their ages on arrest warrants in order to prosecute them as adults.

Prisons in Nigeria offer little educational or vocational training or recreational facilities. For a while, Nkeiruka was

Convention on the Rights of the Child, except in countries where the age of majority is lower.) The corresponding figures in the 29 countries surveyed for Africa and 8 countries for Latin America and the Caribbean are 42 per cent and 29 per cent, respectively.[31] The incidence varies widely between countries as well as continents: In sub-Saharan African countries surveyed, for instance, Niger had the highest rate of women between 20-24 who were married by age 18 (77 per cent); in contrast, this rate dropped to 8 per cent in South Africa.[32]

Some of these girls are forced into marriage at a very early age, while others may accept the marriage while being too young to understand its implications or play any active part in the choice of partner. Where early marriage is practised, it is usually a long-established tradition, making protest not just difficult but barely possible. Early marriage tends to ensure that a woman is firmly under male control, living in her husband's household, and also supposedly guards against premarital sex for women. In many societies, the independence that can emerge during adolescence is seen as an undesirable attribute in women, who are expected to be subservient: Early marriage is therefore convenient because it effectively cancels out the adolescent period, quenching the sparks of autonomy and strangling the developing sense of self.

Poverty is another factor underpinning early marriage. Marriage can be seen as a survival strategy for a girl – particularly if she marries an older and wealthier husband. In West Africa, for example, a UNICEF study in 2000 showed a correlation between economic hardship and a rise in early marriage, even among some population groups that do not normally practise it.[33] There are also

taught soap-making and knitting, but she says the classes abruptly stopped in 2003. Limited or no counselling services are available to detained juveniles. While in detention, about 90 per cent of young people do not get proper meals, bedding or access to toilets and bathing facilities, making them vulnerable to sickness and disease. Nkeiruka and her mother were lucky to share the cell with women. Many other female prisoners are housed in mixed cells, increasing the risk of sexual abuse and exploitation.

Where juvenile courts do not exist, children and youths are tried in adult courts. Lacking the means to secure legal representation, or to pay bail, they often languish in jail for long periods. Juveniles in prison are often cut off from family and friends, as a deep-seated fear and distrust of the police and justice system leads people to shun those who come in contact with the law, whether as perpetrators or victims. Stigmatization and rejection by society further affect the reintegration of victims. During the five and a half year incarceration, Nkeiruka received only one visitor, a sibling, in the week before her scheduled release date.

Since 2003, UNICEF Nigeria has helped to promote improved treatment and legal aid for juveniles in conflict with the law. As part of the Juvenile Justice Administration project – undertaken in partnership with the National Human Rights Commission, the Nigerian Bar Association and local non-governmental organizations – a pro bono service was introduced and institutionalized for lawyers renewing their licences with the association. UNICEF has assisted in supporting the training of magistrates, police, prison officers, lawyers and social workers in juvenile justice administration, which has strengthened the provision of free legal services for children, young people and women.

The project, which aims to reduce the number of children being detained, was started in three pilot states in southern Nigeria. By mid-2005, almost 600 children had benefited from the project in these states, either by being released from prison or detention centres, being granted bail, having their cases dismissed or settled out of court, receiving counselling or having the project handle their ongoing case.

The number of children and young people in detention has decreased as a result of the project. The training of magistrates has facilitated more careful use of custodial sentencing of juveniles to prison terms for minor offences. Police officers are exercising restraint in detaining juveniles in police cells for minor offences and instead immediately take them to court for processing. Given its success, the project is now being implemented in nine additional states throughout the country in a strong partnership with the Nigeria Police Service.

See References, page 92.

Figure 3.3: Early marriage* in the developing world

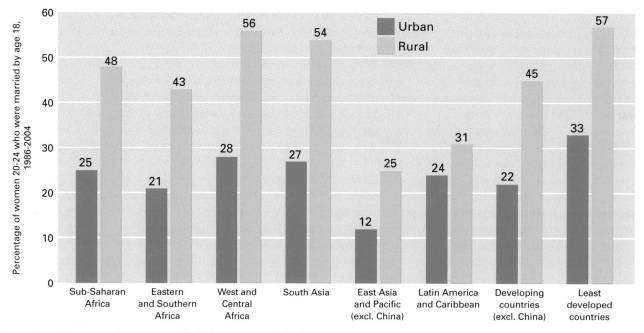

y-axis: Percentage of women 20-24 who were married by age 18, 1986-2004

Legend: ■ Urban ■ Rural

Region	Urban	Rural
Sub-Saharan Africa	25	48
Eastern and Southern Africa	21	43
West and Central Africa	28	56
South Asia	27	54
East Asia and Pacific (excl. China)	12	25
Latin America and Caribbean	24	31
Developing countries (excl. China)	22	45
Least developed countries	33	57

* Early marriage: Percentage of women aged 20-24 that were married or in statutory or customary union recognized as marriage before they were 18 years old.

Regional averages: These aggregates do not include all countries in each region. However, sufficient data was available for more than 50 per cent of the target population to generate the averages for the regions shown. Averages for East Asia and Pacific and the developing countries do not include China.

Data range: Data refer to the most recent year available during the period specified.

Sources: Multiple Indicator Cluster Surveys (MICS), Demographic and Health Surveys (DHS) and other national surveys.

reports from East Africa that girls orphaned by HIV/AIDS are increasingly being steered towards early marriage by caregivers who find it hard to provide for them.[34]

However it arises, early marriage jeopardizes the rights of children and adolescents. The right to free and full consent to marriage is recognized in the Universal Declaration of Human Rights, while Article 16 of the Convention on the Elimination of All Forms of Discrimination against Women stipulates that "the betrothal and the marriage of a child shall have no legal effect...".[35] Early marriage can put an end to all educational development and opportunities for children. All too often it is the gateway to a lifetime of domestic and sexual subservience.

Early marriage also has physical implications for young girls, notably premature pregnancy and childbirth, which entail vastly increased risks of maternal and neonatal mortality. Pregnancy-related deaths are the leading cause of mortality for 15- to

19-year-old girls worldwide, whether they are married or not. Those under 15 are five times more likely to die than women in their twenties.[36] Their children are also less likely to survive: If a mother is under 18, her baby's chance of dying in the first year of life is 60 per cent higher than that of a baby born to a mother older than 19.[37]

Children engaged in hazardous forms of labour risk serious injury and often miss out on an education

An estimated 246 million children between 5 and 17 are engaged in child labour, according to the latest estimates from the International Labour Organization (ILO). Of these, nearly 70 per cent or 171 million children were working in hazardous situations or conditions, such as in mines, with chemicals and pesticides in agriculture or with dangerous machinery. Some 73 million of them are less than 10 years old.[38] Their physical immaturity leaves them more exposed to work-related illnesses and

Early marriage and fistula

At least 2 million young women in the developing world suffer the painful, humiliating and devastating consequences of obstetric fistula. Caused by complications during childbirth, usually because the young woman's pelvis is too small or because the baby is too big or badly positioned, obstetric fistula manifests itself as a hole between a woman's vagina and her bladder, rectum or both, creating a constant leakage of urine or faeces. Girls and young women suffering from fistulas are ostracized by their communities and often abandoned by their families, forcing many to become desperate beggars.

Once widespread in Europe and America, fistulas were eradicated by modern medical care early in the 20th century. They are still common in the developing world, however, where malnutrition and stunted growth make obstructed labour more likely, where cultural practices and poverty lead to early marriages and early pregnancies, and where health care is largely unavailable or extremely limited.

Young girls are often pressured to get pregnant soon after marriage and may face a variety of barriers to accessing contraceptive services. In spite of laws against early marriage in many countries, 82 million girls in developing countries will be married before they turn 18. Worldwide, some 14 million women and girls between 15 and 19 give birth each year.

Teenage pregnancies are risky, and the younger the girl, the higher the risk. Girls under 15 are five times more likely to die in childbirth than women in their twenties. Many of those who survive days of obstructed labour end up with fistula. Thus, delaying a girl's first pregnancy is a critical strategy for reducing fistula and maternal death, as well as an important public health issue.

Fistula is preventable, and also treatable through surgery that costs under $300. In 2003, the United Nations Population Fund (UNFPA) launched a Global Campaign to End Fistula in response to emerging evidence of the devastating impact obstetric fistula has on women's lives. The campaign involves a wide range of partners and currently operates in some 30 countries in sub-Saharan Africa and South Asia and in some Arab States. The long-term goal is to make fistula as rare in developing nations as it is in industrialized countries today.

The campaign works to prevent fistula from occurring, treat women who are affected and help women reintegrate into their communities once they are healed. In Niger, 600 community health agents have received basic training on fistula prevention. In Nigeria, 545 women have received surgery and dozens of doctors and nurses have been trained in fistula care. In Chad, hundreds of women have been taught new skills and received small grants following surgery through an income-generation project.

Each country that joins the campaign passes through three steps. First, national needs are assessed to determine the extent of the problem and the resources required. Next, a national response is formulated based on needs identified. Finally, programmes focusing on prevention, treatment and reintegration of cured patients into their communities are implemented.

See References, page 92.

injuries than adults, and they may be less aware of the risks involved in their occupations and place of work. Illnesses and injuries include punctures, broken or complete loss of body parts, burns and skin disease, eye and hearing impairment, respiratory and gastro-intestinal illnesses, fever and headaches from excessive heat in the fields or in factories. Although the numbers of illnesses and injuries from hazardous child labour are highest by far for children working in the agriculture sector – which employs two thirds of all working children – the incidence of injuries for children is highest in construction and mining. One boy in every four and more than one in every three girls working in construction suffers work-related injuries and illness; the corresponding incidences for mining are a little more than one in every six boys and one in every five girls.[39]

But it is not only injury, sickness and even death that children risk when involved in hazardous labour. They also often miss out on an education that would provide the foundation for future employment as an

Figure 3.4: Total economic costs and benefits of eliminating child labour over the period 2000-2020

	US$ billion, at purchasing power parity
Economic costs	
Education supply	493.4
Transfer implementation	10.7
Interventions	9.4
Opportunity costs	246.8
Total Costs	**760.3**
Economic benefits	
Education	5,078.4
Health	28.0
Total benefits	**5,106.4**
Net economic benefit (total benefits – total costs)	**4,346.1**
Transfer payments	213.6
Net financial benefit	**4,132.5**
(net economic benefit – transfer payments)	

Source: International Labour Organization, *Investing in Every Child: An economic study on the costs and benefits of eliminating child labour,* International Programme on the Elimination of Child Labour, ILO, Geneva, 2004.

adult in less dangerous occupations. As Figure 3.4 clearly attests, the net economic benefits of eliminating child labour, hazardous or not, for individuals and societies would heavily outweigh the economic costs.

The scale of the worst forms of child labour makes it an urgent issue for the Millennium agenda, especially in the area of education. Unless millions of children currently working in hazardous conditions are reached, the goals of attaining universal primary education (MDG 2) and gender parity in primary and secondary education (a key indicator for MDG 3) will not be reached. A key starting point will be to step up efforts to eliminate immediately the worst forms of child labour, as stipulated by the International Labour Organization's Convention No. 182. Education that is safe, accessible and of a high quality is the best way to encourage families to send their children to school and to prevent children from engaging in hazardous labour.

Exploitation of children

In the aftermath of the Indian Ocean tsunami that struck in late December 2004, there were fears that children, particularly those separated from their parents, were at risk of being trafficked and exploited. Protection measures were immediately adopted by international agencies and national governments to prevent widespread abuse. Nonetheless, incidents of exploitation were reported, including a growth in the recruitment of child soldiers. These incidents underline the increased vulnerability of children to exploitation when they are deprived of family protection.

Preventing the exploitation of children and bringing the perpetrators to justice is one of the most pressing issues on the international agenda, but one that is not being given sufficient attention. In particular, the trafficking of children – who are then often forced into commercial sex work, hazardous labour or domestic service – is a widespread aspect of the problem and merits special attention by both national governments and the international community. Children who are victims of exploitation are arguably among the most invisible, as their abusers will prevent them from accessing services even if these are made available.

Trafficking causes multiple rights violations for children

Trafficking of children takes many different forms. Some children are forcibly abducted, others are tricked and still others opt to let themselves be trafficked, seduced by the promise of earnings but not suspecting the level of exploitation they will suffer at the other end of the recruiting chain. Trafficking always involves a journey, whether within a country – from the rural areas to a tourist resort, for example – or across an international border. At the final destination, trafficked children become part of an underground world of illegality into which they effectively disappear.

The relocation takes children away from their families, communities and support networks, leaving them isolated and utterly vulnerable to exploitation. Often they are even

Figure 3.5: Forced commercial sexual exploitation

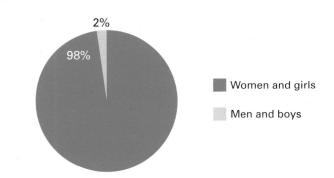

- Women and girls
- Men and boys

Source: International Labour Organization, 'A Global Alliance against Forced Labour', ILO, Geneva, 2005.

more disempowered by being transported to a place where they do not speak the local language, making it much more difficult for them to seek help or escape. Because they are there illegally and without documents, they may feel unable to trust the police or other officials or to access the rights of citizens that entitle them to services.

Trafficked children are also almost invisible to the eye of the statistician. Collecting data

© UNICEF/HQ01-0423/ Donna Decesare

Figure 3.6: Child labour* in the developing world

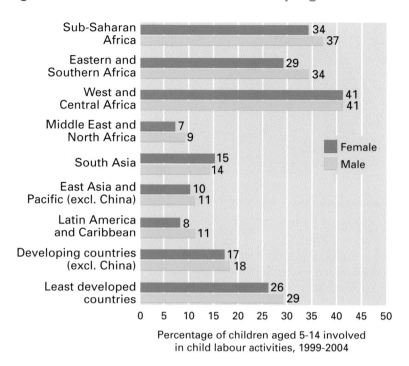

Percentage of children aged 5-14 involved
in child labour activities, 1999-2004

* Child labour: A child is considered to be involved in child labour activities under the following classification: (a) children 5 to 11 years of age that during the week preceding the survey did at least one hour of economic activity or at least 28 hours of domestic work; (b) children 12 to 14 years of age that during the week preceding the survey did at least 14 hours of economic activity or at least 42 hours of economic activity and domestic work combined.

Regional averages: These aggregates do not include all countries in each region. However, sufficient data was available for more than 50 per cent of the target population to generate the averages for the regions shown. Averages for East Asia and Pacific and the developing countries do not include China.

Data range: Data refer to the most recent year available during the period specified.
Source: Multiple Indicator Cluster Surveys (MICS) and Demographic and Health Surveys (DHS).

those countries affected by conflict, they can be directly abducted by militias.

- In East Asia and the Pacific, most trafficking is into child prostitution, though some children are also recruited for industrial and agricultural work. It is largely driven by poverty and especially by the pull of the wealthier countries in the region. Girls are also recruited as mail-order brides and for domestic service.

- In South Asia, trafficking forms part of the immense child labour problem in the subcontinent, often related to debt bondage, whereby a child is in effect 'sold' to pay off a debt, frequently a debt deliberately imposed by the exploiter with this in mind. In addition, significant numbers of children are trafficked for other purposes, including into prostitution, carpet and garment factories, construction projects and begging.

- In Europe, children are mainly trafficked from east to west, reflecting the demand for cheap labour and child prostitution in the richer countries of the continent. There are organized criminal gangs exploiting the open borders to channel children into unskilled labour, work in the entertainment sector and prostitution.

- In the Americas and the Caribbean, much of the visible child trafficking is driven by tourism and focused on coastal resorts, again feeding a demand for child prostitution and easily exploitable labour. Criminals who move drugs across borders are reportedly becoming involved in human trafficking as well.[41]

Often children trafficked into one form of labour may be later sold into another, as with girls from rural Nepal, who are recruited to work in carpet factories or hotels in the city, but are then trafficked into the sex industry over the border in India. In almost all countries, the sex trade is the predominant form of exploitation of trafficked children, a practice that entails systematic, long-term physical and emotional abuse.[42]

Children in forced labour and domestic service are among the most invisible

An estimated 8.4 million children work under horrific circumstances: They are

about these children is notoriously difficult. Although reliable global statistics are impossible to compile, it is estimated that trafficking affects about 1.2 million children each year.[40]

Though the trafficking of children is a shadowy practice with neither particular rules nor predictable sequences, some dominant regional patterns are identifiable:

- In West and Central Africa, the most common form of trafficking is an extension of a traditional practice – often a survival strategy – whereby children are 'placed' in marginal positions within other families. Increasingly, this practice is being used to exploit children's labour, both within and outside the home. Children are also trafficked into plantations and mines, and in forced into debt bondage or other forms of slavery, into prostitution and pornography or into participation in armed conflict or other illicit activities.[43]

According to the ILO, "forced labour is present in all regions and kinds of economy.... The offence of exacting forced labour is very rarely punished.... For the most part, there is neither official data on the incidence of forced labour, nor a widespread awareness among society at large that forced labour is a problem. It remains, with very few exceptions, one of the most hidden problems of our times."[44]

Debt bondage, whatever the origin of the debt, leaves children under the complete control of a landowner, entrepreneur or moneylender in a state little distinguishable from slavery. They may be making gravel in Latin America or bricks in South Asia, or quarrying stone in sub-Saharan Africa.[45] The work is often hazardous and much too heavy to be appropriate for children; the conditions of service betray every aspect and principle of human rights, let alone any conception of childhood.

Children in domestic service are also among the most invisible child labourers. Their work is performed within individual homes, removed from public scrutiny, and their conditions of life and labour are entirely dependent on the whims of their employer. The number of children involved in domestic service around the world is unquantifiable because of the hidden nature of the work, but it certainly runs into the millions. Many of these children are girls, and in many countries domestic service is seen as the only avenue of employment for a young girl, though in some places, such as Nepal and South Africa, boys are more likely to be domestic workers than girls.[46] Children exploited in domestic service are generally paid little or nothing over and above food and lodging. Many are banned altogether from attending classes or have such restrictions placed on their school attendance that it becomes impossible. All too often domestic service becomes a 24-hour job, with the child perpetually on call and subject to the whims of all family members.[47]

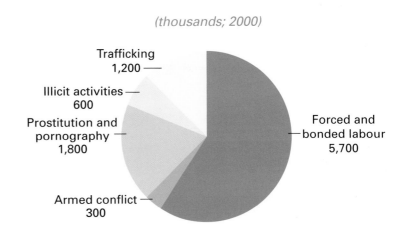

Figure 3.7: Children in unconditional worst forms* of child labour and exploitation

(thousands; 2000)

Trafficking 1,200

Illicit activities 600

Prostitution and pornography 1,800

Armed conflict 300

Forced and bonded labour 5,700

* Unconditional worst forms of child labour: These forms of labour correspond to those outlined in Article 3 of the International Labour Organization Convention No. 182.

Source: International Labour Organization, *Every Child Counts: New global estimates on child labour,* ILO, International Programme on the Elimination of Child Labour, Statistical Informational and Monitoring Programme on Child Labour, April 2002.

In addition, children in domestic service are especially susceptible to physical and psychological harm. Many are forced to undertake tasks that are completely inappropriate for their age and physical strength. The food they are given is often nutritionally inadequate, vastly inferior to the meals eaten by the employing family. In Haiti, for example, 15-year-old domestic workers were found to be on average four centimetres shorter and 40 pounds lighter than 15-year-olds not in domestic service in the same area.[48] Children frequently suffer physical abuse as punishment for a task performed at a lower standard than demanded or simply as a routine means of ensuring their submission. They are also at extreme risk of sexual abuse. Rapid assessment research in El Salvador found that 66 per cent of girls in domestic service reported having been physically or psychologically abused, many of them sexually, and that the threat of sexual advances from employers was ever present.[49]

Making children visible by creating a protective environment

All children have the right to grow up in a protective environment in which all elements work, individually and collectively, to secure them from violence, abuse and

The protective environment

The protective environment is made up of interconnected elements that individually and collectively work to protect children from exploitation, violence and abuse. While much of the responsibility for the creation of a protective environment lies with the government, other members of society also have duties. The key elements of the protective environment include:

- **Capacity of families and communities:** All those who interact with children – parents, teachers and religious leaders alike – should observe protective child-rearing practices and have the knowledge, skills, motivation and support to recognize and respond to exploitation and abuse.

- **Government commitment and capacity:** Governments should provide budgetary support for child protection, adopt appropriate social welfare policies to protect children's rights and ratify with few or no reservations international conventions concerning children's rights and protection. Ratification

of the two Optional Protocols to the Convention on the Rights of the Child would be an important demonstration of the commitment to protect children from armed conflict and exploitation.

- **Legislation and enforcement:** Governments should implement laws to protect children from abuse, exploitation and violence, vigorously and consistently prosecute perpetrators of crimes against children and avoid criminalizing child victims.

- **Attitudes and customs:** Governments should challenge attitudes, prejudices and beliefs that facilitate or lead to abuses. They should commit to preserving the dignity of children and engage the public to accept its responsibility to protect them.

- **Open discussion by civil society and the media:** Societies should openly confront exploitation, abuse and violence through the media and civil society groups.

- **Children's life skills, knowledge and participation:** Societies should ensure that children know their rights – and are encouraged and empowered to express them – as well as give them the vital information and skills they need to protect themselves from abuse and exploitation.

- **Essential services:** Services for victims of abuse should be available to meet their needs in confidence and with dignity, and basic social services should be available to all children without discrimination.

- **Monitoring, reporting and oversight:** There should be monitoring, transparent reporting and oversight of abuses and exploitation. Key to building the protective environment is responsibility: All members of society can contribute to protecting children from violence, abuse and exploitation.

See References, page 92.

neglect, as well as from exploitation and discrimination. Without this, children are at risk of being excluded and becoming invisible. Furthermore, the persistence of child protection abuses threatens to jeopardize every one of the MDGs *(see Panel: The links between child protection and the Millennium Development Goals, page 53).*

There are numerous obstacles to ensuring that children's right to protection is not violated. Traditional practices, lack of national capacity to administer programmes for even those children who are readily reachable and the absence of rule of law are just three examples of impediments to protecting children. Broad and systemic protection strategies are required to both prevent abuses and address the failures that occur.

In an ideal society, children are manifestly protected because all forms of violence, abuse and exploitation against them are considered socially unacceptable and because customs and traditions respect the rights of women and children. However, in the majority of countries and societies, this ideal is not yet fully in place. Article 5 of the Convention on the Elimination of All Forms of Discrimination against Women calls on all States parties to adopt measures that will help modify the social and cultural patterns of men and women, with the aim of eliminating prejudices and customary practices based on gender inequality and stereotypes. The recommendations of the Convention on the Rights of the Child also underline the importance of modifying social practices and patterns to safeguard children's rights.[50]

The links between child protection and the Millennium Development Goals

Millennium Development Goal	Child Protection Consideration
MDG 1: Eradicate extreme poverty and hunger	• **Child labour** squanders a nation's human capital. • **Armed conflict** depletes a nation's physical, economic and human resources and leads to the displacement of populations. • Accurate and complete **birth registration** information is a prerequisite for all economic planning to address poverty and hunger issues. • Poverty and exclusion contribute to **child abandonment** and to the overuse of formal and informal fostering arrangements or institutional care, leading to poor child development. • Legal systems that do not take into account the child's age and fail to promote reintegration into the community of **children in conflict with the law** increase the likelihood of their poverty and marginalization.
MDG 2: Achieve universal primary education	• **Armed conflict** disrupts education. • **Child labour** prevents children from attending school. • **Violence** is an obstruction to a safe and protective learning environment. • **Child marriage** leads to the removal of girls from school. • **Children without parental care** must be placed in an appropriate family environment to increase the likelihood they will receive an education.
MDG 3: Promote gender equality and empower women	• Girls are disproportionately engaged in **domestic work,** which compromises their school participation. • **Child marriage** leads to the removal of girls from school and may limit their opportunities to participate in the public life of their communities. • **Violence and harassment in schools** are obstacles to gender equality in education. **Sexual violence, exploitation and abuse** undermine efforts to empower women and girls.
MDG 4: Reduce child mortality	• **Violence** against children can lead to child mortality. • **Child marriage** and early childbearing lead to higher risks of maternal mortality and morbidity. • **Children separated from their mothers** at an early age, especially those who remain in institutional settings for long periods of time, are at greater risk of early death.
MDG 5: Improve maternal health	• **Child marriage** jeopardizes both maternal and infant health. • **Sexual violence** can lead to unwanted pregnancies and puts women at risk of HIV/AIDS infection. • **Female Genital Mutilation/Cutting** increases the chance of maternal mortality during delivery and complications thereafter.
MDG 6: Combat HIV/AIDS, malaria and other diseases	• Many of the worst forms of **child labour** are a cause and consequence of the HIV/AIDS pandemic. • **Sexual exploitation, abuse and violence** can lead to the infection of girls and boys. • Children in HIV/AIDS-affected families are particularly at risk of **losing the care and protection of their families.** • **Children in detention** are vulnerable to HIV infection, given the high rates of transmission in prisons.
MDG 7: Ensure environmental sustainability	• **Armed conflict** leads to population displacement and potential overuse of environmental resources. • Environmental disasters increase household vulnerability and increase the potential for **child labour**, as well as for sexual exploitation and child marriage.
MDG 8: Develop a global partnership for development	• **Child protection** requires inter-sectoral cooperation at the national and international level to create a protective environment for children.

See References, page 92.

In countries where these discriminating patterns have been challenged, the results have been significant. In Somalia, for example, following a study on sensitive child protection issues in which more than 10,000 children and adults participated, child protection coordination networks have been established in Bari, Nugal, Benadir, Lower Shabelle and Hiran regions, with similar initiatives now under way in other regions, including Somaliland. The networks have agreed on priority areas of focus for their work, such as improving the situation of street children, increased efforts to eradicate female genital mutilation and the protection of internally displaced children.[51]

Children may be able to reduce their own risk of exploitation when they know that they have rights and about the options they have to protect themselves against violations. Health workers, teachers, police

officers, social workers and others who work with children should be equipped with the motivation, skills and authority to identify and respond to child protection abuses. Parents and communities need to be provided with the tools and capacity to protect their children.

Monitoring systems that record the incidence and nature of child protection abuses and allow for informed and strategic interventions are also required. Such systems tend to be most effective when they are participatory and locally based. One such example is provided by Benin, where village committees have been set up to combat child trafficking. The first such committees were set up in 1999 in the area in the south most affected by trafficking, and there are now more than 170.[52] Among their activities are raising awareness about child protection issues among parents, children and the general population, reporting cases of abuse or disappearance and monitoring the reintegration of trafficked children when they return to the village. The committees provide an effective early warning system that genuinely strengthens children's protection by investigating when a child leaves the village and alerting the Juvenile Protection Squad, thwarting the transportation of many children to neighbouring countries.[53]

Another example of where evidence-based risk factors can be used to guide programming is seen in Moldova, where UNICEF has been supporting a life-skills education project for children growing up in residential care institutions. Research indicates that children in these institutions were several times more vulnerable to trafficking than the rest of the child population. The project uses participatory methods and a life-skills-based approach to raise children's awareness of the dangers of trafficking and build their capacity to understand and exercise their rights.[54]

Creating an environment that protects children requires ongoing and sustained efforts by individuals and organizations at all levels of the international community, from the family to the largest multinational corporation operating in the globalized economy. While families and governments bear the primary responsibility for ensuring that children are included in essential services and protected from harm, they require the support of others – civil society, donors, international agencies, the media and the private sector – to confront and stamp out abuses, challenge attitudes and prejudices and monitor and evaluate exploitation. The roles that these actors play, as discussed in Chapter 4, will be critical to ensuring that all children become visible, not only in official statistics, budgets, programmes and legislation, but also in their societies and communities.

Signing human rights treaties and passing progressive legislation by governments is critical but must be seen as only the beginning: To truly protect all children against violence, exploitation and abuse, behaviour and attitudes that devalue some children must be changed. A partnership across levels of society must be forged to ensure that each child's right to a protective environment is fulfilled, that impunity for abuses against children is challenged, and that each child has the opportunity to reach his or her full potential.

Making Every Child Count

The ability to prove age and nationality is key to guaranteeing a child's rights. Article 7 of the Convention on the Rights of the Child establishes the right of every child to a name and nationality, stipulating that boys and girls should be registered immediately after birth. Yet in many countries, birth registration is neither accessible nor affordable to large portions of the population.

A formal record of age may help to protect a child's right to a childhood. Children forced into the labour market, who serve as combatants or who enter into marriage take on adult roles. Unable to prove their age, unregistered children and those seeking to assist them often find it difficult to claim their rights as children or prove that these rights have been violated.

Birth registration guarantees the right to be counted in official statistics and acknowledged as a member of society. It also increases the chances that children from poor and marginalized families will be included in national-level planning and decisions. An accurate count of the number of children in a given community, village or region provides a basis on which to demand that resources be distributed to fulfill the rights of children and that proportionate basic services are available. Because those excluded from birth registration tend to be those who are excluded from other essential services, universal birth registration should be seen as the first step towards including all children.

Girls in rural areas are more likely to be married by age 18 than their urban peers

Peru
Viet Nam
South Africa
Togo
Egypt
Indonesia
Burkina Faso
Ghana
India
Tanzania, United Republic of

2 times as likely   3 times as likely

Source: Demographic and Health Surveys.

Protecting Childhood

Proportion of women aged 20-24 who were married or in union before their 18th birthday

⊘ 15% or less
⊘ 16% - 30%
⊘ 31% - 50%
⊘ 50% or more

Source: Demographic and Health Surveys, as reported in Statistical Table 9, pp. 130-131.

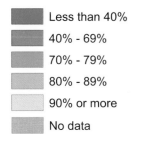

Proportion of children under 5 years of age who are registered:

- Less than 40%
- 40% - 69%
- 70% - 79%
- 80% - 89%
- 90% or more
- No data

Sources: Demographic and Health Surveys and Multiple Indicator Cluster Surveys, as reported in Statistical Table 9, pp. 130-131.

This map does not reflect a position by UNICEF on the legal status of any country or territory or the delimitation of any frontiers. Dotted line represents approximately the Line of Control in Jammu and Kashmir agreed upon by India and Pakistan. The final status of Jammu and Kashmir has not yet been agreed upon by the parties.

4

Including Children

The principles of universality and non-discrimination must govern our interventions for children

A human rights-based approach to development demands that every effort be made to reach all children without exception. The principle of universality, the foundation of all human rights treaties, and the related principle of non-discrimination (on the basis of race, colour, gender, language, opinion, origin, disability, birth or any other characteristic) as expressed in Article 2 of the Convention on the Rights of the Child, must apply to all actions to support, protect and care for children.

How can we reach the children who are the most vulnerable to ensure their inclusion in essential services and protect them from harm, exploitation, abuse and neglect? How can we ensure that we will know enough about them to guarantee their rights?

A 'business as usual' approach will never reach excluded and invisible children

The first answer is that they will never be reached through a 'business as usual' approach. Routine development initiatives pitched at the general population, aiming to include as many children as possible, risk failing to reach excluded and invisible children. Understanding their plight and the factors behind their marginalization, and then targeting initiatives towards these children, must therefore form an integral part of national strategies on child rights, development and well-being, as well as those on reaching the goals of the Millennium agenda. The disaggregation of indicators – by age, sex, household income, geographic area and other factors – permits the assessment of discrimination and inequality and is therefore essential for formulating policies and programmes that can reach the most disadvantaged children.

SUMMARY

ISSUE: Our commitments to children demand that every effort be made to reach them. But how can we reach those children living in the shadows? How can we ensure their inclusion in essential services and their visibility by protecting them from harm, abuse and violence and encouraging their participation in society? Three conclusions emerge:

- Understanding the plight of excluded and invisible children and the factors behind their marginalization, and then focusing initiatives on these children, must form an integral part of national strategies on child rights and development.
- The root causes of exclusion and the factors making children invisible must be directly addressed. Even well funded, well targeted initiatives for disadvantaged families and children risk failure if the overall conditions that foster poverty, armed conflict, weak governance, the uncontained spread of HIV/AIDS, inequalities and discrimination are not addressed.
- All elements of society must recommit to their responsibilities to children, including the creation of a strong protective environment.

ACTION: Governments bear the primary responsibility for reaching out to excluded and invisible children and need to step up their efforts in four key areas:
- **Research:** Strong research is essential to effective programming, but reliable data on these children is currently in short supply.
- **Legislation:** National legislation must match international commitments to children. Legislation that entrenches discrimination must be amended or abolished.
- **Financing and capacity-building:** Legislation and research on excluded and invisible children must be complemented by child-focused budgets and institution-building.
- **Programmes:** Service reform to remove entry barriers to essential services for excluded children is urgently required in many countries and communities. Packaging services can increase access, as can the use of satellite and mobile services for children in remote or deprived locations.

Other actors also have a role to play. Donors and international organizations must create an enabling environment through bold and well conceived policies on aid, trade and debt relief. Civil society must acknowledge its responsibilities to children and be part of the solution. The private sector must adopt ethical corporate practices that ensure that children are never exploited. The media can become a vehicle for empowerment by providing people with accurate information and by challenging attitudes, prejudices and practices that harm children. Finally, children themselves can play an active part in their own protection and that of their peers.

59

Second, the root causes of exclusion and the main factors that contribute to making children invisible must be tackled. Eradicating extreme poverty, combating HIV/AIDS, promoting conflict resolution, providing special assistance to and protection for children caught up in conflict, maintaining assistance to children in fragile States, and addressing discrimination on the basis of ethnicity, gender or disability would go a long way towards eliminating the background conditions that foster exclusion and invisibility.

The final requirement is that all duty bearers recommit to ensuring that no child is excluded and that all children are protected and made visible. The primary duty will inevitably fall upon national governments, since they bear the statutory responsibility for providing for and protecting their citizens. But all sectors of global society and national constituencies also have a part to play. Donors and international organizations must create an enabling environment through equitable policies on aid, development, debt relief and trade aimed at including the most impoverished and excluded countries, communities and groups. Civil society, in all its diversity, must acknowledge its responsibilities to children and be part of the solution. The private sector must

become a partner for human development by adopting responsible corporate practices and by ensuring that its actions do not harm or exploit children. The media must aid in empowering people by providing accurate information on the exclusion and invisibility experienced by children, and by scrutinizing and challenging behaviours and attitudes, prejudices and practices that harm them. Finally, children themselves should be able to play an active part in their own protection and empowerment – and that of their peers.

Research

Strong research is essential to effective programming

An assessment of capacities, vulnerabilities and needs is the first step in formulating appropriate responses targeted at reaching excluded and invisible children. However, reliable data on excluded and invisible children are usually in short supply, often because of significant practical difficulties for data collection. This inevitably complicates the development of evidence-based interventions.

Detailed situation analyses of the plight of these children, and its root and proximate causes, are vital complements to statistical

Statistical tools for monitoring the Millennium agenda for children

Measuring impact and progress is crucial to ensure that programmes and policies lead to the desired effects on the ground. By supplementing official national data, household surveys provide nationally representative information on the status of individual women and children, allowing for monitoring across a range of social stratifiers. As a result, international organizations, researchers and national governments often use household surveys such as the Demographic and Health Surveys – which gather information through questionnaires that can take from half an hour to an hour to administer. One household survey tool, the Multiple Indicator Cluster Surveys (MICS), was originally developed to measure progress towards the goals that emerged from the 1990 World Summit for Children. The first round of MICS was conducted around 1995 in more than 60 countries, with a second round of surveys five years later.

A third round of MICS was conducted in more than 50 countries during the year 2005. MICS-3 has collected information on some 20 of the 48 MDG indicators, offering the largest single source of data for MDG monitoring. In addition, the current round of MICS is also providing a monitoring tool for 'A World Fit for Children' compact, as well as for other major international commitments such as the United Nations General Assembly Special Session on HIV/AIDS and the Abuja targets for malaria.

Questionnaires

Household surveys are based on questionnaires that can be easily customized to the needs of a country. For example, the MICS consists of a household questionnaire, a questionnaire for women aged 15-49, and a questionnaire for children under the age of five (to be completed by the mother or other caregivers). The surveys contain many questions and indicators directly related to the causes and implications of a child being excluded or invisible, including birth registration, orphaned and vulnerable children, child disability, age of marriage and questions related to health, education, shelter, water and sanitation, HIV/AIDS and early child development. Each survey takes around an hour to complete, depending on whether optional modules are included, and the responses from each household provide crucial information for planners, programmers and policy makers.

Survey results

Results from the surveys, including national reports, standard sets of tabulations and micro level data sets, will all be made widely available after completion and collation. Survey results for most countries are expected to be completed by early 2006 and will be made available through DevInfo, a statistical database designed to monitor progress towards the Millennium Development Goals. DevInfo facilitates the presentation of data in tables, charts and maps to illuminate where disparities exist, making visible the factors of exclusion and the existence of those who might otherwise go unseen. Data can be accessed at the local level to improve the capacities of local authorities and civil society organizations to assess the situation of children, or databases can be compiled regionally or globally to allow for cross-country comparisons.

Mapping data trends geographically is an immensely useful tool for visualizing disparities across geographical regions. For example, a map can demonstrate the differences between the number of children registered in the capital city compared to the province in which it sits, or the number of girls in school across several provinces, indicating clearly where further efforts are required. Combining data collection, analysis and mapping technology allows researchers to create an evidence base for programmers to use in implementing the most efficient and effective programmes and ensuring that those most in need are identified.

See References, page 93.

information. Studies that are based on the direct experiences of individuals are particularly valuable. Lessons learned – often from the experiences of other countries and regions – can be integrated with accurate local knowledge, including the root causes of exclusion and of protection violations that make children less visible, to produce the most effective response. Monitoring and evaluation is also required to ensure that those most in need are being reached and to make adjustments over time as their situation changes.

Collecting accurate data and compiling qualitative studies on excluded and invisible children is clearly fundamental to the assessment process. Agreeing on definitions is often the first step towards gathering comparable data and information in areas where systematic research is in early stages. For example, the consensus around the Palermo Protocol definition of trafficking in 2000 provides a consistent basis for researchers, policymakers, legislators and programme developers across different contexts.[1]

Census and household surveys can be immensely useful in identifying factors that increase the risk of exclusion

The results of censuses or nationally representative household surveys such as the Demographic and Health Surveys (DHS) and Multiple Indicator Cluster Surveys (MICS) are being employed by governments and international agencies to construct a clearer picture of how disparities within countries affect children's quality of life. Statistical tools, such as multivariate analysis, can help uncover significant contributing elements to a particular material deprivation or protection violation such as non-registration at birth. They are increasingly used to identify factors that make some children vulnerable to exclusion and invisibility, and to pinpoint where interventions might be most effective. These analyses have shown, for example, that lack of education, particularly at the secondary level, plays a significant role in whether a girl will be married before 18, and whether, as a mother, her own children will attend school.[2]

While household surveys are immensely useful tools, they are limited in that some of the most excluded and invisible children and families will be left out – for example, nomadic tribes that have no formal abode, children living outside a household and internally displaced people. Despite these limitations, surveys can illuminate key risk factors that make a child particularly prone to exclusion from essential services. Survey designs should be continually strengthened to ensure that their coverage is as broad and inclusive as possible.

Using household survey data in tandem with qualitative information on the state and condition of children's lives will provide a more complete picture of exclusion in particular. Quantitative analyses often point to issues or geographical areas where more detailed and qualitative investigation is required. In this regard, pilot studies with small groups of excluded or invisible children and community-led surveys and consultations can make a valuable contribution to understanding the plight of the children hardest to reach.

Many gaps in data gathering and qualitative analysis remain that must be urgently addressed. Key examples include child trafficking, child labour and children caught up in conflict.

- **Child trafficking:** In the field of child trafficking, there is no single research methodology that is universally applicable and reliable, although the action against trafficking formulated by the Economic Community of West African States (ECOWAS) specifically includes expanded efforts to collect and share data.[3]

- **Child labour:** The International Programme on the Elimination of Child Labour (IPEC) of the International Labour Organization has successfully used rapid assessments to gain local snapshots, but these are not easily comparable across locations. In practice, information is gathered from multiple sources, and programmes tend to be quite small.[4]

- **Children caught up in conflict:** There has been a high pitch of international concern about child soldiers and other children caught up in conflict since the landmark UN report on the subject by Graça Machel in 1996.[5] But firm estimates on the number of child soldiers have been difficult to obtain. The latest approximations, announced in a statement from the then UN's Special Representative on Children in Armed Conflict, Olara Otunnu, to the UN Security Council Meeting on Children and Armed Conflict held in February 2005, suggest that over 250,000 children are currently serving as child soldiers.[6]

Lack of firm quantitative data is not an excuse for inaction by policymakers

While data collection and analysis are certainly important, it is also imperative to

Figure 4.1: Status of ratification of major international treaties*

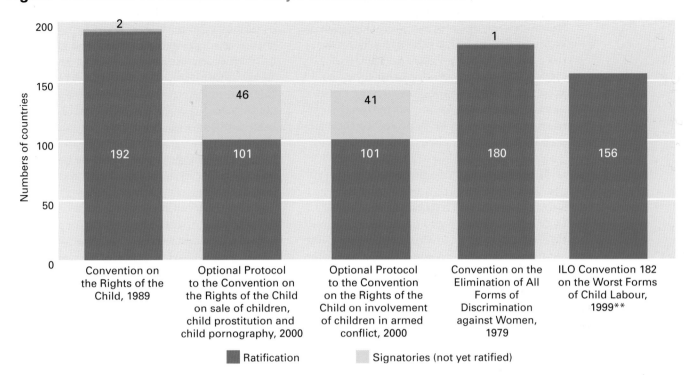

* As of September 2005
** The International Labour Organization (ILO) database includes lists of conventions ratified, non-ratified and denounced.
Sources: United Nations Treaty Collections Databases and ILOLEX of International Labour Standards.

take judicious action based on human rights principles in areas where quantitative data is still lacking. The absence of an updated estimate of the number of children involved in armed conflict, for example, is not a reason to delay programme development and expansion of capacity to address the known needs of those children, or for governments not to sign and ratify the Optional Protocol to the Convention on the Rights of the Child on the involvement of children in armed conflict. Efforts must proceed on simultaneous tracks, both to learn more about children who are excluded or less visible through quantitative research and through further and more detailed qualitative assessments of their situation and circumstances.

Enforcement, monitoring, evaluation and follow-up are also vital to ensure that legislative, programmatic and budgetary efforts effectively reach those they seek to benefit. Given the current dearth of knowledge on how to provide access to quality essential services for the most excluded and invisible

children and their families, it is important that any lessons learned from experience be scrupulously evaluated and documented. And because most strategies to reach such groups require special efforts over and above the norm, they require rigorous monitoring to ensure that the target group is being reached.

Legislation

National laws must match international commitments for children

The Convention on the Rights of the Child commits governments to guaranteeing the rights of all children. Ratification of this international convention, its Optional Protocols and other international legislation that protect the rights of children and women means little, however, unless their principles are enshrined in national law. This process of reforming national legislation to meet the standards established by the Convention on the Rights of the Child has been important in making more children visible.

In Latin America, for example, ratification of the Convention on the Rights of the Child has involved changing the prevailing legal doctrine of 'irregular situation', which was codified in legislation enacted across the continent in the 1920s and 1930s. Under this system, children could be accused of 'antisocial behaviour' or criminalized simply for having no material resources, and then be deprived of their liberty by a judge 'for their own protection'. The doctrine was clearly incompatible with the principles of universality and non-discrimination that undergird the Convention on the Rights of the Child. Legislative reform was initiated to eliminate this legal approach towards children. These changes are still in progress and have potentially profound implications for juvenile justice and social protection, and for keeping children visible.

In 2003, the Philippines adopted an act against trafficking in persons that incorporates into domestic law the Protocol to Prevent, Suppress and Punish Trafficking in Persons, Especially Women and Children, supplementing the United Nations Convention against Transnational Organized Crime. The law imposes higher sanctions for trafficking in children and includes provisions related to the rights of victims of trafficking by requiring the Government to make available appropriate social services for their recovery, rehabilitation and reintegration.

Legislation that entrenches or fosters discrimination must be altered or abolished

Many national laws exist that entrench and encourage exclusion. Among these are laws determining the legal age of marriage. In keeping with the spirit of the Convention on the Rights of the Child, an increasing number of national laws fix the minimum age for marriage at 18 – a threshold also suggested by both the Committee on the Elimination of Discrimination against Women and the UN Special Rapporteur on Violence against Women.[7] Yet the majority of nation states – including many industrialized countries – allow marriage at younger ages. Particularly discriminatory are national laws that enshrine a younger marriageable age for girls than for boys.

In other cases, new legislation is required to ensure that the rights of boys and girls are fulfilled. For example, at the end of 2004, Bangladesh passed the Births and Deaths Registration Act, marking the first time the country had recognized birth certificates as legal proof of age. As only 7 per cent of children in Bangladesh are registered at birth,[8] the change in law must be accompanied by capacity building, social mobilization and budgetary allocation to finance the registration of children if the law is to have the intended effect. The benefits of the legislation will facilitate the implementation of other laws requiring proof of age, such as issuance of passports, registration of marriage and the preparation of voters' lists. In addition, to ensure that the new legislation has positive outcomes for children, there is also the need to review other legislation – such as on education, marriage and labour laws – to guarantee compatibility.

Changing legislation is vital if entrenched prejudices are to be challenged

Positive examples from around the world show how legislation can improve the position of disadvantaged children and adults. Legislation on the rights of physically disabled people in industrialized countries, for example, has in recent years transformed their access to many public buildings and resulted in a more inclusive approach by schools. Antidiscrimination legislation enhances the rights of women and children. But enacting a law against discrimination – whatever the basis – is only a beginning, a necessary prerequisite that requires consolidation through rigorous monitoring, enforcement and active campaigning on behalf of the communities suffering the discrimination.

Traditional practices, although not entrenched in law, can also harm children and need to be addressed at the national level through legislation. Female genital mutilation/cutting (FGM/C) is one such practice. In countries where FGM/C persists, where governments have taken a strong lead, running public education campaigns and pointing out the appalling health risks involved, the incidence has been reduced – though, again, legislative direction from the top must be supported by active promotion by civil society and echoed by grassroots support.

The very strong lead taken by the Government of Burkina Faso over a 13-year period, for example, seems now to be making a difference. Burkina Faso started major public education campaigning against the practice in the mid-1990s and then formally outlawed FGM/C in 1996. Before the practice was outlawed, around two thirds of girls were being mutilated. The law stipulates that anyone performing FGM/C risks a prison term of up to three years, which can rise to 10 years if the victim dies of the procedure. A national telephone hotline that people can phone anonymously to report violations or when a girl is threatened with being cut was established. Strong advocacy and a clear legislative lead has succeeded in reducing the incidence of cutting of girls to 32 per cent, according to the latest UNICEF estimates.[9]

Domestic law reform, though necessary, needs to be supported by social policies, institutional changes and budget allocation to be truly effective in reaching excluded and invisible children. Changing legislation does not conclude the legal reform process, and attention must be paid to ensure that the institutions and capacity for implementation are established. Duty bearers must be made aware of the law, people should know their rights, and the mechanisms to implement and enforce them need to be established.

Financing

Legislation and research must be supported by budgetary allocations, institution building and reform

Stronger legislation and better and more extensive research on excluded and invisible children will mean little if the financial resources to implement and enforce new laws and policies are not forthcoming or inadequate to fulfil commitments to these children. Few countries currently incorporate a children's rights perspective into their budgetary processes – and few donors demand it when working with countries on

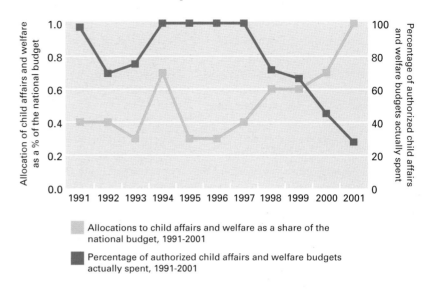

Figure 4.2: Budgeting for a child's right to protection and development* in Zambia, 1991-2001

Allocation of child affairs and welfare as a % of the national budget

Percentage of authorized child affairs and welfare budgets actually spent

Allocations to child affairs and welfare as a share of the national budget, 1991-2001

Percentage of authorized child affairs and welfare budgets actually spent, 1991-2001

* This is a composite spending area made up of budget programmes relating to children in institutional homes; children living or working on the streets; child sports and recreational activities; child labour interventions; and poverty reduction programmes aimed at guardians or parents of children.

Source: Institute for Democracy in South Africa and Save the Children Sweden, *Children and the budget in Zambia,* 2004.

poverty-reduction strategies or similar policy frameworks. Financing deficiencies may be the result of constraints on the overall resources available, lack of information and knowledge about demands for financial resources, practical obstacles in the budget process or lack of political will. In Zambia, for example, although the share of the national budget apportioned to children increased steadily in the decade preceding 2001, the percentage of these funds that was actually spent declined *(see Figure 4.2)* – suggesting a lack of capacity to implement programmes for children. Children, who lack a political voice, have limited ability to bring pressures to bear on national budgetary processes.

Child-focused budgets draw growing interest across the world

On a more optimistic note, there is growing worldwide interest in child-focused budgets. In most cases, this does not imply a children's budget separate from the main financial programme outlined by a government. Instead, it entails detailed and expert analysis of mainstream budget measures in order

Monitoring the effectiveness of budgets in meeting children's rights in South Africa

While monitoring government budgets is a relatively new area, experience is already showing how such analysis can uncover whether sufficient resources are being dedicated to realize children's rights and if they are being used effectively. One example is in South Africa, where the Children's Budget Unit of the Institute of Democracy in South Africa (IDASA) – an independent public interest organization committed to promoting sustainable democracy – focuses on conducting research of the government's budget and disseminating its findings.

In the initial phase of South African democracy, the Children's Budget Unit (CBU) tracked the government's ratification of the Convention on the Rights of the Child and the African Charter on the Rights of the Child. Since then the focus has shifted to how well the government is realizing these rights. In the first 10 years of democracy in the country, the CBU identified significant progress in South Africa in funding programmes to provide services to vulnerable children, including a child support grant for children up to 14 years old who pass an income-means test; primary school feeding plans to promote child nutrition; a programme to provide free basic health care for young children and pregnant mothers; a means-tested health-care

provision for all children; and a programme that identifies and assists children made vulnerable by HIV/AIDS.

The CBU also identified key areas where considerable work was needed, such as the underfunding of non-governmental organizations that deliver critical services to vulnerable children; the extension of the child support grant to cover children aged 15-18; the need to make clear the government's obligation in funding 100 per cent of statutory services; and the development of norms and standards for early childhood development.

The CBU has also assessed the 2005 budget, indicating the areas where it considers progress has been made and those where challenges remain. One positive focus of the budget was that it aims to strengthen economic growth, which the CBU indicates will help children by increasing the incomes of vulnerable families. It also allows for more direct investments in social infrastructure, social services and grants to address poverty and vulnerability at the household level, and additional investments in child-specific social services and grants. Despite these improvements, significant gaps remain. It was far from clear that additional funds allocated in the

budget for extending delivery of welfare services are sufficient for addressing the service needs of excluded children and their families. In particular, there was no new funding for non-governmental organizations, which puts increasing pressure on provincial budgets to make up shortfalls, and no mention of extending the child support grant to cover children 14-18 or clarification on the Government of South Africa's obligation to pay 100 per cent of statutory services for children.

Such analysis is extremely effective in outlining to governments and advocates for children's rights where further action and financial resources are urgently required. But effective budget analysis requires specialized skills and knowledge. Along with undertaking research on government budgets, the CBU also builds capacity in budget analysis. In partnership with four South African youth organizations, the unit is teaching and assisting young people from all walks of life to build their capacity to monitor local- and provincial-level budgets, empowering South African children to improve their own lives, both now and in the future.

See References, page 93.

to understand their specific impact on children and suggest methods for targeting the budget more accurately and effectively.[10]

Child-focused, targeted budgets inevitably depend upon gathering and processing accurate information. This was one of the main conclusions drawn by an in-depth study of social public expenditure targeted to children

in Peru between 1990 and 2003. The study found that children were essentially invisible as part of the budget process. The result was that no more than 25 per cent of the public budget was targeted to children rather than the 45 per cent that would have been appropriate given their presence in the population. In addition, the funds allocated did not reach the extreme poor, nor the most socially and geographically excluded, such as the children of the rural Sierra and the jungle. Children living in high-risk situations, on the streets or working in hazardous conditions were also, in effect, invisible to policymakers. The research team therefore designed a methodology for 'visualizing children', the starting point of which was not only gathering data effectively but also then processing the indicators. The methodology involved upgrading the use of information technology and training staff in the relevant institutions.[11]

There is also increasing interest in budget processes that involve children's participation. One of the best examples of this is the children's budget in the Brazilian city of Barra Mansa. The city has a children's participatory budget council of 18 boys and 18 girls who have the task of ensuring that the municipal council addresses children's needs and priorities. These representatives had previously been elected by their peers in their neighbourhood and district assemblies. This council determines how a proportion of the municipal budget – equivalent to around US$125,000 a year – is spent on addressing children's priorities, and its child councillors also participate in other aspects of government. The elected children learn how to represent their peers within democratic structures, to prioritize actions based on available resources, and then to develop projects within the complex and often slow political and bureaucratic process of city governance. Other cities in Latin America are being inspired to follow Barra Mansa's example as its success becomes better known. Among the other cities around the world that are experimenting with participatory budgeting for children are Córdoba in Spain, Essen in Germany and Tuguegarao City in the Philippines.[12]

Reaching excluded and invisible children will require greater and more targeted financing for services to support them

Including excluded and invisible children is likely to cost more money per child, largely because of the obstacles these children face. Programmes that are more narrowly and specifically targeted, through careful research and project design, are inevitably likely to cost more than general initiatives. It is also costly to expand existing initiatives

to meet the particular needs of these children. But the higher unit cost for extending a service to these children is justified on the grounds that they have benefited less than other children from past public expenditures on essential services. This is acknowledged by the Government of Namibia, which concluded that: "Marginalized children are entitled to their share of the educational budget. As they have been denied their educational rights earlier, the additional costs of including them must be accepted."[13]

The resources required to reach excluded children may also result from better targeting of public funds towards the priority needs and rights of children, harnessing the same amounts of money but directing them in a more cost-effective way. In South Africa, for example, a costing exercise of the Child Justice Bill projected its impact on various government departments, illustrating how savings generated by implementation of the bill, through reduced costs of legal representation due to decreased numbers of children going to trial, could be reallocated to ensure respect for the rights of children in conflict with the law. The bill expanded the legal mechanisms to avoid detention before trial by redirecting children to programmes that contained an element of restorative justice and increased the range of sentencing options, including alternatives to imprisonment.[14]

Budget initiatives can also serve to raise public awareness of discrimination. Developing Initiatives for Social and Human Action (DISHA), an Indian organization of tribal and forest workers in Gujarat, studies the codification of sectors, programmes and schemes in the state-level budget and analyses the levels of social expenditures in the poorest areas relative to other areas. The analysis demonstrated that these areas were being neglected, and the findings were disseminated in the local language and distributed to members of the legislature, the press, opposition parties and public-cause advocates. The government was encouraged to address the analysis of socio-economic conditions and expenditures in the tribal areas. The analysis led to increased allocations and expenditures in subsequent budgets.[15]

Photo credit (vertical, right margin):
© UNICEF/HQ00-0595/ Jose Hernandez-Claire

Capacity building

Capacity building empowers marginalized children, families and communities

Marginalized groups are often excluded from power within the political system. Removing the obstacles and strengthening their capacity for political participation is, therefore, a requirement for their inclusion. In Latin America, indigenous peoples are becoming increasingly involved in representing their own interests and defending their rights on the national political stage. Indigenous children and young people are playing an important role in countries like Venezuela, where the Fourth National Meeting of Native American Youth took place in the province of Amazonas in August 2003. The *Encuentro* involved 62 young people from 17 different indigenous groups who focused on cultural identity, identifying the key aspects of life for each indigenous group, and electing a new board of directors for the National Network of Native American Youth.

Building capacity at the local level is essential to the success of initiatives to further the rights of children. Communities play a significant role in identifying their most vulnerable children – and, where possible, in distributing the goods and services to them. In societies with strong traditional systems of mutual support, as in much of Eastern and Southern Africa, villagers may be able to reach out to orphans and other vulnerable children with relatively little help from outside. In Swaziland, for example, a system of volunteers provides protection, and emotional and material support. They intervene in cases of child exploitation and sexual abuse, provide comfort to victims, consult with relatives and sometimes talk to the abusers or inform the police.[16]

Programmes

Programmatic interventions are no substitute for addressing the root causes of marginalization and discrimination, or for creating a strong protective environment.

Nevertheless, there are many strategies that facilitate reaching children who are at risk of being excluded or suffering protection violations that must be enacted as interim solutions. These will respond to their immediate needs as well as pave the way for future action to reduce their exclusion in many dimensions.

One of these strategies is providing exemptions and subsidies for marginalized communities and families, including the adjustment of service standards in line with their particular situation. Direct subsidies or stipends to individual children and families have been offered to encourage children to attend school rather than be sent to work. In Brazil, for instance, families are paid a monthly stipend of about US$8 for each child who attends school under the National Programme for the Eradication of Child Labour.[17] School feeding programmes are another method often used to bring hard-to-reach children into the education system.

Removing entry barriers to essential services will encourage usage

Reform is often required to remove entry barriers to essential services. These barriers can include the failure to provide services in the local language, prejudice among staff, or the requirements to produce identity cards or proof of address in order to access services. For example, more than 85 per cent of Bolivians living in rural indigenous communities lack the official documentation that would allow them to inherit land, register their children in school or vote.[18] In countries with historical or current repression by the state, marginalized peoples might be reluctant to come into contact with government-related bodies. Lack of knowledge or trust and cultural distance may also prevent people from knowing that a service exists, what its benefits might be, or that it is free or affordable. Removing these barriers can be an effective strategy to reach and include marginalized children and families, as illustrated by the decision of the Government of the Dominican Republic in 2001 to eliminate the requirement for children to produce birth certificates in order to enter school.[19] Social mobilization campaigns to publicize

services and their benefits can spread accurate information about the available options.

Packaging services together increases access

Another way to make services more user-friendly is to package them, creating a single location where multiple services can be accessed. In southern Sudan, for example, child immunization programmes have been combined with campaigns to vaccinate cattle against rinderpest. This combination was particularly successful as young children typically lived in the cattle camps and the logistics of keeping the two different vaccines cold were similar.[20] In like manner, efforts to make schools the centre of communities by locating water points at schools both decrease the additional distance that girls must travel to get water and can help bring those girls to school.

Satellite and mobile services provide services to children in remote or deprived geographic locations

In some places, satellite services may be required as a stopgap measure until comprehensive services can be provided. In Sarawak, Malaysia, remote from the mainland, it is currently too expensive to maintain permanent health clinics. Health care on the island is provided through a combination of outreach and community-based services. Since the road network is poor, mobile health teams usually travel along the rivers or by air in a 'flying doctor' service that is complemented by village health assistants who are trained in first aid, health promotion, disease prevention, curative care and community development, with a particular focus on infant and child health. The Government provides incentives in the form of recognition certificates, logistical support and further training opportunities.[21]

Satellite and mobile facilities are often very important in reaching poor families or those living in remote areas, many of whom are currently excluded from essential services. The distance to services is often cited as the reason women give birth at home and children are not registered, taken to the doctor

The Child Rights Index: Assessing the rights of children in Ecuador and Mexico

In Ecuador and Mexico, national observatories focused on children and adolescents are working to ensure that the rights of children are met in practice. In both countries, the participation of different sectors of civil society has been an essential element in promoting a national consensus aimed at the universal fulfillment of child rights.

In 2001, Ecuador's *Observatorio por los Derechos de la Niñez y Adolesencia* (Observatory for the Rights of Children and Adolescents) took the first successful steps towards the establishment of the Child Rights Index, which measures the degree of fulfillment of rights to survival, health, adequate nutrition and an education during every phase in the lives of children and adolescents. The *Observatorio* recently led an effort to commit local elected authorities to implement actions that would raise the Child Rights Index in their communities.

In Mexico, the *Consejo Consultivo de UNICEF Mexico* (Advisory Board), composed of prominent citizens from various walks of life including the business community, academia, politics, media and entertainment, has been a key actor in sensitizing public opinion and mobilizing society around the issue of child rights, specifically through the construction and publication of the Child Rights Index. The Advisory Board, in partnership with UNICEF Mexico and the *Observatorio Ciudadano de Políticas de Niñez, Adolescencia y Familias* (Citizens' Observatory of Policies on Children, Adolescents and Families), an NGO, set up the index in 2004.

Since the challenges children face in their physical, emotional and intel-

Child Rights Indices in Ecuador and Mexico: Parameters employed to assess survival, health and education in early childhood

Rights	Indicators	Policy priorities
Early childhood (0-5 years)		
The right to survival.	Under-five mortality rate. Mortality rate of women from causes related to pregnancy and childbirth.	Guarantee universal access to maternal and child health care, including prenatal care and care during childbirth.
The right to a healthy and safe development.	Low weight for age.	Guarantee healthy residential environments, including decent housing, safe water and sanitation.
	Mortality due to malnutrition.	Guarantee universal access to good nutrition, including nutrition education for children and their families, as well as supplementary feeding programmes.
The right to intellectual and emotional development and the right to education.	Preschool non-attendance. Mother's education. Illiteracy rate in women over age 15.	Guarantee universal access to early education and stimulation, including information services and support for parents.

Note: The table is a compilation of indicators from the Mexican Child Rights Indicator and the Ecuador Rights of Children Indices related to the early childhood period of the life cycle.
Source: Child Rights Indices for Ecuador and Mexico.

lectual development vary with their age, the Mexican and Ecuadorian indices are sensitive to children's developmental stages. To account for the changing priorities in the fulfillment of children's rights, the indices are calculated for three developmental stages – early childhood (0-5), school-aged children (6-12) and adolescents (13-18).

The indices measure the extent to which the country is fulfilling the rights of children and adolescents in survival, health and education, and help reveal where social, economic or cultural barriers prevent the exercise of children's rights. They measure aspects of the welfare of children that are sensitive to changes in social spending and interventions, and summarize large amounts of information into one single measure to provide a comprehensive view of the situation. After compiling data from various sources, the indices convert all indicators to a scale of 0-10, with 0 representing the worst values of the indices for each indicator and 10 indicating that the right is being fully exercised by all children. A simple average is calculated for each right considered, and the final result is the average of the resulting figures.

The indices in Ecuador and Mexico provide a tool for society to measure and track progress over time. They also serve to identify disparities in children's well-being within the respective countries. According to the Mexican Child Rights Index, in aggregate terms there has been gradual improvement in the fulfillment of the rights of the country's children. The index stood at 4.68 in 1998, 5.25 in 2000 and 5.71 in 2003, with the majority of the states also showing improvement. But the index also illustrates wide disparities between states and points out that those with the lowest levels of fulfillment of rights also have the highest percentage of indigenous populations. Similarly low scores for provinces with the largest indigenous populations were observed in Ecuador, where the probability of children's rights remaining unmet, as measured by the index, was nine times higher in the impoverished provinces of Cotopaxi and Chimborazo than in Galápagos, the province with the highest score. Significant gaps were also observed between urban and rural areas. Overall, the index for early childhood showed improvement in Ecuador, increasing from 3.4 to 3.6 between 2002 and 2003.

By gathering official data and analysing and disseminating this information, the indices provide families and communities with an assessment of how well their children's rights are being fulfilled. The aim is that the public will be able to monitor the index's progress and advocate for public policies oriented towards universal guarantee of these rights.

To improve the index rating, governments must take swift and decisive action in partnership with families and communities, civil-society organizations, the media and the private sector. The union of their efforts is essential for ensuring the sustained application of public policies for reducing the number of preventable children's deaths, decreasing malnutrition and guaranteeing access to pre-school education for children. There are already a number of encouraging signs that such partnerships are forming. In the states of Michoacán and Zacatecas in Mexico, for example, the government has taken the initiative to launch a 'social dialogue for children', aimed at building broad-based consensus on goals for fulfilling child rights (including improvement of the index), and promoting the support of all sectors of society for concrete actions to achieve these goals.

In the province of Carchi in Ecuador, the index rose from 2.8 to 3.9 after actions were taken by a local assistance programme. The under-five mortality rate fell, and school enrolment in the first grade of basic education increased. The local programme was scheduled to be discontinued but, thanks to the positive impact it had on the situation of children and the timely intervention of the *Observatorio*, the government decided to give this type of initiative a permanent budget.

See References, page 93.

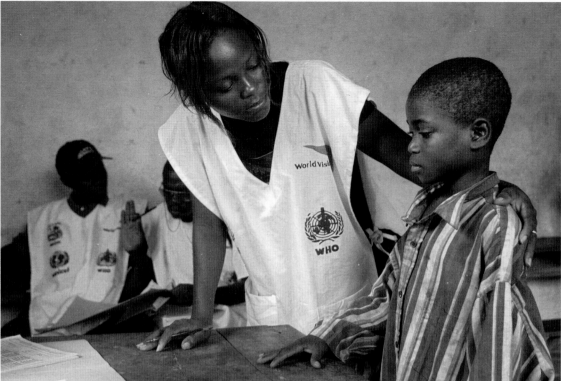

or immunized. Outreach efforts and door-to-door campaigns are effective strategies used for immunization that might be expanded to other areas. For example, UNICEF has worked with the Serbian Health Ministry and the Public Health Institute to send mobile teams to different parts of the country to identify and register unregistered children, and then to immunize them against major killer diseases, including tuberculosis, diphtheria, tetanus, pertussis (whooping cough), measles and polio.[22]

Civil society

The involvement of civil society will help to broaden the scope of interventions

'Civil society organizations' refers to a broad group of institutions and actors including, but not limited to, community-based organizations, non-governmental organizations, think tanks, social movements, religious organizations, women's rights movements, grassroots and indigenous people's movements, and voluntary organizations.[23] The United Nations has recognized the importance of engaging civil society in governance and development and has made it part of its reform process. The Secretary-General highlighted this impor-

tance in his report to the General Assembly in 2002, and the subsequent year he created a panel of experts to produce a set of practical recommendations on how the UN's relationship with civil society, as well as with the private sector and parliaments, could be improved. Since then, the engagement of civil society has been prominent on the UN agenda.

International non-governmental organizations (NGOs) play a vital role by bringing issues to the attention of governments and the global community and by providing large-scale programmes and projects. For example, Plan International has been responsible for a global campaign calling on governments to ensure all children are registered at birth. They have been working with local partners in more than 40 countries worldwide to boost the rates of child registration, with some major successes. In Cambodia, for example, Plan International's Mobile Registration Project, in partnership with the government and UN volunteers, has recently registered 1.5 million people in two months. It aims to register the whole population of some 13 million people in the coming year. In India, Plan International has successfully registered 3.2 million children in the state of Orissa alone.

Local civil society organizations can perform many tasks to assist excluded and invisible children

Civil society organizations composed of members of the local community are often in the best position within their communities to create development strategies that are tailor-made for the children who are hardest to reach. They can contribute to the inclusion of these children in a variety of ways, including situation analyses and public advocacy, policy design and scaling up service delivery, monitoring and evaluation, and fund-raising. In addition to these activities, civil society organizations play a key role in raising awareness in communities, challenging social taboos, promoting open discussion on important issues and ultimately changing public behaviour.

Professional associations are one area in which civil society organizations have been actively promoting children's rights issues. The Mutawinat Benevolent Company, an NGO of women lawyers in Khartoum, has for years offered free legal services to women and children, most of them internally displaced people living in extreme poverty. It has helped focus attention on the plight of women in prison – often with their children alongside them – and has worked to educate judges and police on the implications of the Convention on the Rights of the Child.[24] In a similar initiative in rural Nepal, community paralegal committees, made up primarily of women, monitor violence against women and children by facilitating the reporting of any incidents.[25]

The participation of religious leaders and organizations is vital to addressing sensitive issues related to children

Religion plays a central role in social and cultural life in most developing countries, and religious leaders and faith-based organizations are greatly respected and listened to. They are in a very strong position to raise awareness and influence behaviour. All over the world, religious leaders and organizations are working to combat the spread of HIV/AIDS, fight poverty and end harmful traditional practices such as female genital mutilation and cutting. They also advocate

for children's rights, such as the right to an education for all children.[26]

They do this through speaking out about these sometimes sensitive or taboo issues in their communities. Inter-religious councils in different regions provide a forum for discussion and creation of frameworks of action. Where religious leaders have acted to fight the spread of HIV/AIDS, particularly in partnership with national governments and NGOs, there have been significant successes in preventing HIV and alleviating the suffering from AIDS.[27]

For the past 21 years, the *Pastoral da Criança* (Children's Pastoral) project has been working to reduce child deaths and hunger in the poorest communities of Brazil and 14 other Latin American and African countries, relying on a huge network of some 240,000 volunteers. Supported by the Catholic Church, UNICEF and other organizations, the initiative received the King of Spain's first Human Rights Award in January 2005 in recognition of its innovative

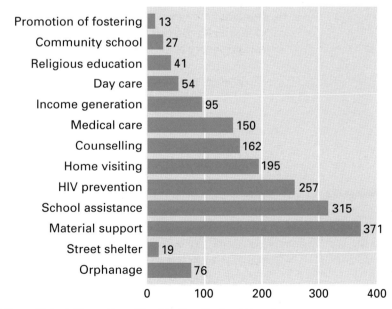

Figure 4.3: Main activities of faith-based organizations for orphans and vulnerable children in southern and eastern African countries*

* Kenya, Malawi, Mozambique, Namibia, Swaziland and Uganda.

Source: World Conference of Religions for Peace and United Nations Children's Fund, *Study of the response by faith-based organizations to orphans and vulnerable children,* January 2004.

efforts on behalf of children's rights.[28] Similar projects operate in other parts of the world. In Thailand, for instance, the Sangha Metta project has trained more than 3,000 Buddhist monks, nuns and novices to work with their communities in preventing HIV infection, providing support for families and prevent prejudice and discrimination. These efforts have had a marked impact on challenging stigmatization associated with HIV/AIDS, resulting in the integration of HIV-positive women and children into groups and schools from which they were previously excluded, and the return of children to the care of mothers living with HIV/AIDS.[29]

Civil society organizations can contribute to identifying and targeting priority areas and communities, designing effective implementation strategies, setting national and local budget priorities, and involving women and children in the design and implementation of these strategies. Because they have first-hand information on the needs and constraints at the local level, they make an invaluable contribution to the policy debate. Excluded children and their families often depend on grassroots organizations to make their concerns known in policy circles. A model of civil society engagement in policy design is offered by the Global Fund to Fight AIDS, Tuberculosis and Malaria. The fund calls for country-level partnerships including civil society organizations to submit grant proposals based on priority needs. Once grants are approved, these partnerships oversee programme implementation.[30]

Encouraging children to participate will also help to empower them

Children are not passive recipients of our charity or protection, but active citizens with rights who should be able to participate in their communities and societies. But, lacking a political voice or representation, children are easily left out of discussions on public policies. Policymakers should ensure that the views of all children, and those of excluded and invisible children in particular, are heard and taken into account. The fullest measure of our success in including marginalized children will be their participation, their new visibility. Participation of children should be

developed and supported in line with the evolving capacities of the children concerned.

The Global Movement for Children exists both to advance children's rights and to foster their participation, seeing the two as inseparable. Launched in the run-up to the UN General Assembly Special Session on Children in 2002, its participants ranged from international organizations to local children's groups. In 2005, representatives of the Global Movement published a report just before the G-8 summit to remind the leaders of the world's most powerful nations of their commitment to end child poverty. They stressed that this is a practical, achievable objective, an economic essential and a moral imperative.

In addition, under the Global Movement umbrella, thousands of children from 13 African countries – working in jobs ranging from domestic labour to shoeshining – published in 2005 the first results of a global survey by children of the world's progress in pursuing child rights. The report states that while there has been some progress in some areas on education and child participation, poverty is still endemic. It also recommends that children around the world work together to ensure that governments are held accountable for the promises they have made.[31]

Youth civil society organizations increasingly contribute to the policy debate through youth forums and parliaments. The Ethiopian Youth Forum, for example, has held seven sessions on a variety of issues, including street children, poverty reduction and youth, HIV/AIDS and, most recently, girls' education. In 2004, the Forum was involved in a child-to-child survey that mapped children out of school and advocated for getting them into school.

Child-to-child surveys in several countries have shown that children can be effective actors in the development process at the local level – and specifically in seeking out excluded or invisible children. In India, for example, the project asked children to draw a map of their village or neighbourhood, marking the houses containing children who do not go to school and including the numbers of girls and boys.[32] The map provided

vital information for local planners and promoted community awareness of both local disadvantage and the importance of education. Children were placed right at the centre of the process, enhancing their sense of empowerment as well as their education.

The media

The media has a unique and vital role in raising awareness and monitoring progress on commitments to children

Media professionals – journalists, writers, broadcasters and programme developers – are the eyes, ears and voices of society and have great influence on how children are visualized and portrayed. They can also help by putting children's rights squarely on the news and media agenda and drawing the attention of the general public and opinion makers to the violations of those rights, using their work to hold governments accountable. As the watchdogs of the public, the media has a unique role to play in ensuring that the rights of children are respected and that violators are brought to justice. Media scrutiny can provide public and independent monitoring of a government's progress towards keeping their commitments to children. Through their work, media professionals can shape public opinion and influence behaviour. They can encourage governments, civil society organizations and individuals to effect change that will improve the quality of people's lives.

Reporting on children's issues must be undertaken with sensitivity and understanding

Excluded and invisible children can often make compelling news stories – from street children to child soldiers – and there is enormous potential for the media to create a social climate that demands their inclusion. But not all media professionals take care to portray such children with the respect and understanding that is their due. The media can sometimes contribute to the exploitation of children – for example, by stereotyping them as powerless victims of abuse, conflict, crime and poverty, as perpetrators of crimes or as charming innocents. Combined with sensationalism, these limited representations can lead to exploitation of children who are experiencing rights violations – for example, by providing identifying details or failing to explore the child's capacities and strengths. Guiding principles such as those under-

UNICEF principles and guidelines for ethical reporting on children

Reporting on children and young people has its special challenges. In some instances the act of reporting on children places them or other children at risk of retribution or stigmatization.

UNICEF has developed principles to assist journalists as they report on issues affecting children. They are offered as guidelines that UNICEF believes will help media to cover children in an age-appropriate and sensitive manner, while respecting their rights under the Convention on the Rights of the Child. The guidelines are meant to support the best intentions of ethical reporters: serving the public interest without compromising the rights of children.

Principles

1. The dignity and rights of every child are to be respected in every circumstance.

2. In interviewing and reporting on children, special attention is to be paid to each child's right to privacy and confidentiality, to have their opinions heard, to participate in decisions affecting them and to be protected from the actuality or possibility of harm and retribution.

3. The best interests of each child are to be protected over any other consideration, including over advocacy for children's issues and the promotion of child rights.

4. When trying to determine the best interests of a child, the child's right to have their views taken into account are to be given due weight in accordance with their age and maturity.

5. Those closest to the child's situation and best able to assess it must be consulted about the political, social and cultural ramifications of any reporting.

6. Do not publish a story or an image that might put the child, siblings or peers at risk even when identities are changed, obscured or not used.

Guidelines for interviewing children

1. Do no harm to any child; avoid questions, attitudes or comments that are judgemental, that are insensitive to cultural values, that place a child in danger or expose a child to humiliation, or that reactivate a child's pain and grief from traumatic events.

2. Do not discriminate in choosing children to interview because of sex, race, age, religion, status, educational background or physical abilities.

3. No staging – do not ask children to tell a story or take an action that is not part of their own history.

4. Ensure that the child or guardian knows they are talking with a reporter. Explain the purpose of the interview and its intended use.

5. Obtain permission from the child and his or her guardian for all interviews, videotaping and, when possible, for documentary photographs. When possible and appropriate, this permission should be in writing. Permission must be obtained in circumstances that ensure the child and guardian are not coerced in any way and that they understand that they are part of a story that might be disseminated locally and globally. This is usually only ensured if the permission is obtained in the child's language and if the decision is made in consultation with an adult the child trusts.

6. Pay attention to where and how the child is interviewed. Limit the number of interviewers and photographers. Try to make certain that children are comfortable and able to tell their story without outside pressure, including from the interviewer. In film, video and radio interviews, consider what the choice of visual or audio background might imply about the child and her or his life and story. Ensure that the child would not be endangered or adversely affected by showing his or her home, community or general whereabouts.

Guidelines for reporting on children

1. Do not further stigmatize any child; avoid categorizations or descriptions that expose a child to negative reprisals – including additional physical or psychological harm – or to lifelong abuse, discrimination or rejection by their local communities.

2. Always provide an accurate context for the child's story or image.

3. Always change the name and obscure the visual identity of any child who is identified as:

   • A victim of sexual abuse or exploitation.

   • A perpetrator of physical or sexual abuse.

   • HIV-positive, or living with AIDS, unless the child, a parent or a guardian gives fully informed consent.

   • Charged or convicted of a crime.

4. In certain circumstances of risk or potential risk of harm or retribution, change the name and obscure the visual identity of any child who is identified as:

   - A current or former child combatant.
   - An asylum seeker, a refugee or an internally displaced person.

5. In certain cases, using a child's identity – their name and/or recognizable image – is in the child's best interests. However, when the child's identity is used, they must be protected against harm and supported through any stigmatization or reprisals.

Some examples of these special cases occur when children:

   - Initiate contact with the reporter, wanting to exercise their right to freedom of expression and their right to have their opinion heard.
   - Participate in a sustained programme of activism or social mobilization and want to be so identified.
   - Engage in a psychosocial programme and claim their name and identity as part of their healthy development.

6. Confirm the accuracy of what the child has to say, either with other children or an adult, preferably with both.

7. When in doubt about whether a child is at risk, report on the general situation for children rather than on an individual child, no matter how newsworthy the story.

See References, page 93.

pinning the Convention on the Rights of the Child, and frameworks such as UNICEF's Principles for Ethical Reporting on Children[33] should be used to ensure that the rights of children are both promoted and respected. In all cases, the best interests of the child should be of primary concern.

A good example of a holistic approach to improving the quality of reporting on children and youth is the Brazilian News Agency for Children's Rights (ANDI).[34] ANDI journalists monitor the media and publish league tables to show which publishers portray children in the most negative light. These tables have contributed to a gradual change in the tone of coverage, with publishers striving to occupy a better position in the league. In addition to monitoring, ANDI offers news guidelines and training for journalists and increases the visibility of social projects aimed at children. Journalist Friends of Children are given awards that have created incentives for sensitive coverage by improving the access that award winners have to children. The model is now being replicated in eight other Latin American countries.[35]

One way to improve the media presentation of children and to empower children in telling their own stories is to encourage their direct participation as programme developers and presenters. In Albania, reports by teenagers on the conditions in an orphanage led to changes in its administration.[36] This illustrates how the media itself, employed judiciously, can be a powerful tool towards helping children to protect themselves.

A constructive and supportive debate is needed on the issue of media images of children. Media organizations should consider appointing children's correspondents with responsibility for covering all aspects of children's lives. Media professionals and organizations need to educate themselves on methods of responsible reporting on children and their rights.

Partnerships with the media can enhance the effectiveness of campaigns

The media can also be used as a vehicle to educate the public on specific issues by

Child labour and corporate social responsibility: The UNICEF-IKEA project to combat child labour

An estimated 14 per cent of children aged 5-14 in India are engaged in child labour activities, including the production of goods, often inexpensive, for direct export by large multinational companies. Most of these children work in the informal economic sector, largely beyond the reach of institutional oversight and often in private homes doing subcontracted work.

What are the implications for corporations and their indirectly employed child labourers? Since the early 1990s, multinationals have begun to include anti-child-labour policies in their corporate codes of conduct. IKEA Group, the multinational that designs, manufactures and sells home furnishings, provides an example of how the private sector can do business in developing countries in a socially responsible manner by using the Convention on the Rights of the Child as a framework.

To ensure that no children are employed at any level of the supply chain, IKEA has specifically designed the 'IKEA Way on Preventing Child Labour', a code of conduct that applies to all its suppliers. The code requires that all contractors recognize the Convention on the Rights of the Child. In addition, to ensure compliance, IKEA employees make regular on-site visits to check that there are no children working on the premises, and unannounced inspections are made at least once a year by independent auditors. As a result, local suppliers who want to attract business have to comply with the corporate codes that are based on existing local and domestic laws concerning children and minimum employment age.

UNICEF and IKEA joined forces to implement this code of conduct in the state of Uttar Pradesh in India. In 2000, UNICEF developed Phase 1 of the Bal Adhikar-IKEA initiative, covering 200 villages where IKEA currently sources carpets. Uttar Pradesh accounts for an estimated 15 per cent of the country's working children. These children are largely employed in the informal sector, working within families or households. The carpet industry of Uttar Pradesh contributes approximately 85 per cent of India's carpet exports and is highly decentralized, with marginalized rural households constituting much of the weaving labour force.

The project has been expanded to 500 villages and is founded on the belief that child labour cannot be eliminated by simply removing a child from work, or terminating a multinational supplier's contract, as the child would simply move on to a different employer. The problem is tackled instead by addressing child labour's root causes, such as indebtedness in marginalized communities, adult unemployment,

bringing information directly to individuals. Television and radio are used in most societies to disseminate information and educate audiences. Media partnerships for education increase the effectiveness of these initiatives. The Global Media AIDS Initiative, an initiative of the UN, UNAIDS and the Kaiser Family Foundation, seeks to engage media companies to combat HIV/AIDS by incorporating messages on the pandemic into short- and long-form broadcasts.[37] More than 20 leading media executives from around the world have joined the initiative and have committed their companies to expanding public knowledge and understanding about HIV/AIDS.

The resources of the Internet are being used by national and international agencies, NGOs and other organizations to highlight the situation of excluded and invisible groups of children and to promote partnerships and action to fulfil their rights. Among these is the AIDS Media Center, a Web-based resource centre for media professionals that includes embargoed materials, contact information, background documents and multimedia materials to facilitate a dialogue between professionals. The Best Practice Media Resource Centre and Database now being established by the British Broadcasting Corporation (BBC) World Service Trust provides HIV/AIDS media materials and training. The BBC is also one of the few international broadcasters with a dedicated and regularly updated section on children's rights and issues on its website.

The private sector

Private-sector organizations, including trade organizations, chambers of commerce and other members of the business community, also have important roles to play in includ-

poverty and children's right to quality primary education.

To that end, IKEA and UNICEF use a two-pronged strategy that simultaneously reaches child labourers and their families. Women within the community, mothers in particular, are tasked with the creation of women's self-help groups. In the Phase 1 villages, 430 such groups, comprising 5,600 women, save about US$3,700 per month. This enables women to escape the exploitative interest rates of local moneylenders. Having their own funds, families are no longer forced to seek help from unscrupulous lenders when they need money to pay for medicines, their children's education, a wedding, or want to start their own businesses. When families are freed from indebtedness, they are less likely to send their children to work.

Children's educational needs are also addressed by both school enrolment campaigns and alternative learning centres. About 75,000 out-of-school children between 6 and 12 years old were identified through a house-to-house survey and brought into the formal school system thanks to these annual campaigns.

Alternative learning centres are a specific, time-bound strategy to reach excluded children, concentrating on 8- to 13-year-olds. With the objective of eventually integrating these children into the formal educational system, 103 alternative learning centres were opened in the Phase 1 villages. Since their inception, about 6,300 children have benefited from them, 4,980 of whom had graduated to the formal education system by June 2005. Efforts are under way to establish alternative learning centres in another 300 villages.

In mid-2002, IKEA, which was already supporting the Bal Adhikar-IKEA Child Labour Initiative in two blocks of the Jaunpur district of eastern Uttar Pradesh, took up the challenge to reach and protect every infant and pregnant woman in all 21 blocks of the Jaunpur district. Its goal was to achieve at least 80 per cent immunization coverage in the district by 2007 and to make it sustainable once external assistance is withdrawn.

IKEA's Add-on Routine Immunization Initiative has achieved immunization coverage of a total eligible population of 52,558 infants and 56,407 pregnant women living in seven blocks, comprising 1,126 villages, in Jaunpur district. With the state government supporting the Routine Immunization Initiative, it is expected that the remaining 14 blocks will be covered in phases over the four-year project cycle.

See References, pages 93-94.

ing children. They serve as partners in building a protective environment for children and by ensuring that their actions never cause children harm or allow them to be exploited. One of the most effective ways that private-sector organizations can do this is through corporate social responsibility, by establishing and abiding by codes of conduct, as well as creating awareness and training staff.

Corporations must ensure that their activities never contribute to excluding children or making them invisible

Recently, many companies have come to accept some form of corporate social responsibility: that they are accountable to all of their stakeholders in all their operations and activities, with the aim of achieving sustainable development not only in the economic dimension but also in the social and environmental dimensions. The publication of corporate social responsibility reports has brought the use of child labour to light and mobilized consumers to demand an end to rights violations. Pressure must continue to be exerted to ensure that hazardous child labour is eliminated, that fair work practices are implemented, and that corporations do not use outsourcing as a means to evade their responsibility to those who produce their profits.

A notable step in the protection of children all over the world was achieved in April 2004 with the launch of the Code of Conduct for the Protection of Children from Sexual Exploitation in Travel and Tourism. The Code of Conduct emerged as a result of collaboration between End Child Prostitution, Child Pornography and Trafficking of Children for Sexual Purposes (ECPAT) and private-sector groups in the

Film-makers shine light on the lives of excluded and invisible children

Film-makers are in a unique position to draw public attention to the plight of excluded and invisible children, and the need to speak for those children who do not have a voice was recently recognized by some of the world's most prominent directors. They collaborated with UNICEF, the World Food Programme and the Italian Government to produce seven short films presented as *All the Invisible Children* during the 62nd Venice Biennale Film Festival. The project aims to raise awareness of the need for a global commitment to help protect the rights of all children everywhere.

The eight directors involved with *All the Invisible Children* portray the lives of children from different regions of the world. Mehdi Charef depicts conditions in Burkina Faso; Emir Kusturica, Serbia and Montenegro; Spike Lee, USA; Katia Lund, Brazil; Jordan Scott and Ridley Scott, UK; Stefano Veneruso, Italy; and John Woo, China. Each episode focuses on children made invisible by poverty, violence, armed conflict, marginalization or HIV/AIDS.

The world of street children is the setting for three of the films. In Lund's short, two siblings scrape together a living by collecting cardboard and scrap metal in the streets of São Paolo, while Veneruso and Kusturica's films show children desperately stealing to get by in Naples and the Serbian countryside, respectively. Lee portrays the tragic story of an HIV-positive Brooklyn teenager facing torment and stigmatization from her peers. In Jordan and Ridley Scott's contribution, a war photographer retreats into reminiscences of his childhood to escape terrifying adult memories. Charef's episode

introduces us to the lives of child soldiers, who manipulate machine guns with practised ease, but who are starved of love and education. The collection ends with Woo's short, which examines the contrasting lives of a rich girl and a poor girl growing up in China.

The characters in *All the Invisible Children* represent millions of their silent off-screen peers: the tens of millions of street children, the hundreds of thousands of children caught up in conflict, the more than 2 million children under 15 living with HIV/AIDS, the many millions who are excluded and made invisible by these and other factors. "Children are being abused and forgotten all around the world, and I hope the film brings recognition to their plight," says Spike Lee.

Director Hanna Polak shares Lee's hope of raising awareness of forgotten children. Her Oscar-nominated documentary, *The Children of Leningradsky*, explores the world of homeless children in Moscow, where an estimated 25,000 to 30,000 children live on the streets. These children are vulnerable to alco and drug addiction, physical sexual abuse, HIV infection, v and exploitation. Polak believ portraying their stories is one tive way of helping them.

"As an individual, I can do on much for these children," she "By giving exposure to their p lems through film and having tell their stories, I hope to influ others to help as well. In fact, ing a film with this subject ma a very practical way to help.... Sometimes people ask me how film the harshest aspects of the

children's lives. The fact of the matter is that these aspects are very much a part of their realities. Without knowing this reality, how can someone become truly aware of their ongoing tragedy and be moved to help them?"

Despite the challenges in reaching the homeless children in Moscow, making the film was very rewarding for Polak and resulted in long-lasting friendships. Her investment is long term; she has established a foundation, Active Child Aid, which uses funds raised by the documentary and other means to help hundreds of children living in the streets.

For Polak, the biggest reward has been showing the children in her film that a different life is possible: "It is wonderful to see the children realize that they have alternatives, that they are not doomed to a life spent on the streets."

DON'T FORGET

coop   WIN-WIN

UNICEF   directors
- publicity   → publicity
about organization   for films
& issues
↳ raise public
awareness

tourism industry.[38] ECPAT is an alliance of organizations working to eliminate the commercial sexual exploitation of children, with Special Consultative Status with the United Nations Economic and Social Council. The Code commits the hotel and travel industry to establishing ethical corporate policies against the commercial sexual exploitation of children, training personnel in countries where children are sexually exploited and providing information on the sexual exploitation of children to travellers.[39]

In the Philippines, the non-governmental organization Coalition Against Trafficking in Women Asia Pacific uses various educational tools to change the sexual attitudes and practices of boys and men that result in the sexual exploitation of women and children in communities known for prostitution.

The way forward

Bringing invisible children out of the shadows and creating inclusive societies requires that all members of the global community – in all their myriad roles – work to ensure that no child is forgotten. International agencies, donors, governments, civil society, the media and the private sector must all take responsibility for the inclusion and protection of children. The principles of the Convention and recommendations of the Committee on the Rights of the Child must be more consistently integrated into development strategies.

Governments must make sure that their laws promote the rights of children and that they are allocating sufficient resources towards ensuring the quality of life of the next generation of citizens, particularly those who have been excluded from receiving social benefits and services. Civil society organizations can provide a forum for the voices of directly affected peoples to be heard. The private sector has made some important strides towards greater corporate social responsibility with regards to children, although continued work and vigilance is required. The media plays a significant role in bringing excluded and invisible children into the light, challenging all to act. Respect for the views of children must be promoted within the family, schools and institutions.

Demographic Challenges

Thirty-eight per cent of the world's population is under the age of 18. In the 50 least developed countries, children account for half of the population. In 91 countries, the proportion of inhabitants under the age of 18 will increase between now and 2015 – the deadline for achieving many of the Millennium Development Goals.

Changes in demographic composition present policy challenges. It is imperative that resources are made available to meet the needs of growing numbers of children in many locations. Individuals' needs vary during their life cycle, and early investment in the next generation is essential for any poverty-reduction strategy to succeed.

Urbanization poses additional challenges as more children are concentrated in large cities throughout the developing world. While population rates are declining, the increased size of urban populations will require significant attention to ensure that children of the urban poor do not miss out on essential services and protection. Simultaneously, attention must be paid to confronting and reversing the inequities faced by rural children.

Strategies being implemented towards achieving the MDGs, as well as forward-looking initiatives that aim to improve the adult lives of the present generation of children, will need to take these demographic trends into account. Children comprise a large, disenfranchised population with limited voice in government decision making. Therefore, it is imperative to ensure that their needs are prioritized in legislation, policies, programmes and, most importantly, resource allocation.

Proportion of the population living in urban areas in the 10 countries with the largest child populations

16%	Ethiopia
25%	Bangladesh
28%	India
34%	Pakistan
40%	China
47%	Indonesia
48%	Nigeria
76%	Mexico
80%	United States
84%	Brazil

Source: Derived from data from the United Nations Population Division as reported in Statistical Table 6, pp. 118-121.

Our Common Future

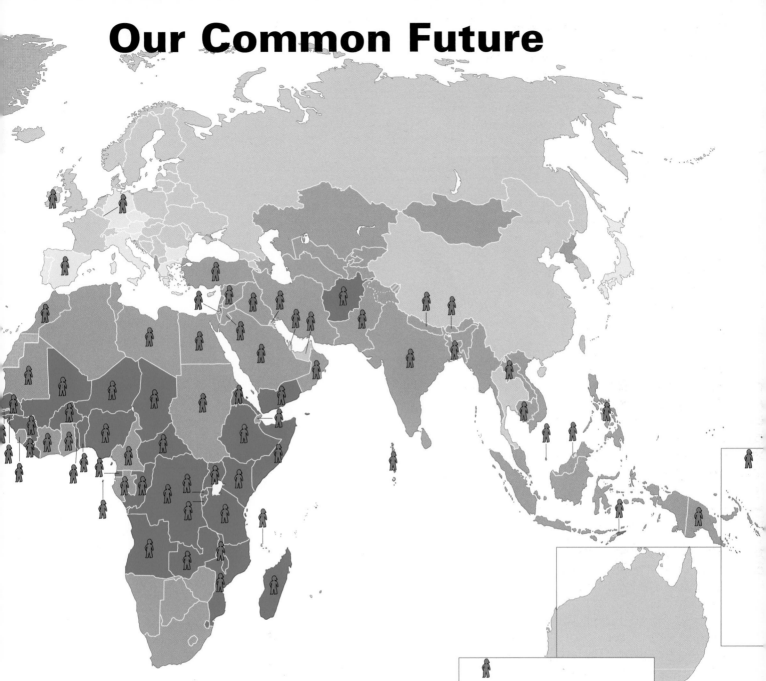

Proportion of the population under the age of 18

	10% - 19%
	20% - 29%
	30% - 49%
	50% or more
	No data

Source: Derived from United Nations Population Division, 2005 as reported in Statistical Table 6, pp. 118-121.

Countries in which the population of children will be larger in 2015

Source: Derived from United Nations Population Division, 2005.

This map does not reflect a position by UNICEF on the legal status of any country or territory or the delimitation of any frontiers. Dotted line represents approximately the Line of Control in Jammu and Kashmir agreed upon by India and Pakistan. The final status of Jammu and Kashmir has not yet been agreed upon by the parties.

Working Together

An unprecedented opportunity

Let us consider a scenario – one in which the world has gone that extra mile to ensure that children, regardless of the country in which they live, their household income, gender, ethnicity or location, have access to essential services and are protected. Countries have made the efforts to reach the last 5 or 10 per cent of children who had been excluded or invisible and are, in many cases, the hardest to reach. Every single child is in school, with all the empowerment and protection against abuse that this implies. Every child is immunized against the main killer diseases, benefiting from the new vaccines currently considered too expensive to be offered to all.[1] No infant loses their life for want of a few simple, inexpensive doses of oral rehydration salts. No child is locked away from the world in a workshop, labouring in conditions approaching slavery.

The benefits of such a world accrue not only to the children but to the whole of humanity. Premature death or debilitating diseases become altogether less of a drag upon the momentum of development. The despair of extreme poverty and the disruption and destruction wreaked by conflict are markedly reduced. Economies benefit as workforces become healthier and more skilled, more adaptable to the challenges of technology and modernity. Democratic systems become more vibrant and sustained as more literate, informed voters demand to have an active voice in the decision-making processes in their countries and keep corruption and authoritarianism in check. Above all, the energy and creativity of children and young people can be channelled into their own development and into their full, active participation in society instead of dissipated in a desperate struggle to survive.

This would indeed be a world fit for children. It may seem impossibly far away, but

SUMMARY

ISSUE: Creating a world fit for children may seem impossibly far away, but achieving it is as simple as this: We must do everything in our power to keep our commitments to children. These commitments are clear and unambiguous. What is now required is the understanding that a commitment is a pledge with both moral and practical obligations. In a moral sense, a commitment signifies a relationship of duty. In practical terms, a commitment binds those making it to a course of action. This was implicitly recognized at the Millennium Summit in 2000, which translated fine words and noble aspirations into time-bound development objectives in the Millennium Declaration – against which the world's leaders undertook to be measured and held accountable.

ACTION: The Millennium agenda for children is eminently attainable. What is needed now is firm and decisive action on three key fronts over the next 10 years.

- **Meet the Millennium Development Goals:** At the September 2005 World Summit, world leaders reaffirmed their commitment to meet the Millennium Development Goals by 2015. Achieving the MDGs must be the first step towards providing universal access to essential services, protection and participation for children. Those countries falling behind on the goals must redouble their efforts, with ample support from donors and international agencies, while those currently on course must strive to go beyond the goals to meet the challenge of eliminating disparities in children's health, education and development.
- **Reach out to the excluded and the invisible:** Our commitments to children demand that we reach out to those most in need of care and protection – the poorest and the most vulnerable, the exploited and the abused. We must confront unpalatable truths about the many disparities and abuses suffered by excluded and invisible children within our countries, societies and communities, and across borders, and do our utmost to eliminate them.
- **Work together:** Making this possible will require more than political will or well intentioned strategies. No government, agency or organization can meet any of the goals by itself; the Millennium agenda will not be achieved without effective, creative and consistent partnerships. We must all not only acknowledge our responsibility to be part of the solution, but also be ready and willing to work together on behalf of children. We must be their partners – seeking to empower them as well as to include and protect them, with the knowledge that realizing the Millennium Declaration's vision of a world of peace, equity, tolerance, security, freedom, respect for the environment and shared responsibility depends on ensuring that no child is excluded or invisible. The children of the world, especially those who so often miss out on the opportunities they need to grow and thrive, are counting on us.

© UNICEF/HQ03-0374/ Ami Vitale

genome to comprehending the origins of the universe – could it really be impossible during the next 10 years to banish child hunger or to keep children from dying of something as easily preventable as diarrhoea?

Reaching all children depends on creative and effective partnerships

Making this possible will require more than political will or well-intentioned strategies. No government, agency or organization can achieve these goals by itself; the Millennium agenda will not be realized without effective, creative and consistent partnerships. Partnering means working in solidarity, not just theoretically but practically. And it requires, as the United Nations Secretary-General's report on enhancing cooperation between the UN and all relevant partners outlines, "voluntary and collaborative relationships in which all parties agree to work together to achieve a common purpose or undertake a specific task and to share risks, responsibilities, resources, competencies and benefits."[3]

There are thousands of people and organizations working on behalf of children around the world, each with its own focus, strength and orientation. But a growing global constituency is uniting around the Convention on the Rights of the Child, the Millennium Declaration, the Millennium Development Goals and 'A World Fit for Children'. Only by pooling strengths can we create a movement with a global voice and political weight that reflects the depth and breadth of these commitments. The children of the world, especially those who so often miss out on the opportunities they need to grow and thrive, the excluded and the invisible, are counting on us.

The concept of partnership is fundamental to UNICEF, whose history provides a powerful illustration of how people and organizations working together, sharing resources and building on one another's ideas can create synergies that produce larger – and more effective – results than might otherwise be imagined. In its founding resolution from the General Assembly,[4] UNICEF was charged to work with relief and child welfare organizations, relation-

it is as simple as this: We must do everything in our power to keep our commitments to children. These commitments are clear and unambiguous. What is required now is the understanding that a commitment is a pledge with both moral and practical obligations. In a moral sense, a commitment signifies a relationship of duty. In practical terms, a commitment binds those making it to a course of action. This was implicitly recognized at the Millennium Summit in 2000, which translated fine words and noble aspirations into time-bound development objectives in the Millennium Declaration – against which the world's leaders undertook to be measured and held accountable.

Politics has been described as the art of the possible. The wonder of the Millennium agenda is that politicians and international organizations have embraced the pledge to make it possible – by 2015 – for every child in the world to complete primary schooling, to cut child mortality rates by two thirds and maternal mortality rates by three quarters, and to not only halt, but send into retreat HIV/AIDS, malaria and other major diseases. In a world with a global economy worth US$60 trillion[2] and rising, all these goals and the other aims of the Millennium agenda are eminently attainable. As humanity continues to push through the frontiers of knowledge, and science advances further every day – from mapping the human

UNGEI: Making the goal of gender equality in education a reality

The majority of the 115 million children out of school are girls. Sustainable development and the eradication of poverty will only be achieved with quality education for all girls and boys alike. A 'business as usual' approach is not an option if universal primary education and gender equality in education are to be achieved by 2015. Since girls face much greater obstacles, additional efforts are needed to get them in school and ensure that they complete their education. One such effort is the United Nations Girls' Education Initiative (UNGEI).

Launched at the World Forum on Education for All in Dakar, Senegal, in April 2000, this global movement for girls' education is an unprecedented partnership that embraces stakeholders and actors at all levels. The movement is being convened by UNICEF and encompasses a broad spectrum of partners who share the same commitment, including governments, UN agencies, donors, development agencies, NGOs, civil-society organizations, the private sector, religious groups, parents, teachers, communities and student organizations.

Rather than creating separate mechanisms and programmes, UNGEI's working principles are based on coordination, pooled resources and strategic alliances that create the synergy needed for maximum impact of girls'

education interventions. UNGEI advocates at global, regional and country levels to influence decision-making and investments that ensure gender equity and equality in national education policies, plans and programmes. The partnership mobilizes resources for projects and country programmes as well as large-scale initiatives targeted at the education system. Its efforts complement and are integrated into existing development structures such as poverty-reduction strategies, sector-wide approaches and United Nations development assistance frameworks.

Making UNGEI work at the country level

Strong partnerships and effective participation in sector-wide processes are required to bolster girls' education at the national level. This process begins with the creation of an UNGEI task force within a country to articulate the importance and effectiveness of its projects and programmes in achieving gender parity in education. UNGEI's plan of action for girls' education includes multiple interventions and initiatives to engage the government and local partners in planning, implementing, monitoring and evaluating programmes and projects.

National strategies to narrow the gender gap in education and to ensure all children obtain their right to quality basic education fall into

two major categories: targeted and systematic interventions.

- Targeted interventions are usually small scale and focus on particular population groups, geographic regions or specific areas of the education system. They often are piloted by civil-society organizations with stand-alone or coordinated funding mechanisms. Targeted interventions may also be large-scale projects that are conducted nationally or across multiple sites within the country.

- Systematic interventions are usually larger in scale and are designed to influence the education system and to serve most population groups. They are frequently joint projects between donor agencies and governments and are usually implemented countrywide or regionally.

Engaging partners is essential to achieving gender equality in education. UNGEI partners work together on targeted and systematic interventions with the goal of building national capacity rather than creating parallel structures. Partner agencies strive to be transparent and realistic about their comparative advantages. Each partner aims to be clear on what it has to offer the initiative, based on its strengths and resources.

See References, page 94.

ships that have been instrumental in sharing information, raising funds and contributing to policy decisions to benefit the world's children. National Committees for UNICEF were established to partner with civil society. In the 1960s, NGOs influenced UNICEF policy decisions related to maternal and child health, education and nutrition. And in the 1970s, it was UNICEF's civil-society

partners who pushed for an International Year of the Child (IYC) – an idea that eventually resulted in the proposal for the Convention on the Rights of the Child. With the firm establishment of children's rights, UNICEF took on the challenge of moving beyond charity-based partnerships – seeking out children and their families as partners and rights-holders to be empowered

KELAS VI.C

and enabled in making their capacities and vulnerabilities known and acted upon.[5]

As part of the United Nations, UNICEF is engaged in the reform process that is redefining the ways UN agencies will work together at all levels to improve the effectiveness and efficiency of the organization. This reflects a new and growing recognition throughout the world that development must involve all actors to be truly effective and sustainable. Boldness and speed are required to strengthen existing partnerships, build new ones and create new mechanisms of accountability. Time is of the essence, not only because the deadline for the Millennium Development Goals is only a decade away, but because millions of children today will miss out on a childhood if we do not act now.

The lives of excluded and invisible children will depend on the actions we take now

Effective partnerships will provide the foundation for achieving the Millennium agenda, which will bring a marked improvement to the lives of millions of children and is a step towards our ultimate aim: creating a world in which every child enjoys a childhood – protected, cared for and loved by their parents, families and communities. This is

possible, but only with the support of national and global partners working together to ensure that children's needs are met and their rights protected under all circumstances. Links between partners will be strengthened as each actor responds to the challenge – from government leaders establishing budgets to voluntary agencies working in slums, from the media as they influence social priorities to communities caring for their children, and from entrepreneurs showing social responsibility to the children themselves, whose talents and energies are just waiting to be released.

It is a bitter irony that the children most at risk of being bypassed by the global march against poverty and disease, illiteracy and exploitation are those whose rights are most abused and undervalued. It is time to reach out to them – not just to those already living on the margins but also to future generations. We must be their partners – not only seeking to include and protect them but also to empower them – with the knowledge that realizing the Millennium Declaration's vision of a world of peace, equity, tolerance, security, freedom, respect for the environment and shared responsibility depends on ensuring that no child is excluded or invisible.

REFERENCES

CHAPTER 1

[1] The term 'childhood' refers to the state and condition of a child's life. The ideal childhood is one where a child's rights under the Convention on the Rights of the Child are fully respected and fulfilled. For a fuller discussion on childhood, see United Nations Children's Fund, *The State of the World's Children 2005*, New York, 2004, Chapter 1.

[2] United Nations, *Millennium Declaration*, New York, 2000, Articles 2, 6.

[3] Derived from Statistical Tables 1, 6, pp. 98-101, 118-121.

[4] United Nations General Assembly, 'A World Fit for Children', New York, October 2002, p. 2.

[5] Ibid., pp. 15-17.

[6] UNICEF projections based on data in Statistical Tables 1-10, pp. 95-137. Notes on the methodology employed can be found in the technical note on this page.

[7] United Nations Millennium Project, *Investing in Development: A practical plan to achieve the Millennium Development Goals*, Earthscan, London/Sterling, VA, 2005, pp. 66-67; United Nations, *In Larger Freedom: Towards development, security, and human rights for all*, Annex, 'For Decisions by Heads of States and Government', New York, 2005; and United Nations, '2005 World Summit Outcome', A/60/L.1*, New York, 20 September 2005, pp. 9-10.

CHAPTER 1 PANELS

Defining exclusion and invisibility of children

[a] Saunders, Peter, 'Can Social Exclusion Provide a New Framework for Measuring Poverty?', *SPRC Discussion Paper No. 127*, Social Policy Research Centre, University of New South Wales, Sydney, October 2003, p. 6.

[b] Atkinson, Tony, 'Social Exclusion, Poverty and Unemployment' in *Exclusion, Employment and Opportunity*, edited by A. B. Atkinson and John Hills, Centre for Analysis of Social Exclusion, London School of Economics, *CASE Paper 4*, London, January 1998, pp. 13-14.

CHAPTER 1 FIGURES

Technical note: The implications for children of meeting the Millennium Development Goals

Figures 1.1 - 1.3 assess progress towards the Millennium Development Goals for five key indicators related to children's well-being and attempt to quantify the potential benefits for children of achieving the MDGs by 2015. The tables explore:

- How many children would benefit between now and 2015 if the MDGs are met (Fig. 1.1.)

- The number of years it will take to meet MDG 4, which aims to reduce under-five mortality by two thirds of its level in 1990, if current trends continue (Fig. 1.2.)

- How many children will miss out if the MDGs are not achieved and current trends continue (Fig. 1.3)

The methodology for projecting progress begins by calculating the current rates of progress towards the goals based on baseline country estimates for 1990 and 2004, or the years closest to these for which data is available, assuming linear progress between the two points.

The *current trends scenario* is calculated by extrapolating these trends to 2015, and then applying population projections relevant to each MDG indicator – e.g., projected birth rates (MDG 4) – to calculate the number of children reached in each category.

The *MDG scenario for 2015* is calculated by projecting the rate of progress required to meet the MDG target – e.g., a reduction in under-five mortality by two thirds from the 1990 rate by 2015 – and interpolating between 2004 and 2015. The number of children reached by meeting the goal is calculated by applying this trajectory to the relevant population indicator.

Calculating the benefits to children of achieving the MDGs and the costs to children of not achieving the Goals

Figure 1.1. The benefits to children of meeting each of the five MDG indicators assessed are calculated by subtracting the estimated number of under-five deaths, children under five who are moderately or severely underweight, children out of primary school, and children without access to improved water and sanitation in 2004 from the respective estimates under the MDG scenario for 2015.

Figure 1.2. The year in which MDG 4 will be achieved on current trends is calculated by extrapolating the current trends scenario until the global under-five mortality rate for developing countries is reduced to two thirds of its 1990 level.

Figure 1.3. The costs of continuing on current trends, thereby failing to achieve the MDGs by 2015, are calculated by subtracting the number of children reached under the MDG scenario for each indicator from its corresponding value under the current trends scenario.

Indicator specific notes

Under-five mortality: Current trends in the global under-five mortality rate (per 1,000 live births) for 1990 and 2004 are calculated from population-weighted national rates and then extrapolated to 2015. Linear interpolation between 2004 and 2015 is used to derive the rate of reduction required to reduce the rate of under-five mortality by two thirds from its 1990 level by 2015. Both of these estimates are then multiplied by projected birth rates from the United Nations Population Division to calculate the number of under-five lives lost based on the current trends scenario and those lives of under-fives lost under the MDG scenario.

Underweight: Current trends are calculated from population-weighted national rates of under-five malnutrition for 1990 and 2004, or the closest years to these, which are extrapolated to 2015. Linear interpolation between 2004 and 2015 is used to derive the rate of reduction required to halve the global rate of under–five malnutrition from its 1990 level by 2015. The number of children reached under each scenario is calculated by applying these trajectories to the estimated under-five population in 1990, 2004 and 2015.

Primary school attendance: Current trends are derived by applying the estimated rate of progress for 1980-2001 to the net attendance ratio for 2004 and extrapolating to 2015. The MDG scenario is calculated as the rate of increase required from 2004 to reach 100 per cent attendance by 2015. The number of children reached under each scenario is calculated by applying these trajectories to the estimated number of primary school-age children in 2004 and 2015.

Access to improved water and sanitation: Current trends calculated from baseline estimates for 1990 and 2002 are interpolated to 2004 and subsequently extrapolated to 2015. Linear interpolation between 2004 and 2015 is used to derive the rate of reduction required to halve the number of under-18s without access to improved water sources or sanitation from 1990 levels by 2015. The number of children reached under each scenario is calculated by applying these trajectories to the estimated under-18 population in 1990, 2004 and 2015. Calculations assumed that the proportion of children under 18 with access to improved water source or sanitation is the same as the general population (analysis of a number of data sets showed that the difference is very small).

CHAPTER 2

1 For a fuller discussion on the threats posed to childhood by poverty, conflict and HIV/AIDS, see United Nations Children's Fund, *The State of the World's Children 2005*, UNICEF, New York, 2004, p.10.

2 International Labour Organization, International Programme on the Elimination of Child Labour, 'Combating Child Labour Through Education', ILO/IPEC, Geneva, April 2004, p. 5.

3 United Nations, Department of Public Information, 'The Millennium Development Goals Report 2005', UN, New York, May 2005, p. 6.

4 United Nations Children's Fund, *The State of the World's Children 2005*, op. cit., pp. 20-22.

5 Derived from Statistical Table 1, p. 98-101.

6 Derived from Statistical Tables 1, 5, 6, pp. 98-101, 114-117, 118-121.

7 United Nations Children's Fund, *The State of the World's Children 2005*, op. cit., pp. 45-46.

8 Derived from Statistical Table 5, pp. 114-117.

9 'Fragile' States are defined in this report as states whose governments are unable or unwilling to deliver core functions to the majority of its people, including the poor. (Department for International Development, DFID, 2005). Generally, one common way to estimate the level of fragility is derived from the World Bank's 2004 Country Policy and Institutional Assessment (CPIA), Overall Rating, Fourth and Fifth Quintiles.

10 United Nations Millennium Project, *Investing in Development: A practical plan to achieve the Millennium Development Goals*, Earthscan, London/Sterling, VA, 2005, p. 113.

11 Derived from Statistical Table 5, pp. 114-117.

12 Joint United Nations Programme on HIV/AIDS, United Nations Children's Fund and the United States Agency for International Development, *Children on the Brink 2004: A joint report of new orphan estimates and a framework for action*, Population, Health and Nutrition Information Project for USAID, Washington, D.C., July 2004, p. 7.

13 Derived from Statistical Table 4, pp. 110-113.

14 Joint United Nations Programme on HIV/AIDS, United Nations Children's Fund and the United States Agency for International Development, *Children on the Brink 2004*, op. cit., p. 14.

15 Derived from the Joint United Nations Programme on HIV/AIDS and World Health Organization, *AIDS Epidemic Update*, UNAIDS/WHO, Geneva, December 2004, p. 1.

16 Huang, Rui., Lilyan E. Fulginiti and E. Wesley F. Peterson, 'Investing in Hope: AIDS, life expectancy, and human capital accumulation', Paper prepared for presentation at the Meetings of the International Association of Agricultural Economists, Durban, South Africa, August 2003, Abstract, p.1.

17 Derived from the Joint United Nations Programme on HIV/AIDS, *2004 Report on the Global AIDS Epidemic*, Geneva, June 2004, p. 93, and the Joint United Nations Programme on HIV/AIDS and World Health Organization, *AIDS Epidemic Update*, op. cit., p. 1.

18 UNICEF calculations based on data from the Demographic and Health Survey (DHS) and Multiple Indicator Cluster Surveys (MICS).

19 United Nations Children's Fund, *Progress for Children: A report card on gender parity and primary education*, Number 2, UNICEF, New York, April 2005, p. 6.

20 Ibid., p. 7.

21 United Nations Millennium Project, *A Home in the City: Task force report on improving the lives of slum dwellers*, Executive Summary, Earthscan, London/Sterling, VA, 2005, p. 10.

22 Ibid., pp. 16-17.

23 United Nations Children's Fund, *Progress for Children*, op. cit., p. 4.

24 Ibid., p. 8.

25 United Nations Population Fund, *State of the World Population Report 2004. The Cairo Consensus at Ten: Population, reproductive health and the global effort to end poverty*, UNFPA, New York, 2004, pp. 34-35.

26 United Nations Development Programme, *Human Development Report 2004: Cultural liberty in today's diverse world*, Oxford University Press for UNDP, New York, 2004, p. 27.

27 NGO/UNICEF Regional Network for Children, Central and Eastern Europe, the Commonwealth of Independent States, The Baltics, 'Leave No Child Out Campaign, Fact Sheets', RNC, 2003, p. 7.

28 United Nations Development Programme, *Human Development Report 2004*, op. cit., pp. 32-33.

29 United Nations Children's Fund, 'Ensuring the Rights of Indigenous Children', *Innocenti Digest No. 11*, UNICEF, Innocenti Research Centre, Florence, 2004, p. 7.

30 Ibid., p. 7.

31 Ibid., pp. 7-10.

32 Ibid., Box 9, p. 9.

33 Ibid., pp. 9-10.

34 Ibid., p.10.

35 Ibid., p. 9.

36 Ibid., p. 9.

37 Ibid., p. 11.

38 United Nations Education, Scientific and Cultural Organization, *EFA Flagship Initiatives*, UNESCO, Paris, 2004, p. 19.

39 NGO/UNICEF Regional Network for Children, 'Leave No Child Out Campaign', op. cit., pp. 18-19.

40 United Nations Children's Fund, *Progress for Children: A Report card on immunization*, Number 3, UNICEF, New York, September 2005, p. 7.

41 World Health Organization, *Nutrition for Health and Development. A global agenda for combating malnutrition*, Progress Report, WHO, France, 2000, pp. 14-15.

42 International Campaign to Ban Landmines, *Landmine Monitor Report 2003: Toward a mine-free world*, Executive Summary, Human Rights Watch, New York, August 2003, p. 53.

43 United Nations General Assembly and Economic and Social Council, 'Implementation of the Programme of Action for the Least Developed Countries for the Decade 2001-2010', Report of the Secretary-General, May 2005, A/60/81-E/2005/68.

44 Otunnu, Olara A., 'Special Comment' on Children and Security, *Disarmament Forum*, No. 3, United Nations Institute for Disarmament Research, Geneva, 2002, p. 2.

45 United Nations Children's Fund, *The State of the World's Children 2005*, op. cit., pp. 56-57.

CHAPTER 2 PANELS

Income disparities and child survival

a Derived from Statistical Table 1, pp. 98-101.

b UNICEF calculations based on data from the Demographic and Health Survey (DHS) and Multiple Indicator Cluster Surveys (MICS).

c United Nations Millennium Project, Task Force on Hunger 2005, *Halving Hunger: It can be done*, Earthscan, London/Sterling, VA, 2005, p. 18.

d United Nations Children's Fund and World Health Organization, *Immunization Summary 2005: A statistical reference*, UNICEF/WHO, New York, February 2005, p. vii.

The marginalization of Roma communities and their children

a Ringold, Dena, Mitchell A. Orenstein and Erika Wilkens, *Roma in an Expanding Europe: Breaking the cycle of poverty*, The International Bank for Reconstruction and Development/The World Bank, Washington, D.C., 2003, p. 12.

b Ibid., pp. 19-20.

c United Nations Development Programme, *The Roma in Central and Eastern Europe: Avoiding the dependency trap*. A Regional Human Development Report, UNDP, New York, 2002, Table 8, p. 47.

d Ringold, et al., op. cit., Box 1, p. 9.

e United Nations Development Programme, *Roma in Central and Eastern Europe*, op. cit., pp. 53-62.

f International Step by Step Association, Open Society Institute, *School Success for Roma Children*, Step by Step Special Schools Initiative, Interim Report, Open Society Institute, New York, 2001, p. 4.

g Ibid., p. 4.

h Ibid., pp. 15-16.

i Proactive Information Services, 'Transition of Students: Roma Special Schools Initiative - Year 4, Final Evaluation Report', prepared for the Open Society Institute, New York, February 2004.

Living with disability

a Osteogenesis Imperfecta Federation Europe, Factsheet, http://www.oife.org.

b Russell, Marta, *Beyond Ramps: Disability at the end of the social contract*, Common Courage Press, Monroe, ME, 1998.

Global Campaign on Children and AIDS

a Joint United Nations Programme on HIV/AIDS, *AIDS Epidemic Update*, op. cit., p. 1.

b Derived from the Joint United Nations Programme on HIV/AIDS, *2004 Report on the Global AIDS Epidemic*, UNAIDS, New York, June 2004, p. 15.

c Barnett, Tony and Gabriel Rugalema, 'HIV/AIDS' in 2020 Focus 5, *Health and Nutrition: Emerging and Reemerging Issues in Developing Countries*, Brief 3, International Food Policy Research Institute, Washington D.C., February 2001.

d Joint United Nations Programme on HIV/AIDS, *Children on the Brink 2004*, op. cit., p. 8.

CHAPTER 2 FIGURES

Figure 2.4 'Fragile' states are among the poorest

'Fragile' States are defined in this report as States whose governments are unable or unwilling to deliver core functions to the majority of their people, including the poor. (Department for International Development, DFID, 2005). The list of countries with weak policy/institutional frameworks is derived from the World Bank 2004 Country Policy and Institutional Assessment (CPIA), Overall Rating, Fourth and Fifth Quintiles. It includes Angola, Burundi, Cambodia, Central African Republic, Chad, Comoros, Congo, Democratic Republic of the Congo, Côte d' Ivoire, Djibouti, Eritrea, Gambia, Guinea, Guinea-Bissau, Haiti, Kiribati, Lao People's Democratic Republic, Mauritania, Nigeria, Papua New Guinea, Sao Tome and Principe, Sierra Leone, Solomon Islands, Sudan, Tajikistan, Togo, Tonga, Uzbekistan, Vanuatu, Zimbabwe.

CHAPTER 3

[1] United Nations Children's Fund, *The 'Rights' Start to Life: A statistical analysis of birth registration*, UNICEF, New York, 2005, p. 3.

[2] Ibid., p.1.

[3] United Nations Children's Fund, 'Birth Registration: Right from the Start', *Innocenti Digest No. 9*, UNICEF Innocenti Research Centre, Florence, March 2002, p. 1.

[4] United Nations Children's Fund, *The 'Rights' Start to Life*, op. cit., p. 1.

[5] Derived from Statistical Table 9, pp. 130-131.

[6] Ibid., pp. 130-131.

[7] United Nations Children's Fund, *The 'Rights' Start to Life: A statistical analysis of birth registration*, op. cit., Table 2, p. 29.

[8] Derived from Statistical Table 9, pp. 130-131; and United Nation's Childrens Fund, 'Birth registration: Right from the start', op. cit., p. 10-12.

[9] Office of the United Nations High Commissioner for Human Rights, *2004 Global Refugee Trends: Overview of refugee populations, new arrivals, durable solutions, asylum-seekers, stateless and other persons of concern to UNHCR*, UNHCR, Geneva, June 2005, p. 2.

[10] Norwegian Refugee Council, *Internal Displacement: Global Overview of Trends and Developments in 2004*, Global IDP Project, Geneva, 2004, p. 9.

[11] United Nations Children's Fund, 'UNICEF and Displacement: A guidance note', UNICEF, Department of Emergency Operations, New York, 2005, p. 2.

[12] Norwegian Refugee Council, *Internal Displacement*, op. cit., p. 23.

[13] United Nations Children's Fund, 'UNICEF and Displacement', op. cit., p. 2.

[14] Executive Committee of the High Commissioner's Programme, 'Agenda for Protection', UNHCR, June 2002, EC/52/SC/CRP.9/Rev.1.

[15] The formal definition of an orphan used here is a child under 18 who has lost at least one parent. A single orphan is a child who has lost one parent, while a double orphan has lost both parents. Joint United Nations Programme on HIV/AIDS, *Children on the Brink 2004*, op. cit., p. 7.

[16] Ibid., p. 7.

[17] Ibid., p. 7.

[18] Kifle, Abiy, 'Ethiopia, Child Domestic Workers in Addis Ababa: A rapid assessment', International Programme on the Elimination of Child Labour, International Labour Office, International Labour Organization, Geneva, July 2002, p. 19.

[19] Musingeh, A.C.S., et al., 'HIV/AIDS and Child Labour in Zambia: A rapid assessment', Paper no. 5, International Programme on the Elimination of Child Labour, International Labour Office, International Labour Organization, Geneva/Lusaka, 2003, pp. vii-viii.

[20] Consortium for Street Children, 'Street Children FAQs',http://www.streetchildren.org.uk/street_children.

[21] United Nations Children's Fund, *The State of the World's Children 2003*, UNICEF, New York, 2002, p. 37.

[22] Casa Allianza, 'Exploitation of Children – A Worldwide Outrage', Casa Allianza, Worldwide Statistics, September 2000, p. 1.

[23] Consortium for Street Children, 'Street Children FAQs', op. cit.

[24] United Nations Children's Fund, 'Factsheet: Child Protection', UNICEF, New York, 2004.

[25] Committee on the Rights of the Child, [Report of] 37th Session, 13 September to 1 October 2004, Geneva, 2004, p. 8.

26 United Nations, 'Violence Against Children in Conflict with the Law: A thematic consultation for the United Nations Secretary-General's Study on Violence Against Children', UN, Geneva, 4-5 April 2005, p. 4.

27 United Nations General Assembly, 'Convention on the Rights of the Child', New York, 1989, Preamble.

28 United Nations Children's Fund, *The State of the World's Children 2005*, op. cit., pp. 41, 44.

29 Ibid., p. 44.

30 Save the Children, 'Forgotten Casualties of War: Girls in armed conflict', Executive Summary, London, April 2005, p.1.

31 United Nations Children's Fund, *Early Marriage: A harmful traditional practice*, UNICEF, New York, 2005, p. 4.

32 Ibid., Table 2, p. 32.

33 Assani, Aliou, 'Etudes sur les mariages précoces et les grossesses précoces au Burkina Faso, Cameroun, Gambie, Liberia, Niger et Tchad', UNICEF Abidjan, 2000. Cited in United Nations Children's Fund, *Early Marriage: Child spouses, Innocenti Digest No. 7*, UNICEF, Innocenti Research Centre, Florence, 2001, p. 2.

34 United Nations Children's Fund, *Early Marriage: Child spouses*, op. cit., p. 2.

35 United Nations General Assembly, 'Convention on the Elimination of All Forms of Discrimination against Women', New York, 1979, Article 16.

36 United Nations Children's Fund, *Early Marriage: Child spouses*, op. cit., p. 11.

37 Ibid., p. 11.

38 International Labour Organization, International Programme on the Elimination of Child Labour, Statistical Information and Monitoring Programme on Child Labour, *Every Child Counts: New global estimates on child labour*, Summary of Highlights, ILO/IPEC/SIMPOC, Geneva, 2002, pp. 8, 12.

39 Ashagrie, Kebebew, 'Statistics on Working Children and Hazardous Child Labour in Brief', International Labour Organization, Geneva, April 1998, pp. 8-12.

40 International Labour Organization, *A Future Without Child Labour*, ILO, Geneva, 2002, p. 32.

41 International Labour Organization, *Unbearable to the Human Heart: Child trafficking and action to eliminate it*, ILO, Geneva, 2002, pp. 14-15.

42 International Labour Organization, International Programme on the Elimination of Child Labour, 'Nepal, Trafficking in Girls with Special Reference to Prostitution: A rapid assessment', Executive Summary, ILO/IPEC, Geneva, 2001, pp. 24, 42.

43 International Labour Organization, *Every Child Counts*, op. cit., pp. 8, 12.

44 International Labour Organization, *A Global Alliance against Forced Labour*, op. cit., p. 17.

45 International Labour Organization, *A Future Without Child Labour*, op. cit., p. 31.

46 International Labour Organization, International Programme on the Elimination of Child Labour, *Helping Hands or Shackled Lives? Understanding Child Domestic Labour and Responses to It*, ILO/IPEC, Geneva, June 2004, p. 20, footnote 25.

47 Ibid., pp. 12, 51.

48 Ibid., p. 51.

49 Organización Internacional del Trabajo, Programa Internacional para la Erradicación del Trabajo Infantil, El Salvador, *Trabajo infantil doméstico: una evaluación rápida*, ILO/IPEC, Geneva, February 2002, p. xi.

50 Landgren, Karin, 'The Protective Environment: Development support for child protection', *Human Rights Quarterly*, Vol. 27, No. 1, Johns Hopkins University Press, Baltimore, 2005, p. 220.

51 Submission from UNICEF Somalia, April 2005.

52 United Nations Children's Fund, 'Child Trafficking in West Africa: Policy responses', UNICEF, *Innocenti Insight*, Florence, April 2002, p. 14.

53 Ibid., p. 14.

54 Submission from UNICEF Moldova, April 2005.

CHAPTER 3 PANELS

Children and young people in detention in Nigeria

Information derived from The Federal Government of Nigeria and United Nations Children's Fund, 'Juvenile Justice in Nigeria', Fact Sheet, UNICEF Abuja, 2003; Submission from UNICEF Abuja, 2005, and group discussions with children held in Enugu, Nigeria, on 14 May 2005.

Early marriage and fistula

Information derived from the United Nations Population Fund, *The Campaign to End Fistula*, 2004 Annual Report, UNFPA, New York, 2005, p. 1, and other material derived from the UNFPA website.

The protective environment

Information supplied by Child Protection Section, Programme Division, UNICEF, New York, 2005.

The links between child protection and the Millennium Development Goals

Information supplied by Child Protection Section, Programme Division, UNICEF, New York, 2005.

CHAPTER 4

1 Inter-Parliamentary Union and United Nations Children's Fund, *Combating Child Trafficking, Handbook for Parliamentarians No. 9*, IPU and UNICEF, France, March 2005, p. 11.

2 United Nations Children's Fund, *Early Marriage: A harmful traditional practice*, op. cit., p. 25; and United Nation's Children's Fund, *Progress for Children*, op. cit., p. 7.

3 Economic Community of West African States, 'ECOWAS Initial Plan of Action against Trafficking in Persons (2002-2003)', ECOWAS, Executive Secretariat, Dakar, December 2001, p. 7.

4 International Labour Organization *Unbearable to the Human Heart*, op. cit., p.67.

5 Machel, Graça, *The Impact of Armed Conflict on Children*, United Nations, United Nations Children's Fund, New York, 1996.

6 Otunnu, Olara A., 'Era of Application: Instituting a compliance and enforcement regime for CAAC', Statement before the Security Council, New York, 23 February 2005, p. 3.

7 United Nations Children's Fund, 'Early Marriage: Child spouses', op. cit., p. 8.

8 Derived from Statistical Table 9, p. 130.

9 UNICEF provides two indicators for female genital mutilation/cutting: (A) Women: the percentage of women aged 15-49 who have been mutilated/cut; (B) Daughters: the percentage of women aged 15-49 with at least one mutilated/cut daughter. Indicator A is indicative of the extent of FGM/C among the female population as a whole, whereas Indicator B is indicative of the extent of new incidence of FGM/C. The figure cited in the text refers to Indicator B and was derived from Statistical Table 9, p. 130.

10 Institute for Democracy in South Africa and Save the Children Sweden, *Report of the Global Seminar on Monitoring Government Budgets to Advance Child Rights and Child

Poverty Alleviation: How far have we come?', Cape Town, 10-14 May 2004, p. 1.

[11] Vásquez, Enrique, and Enrique Mendizabal, 'How to Make Children Come First: The process of visualizing children in Peru', paper presented at the International Conference 'Promoting Human Rights and Social Policies for Children and Women: Monitoring and Achieving the Millennium Development Goals', co-sponsored by the United Nations Children's Fund and the Graduate School of International Affairs of The New School, 28-30 April 2004, New York.

[12] As cited in United Nations Children's Fund, 'A Children's Budget: Ensuring adequate resource commitment and budget analysis for children', Child-Friendly Cities Secretariat, http://www.childfriendlycities.org.

[13] Ministry of Basic Education and Culture, Namibia, 'National Policy Options for Educationally Marginalized Children', 2000, cited in United Nations Children's Fund, 'Guidance Note: Reaching Marginalized Children and Families', UNICEF Organizational Plan 2006-2009, New York, p. 3.

[14] Barberton, Conrad, and John Stuart, *Re-Costing the Child Justice Bill: Updating the original costing taking into consideration changes made to the bill*, Applied Fiscal Research Centre, Executive Summary, (Afrec Pty Ltd), South Africa, May 2001, pp. 11-IV.

[15] Social Development Notes, Environmentally and Socially Sustainable Development Network, 'Case Study 3 - Gujarat, India: Participatory Approaches in Budgeting and Public Expenditure Management', prepared by Wagle, Swarning and Parmesh Shah of the Participation and Civic Engagement Group in The World Bank, Note No. 72, March 2003.

[16] United Nations Children's Fund, UNICEF Efforts to Address the Needs of Children Orphaned and Made Vulnerable by HIV/AIDS: Rwanda, Swaziland, and Tanzania', draft 3, UNICEF, May 2004, New York, p. 8.

[17] United Nations Children's Fund, *Report on the Situation of Children and Adolescents in Brazil*, UNICEF, Brasilia, 2003, pp. 125-126.

[18] Department for International Development, *Departmental Report 2005*, DFID, UK, 2005, p. 128.

[19] Submission from UNICEF Dominican Republic, April 2005.

[20] United Nations Children's Fund, 'Guidance Note: Reaching Marginalized Children and Families', op. cit., p. 17.

[21] Submission from UNICEF Malaysia, May 2005.

[22] Cvekic, Ljiljana, 'Serbia and Montenegro: Immunization to reach the unreached', UNICEF Serbia and Montenegro, January 2004.

[23] United Nations Millennium Project, *Investing in Development*, op. cit., p. 306.

[24] Women's Commission for Refugee Women and Children, 'Only Through Peace: Hope for breaking the cycle of famine and war in Sudan', New York, September 1999, p.10.

[25] United Nations Children's Fund, *Humanitarian Action Report 2005*, UNICEF, New York, 2005, p. 153.

[26] United Nations Children's Fund, World Conference of Religions for Peace and United States Agency for International Development, *What Religious Leaders Can Do about HIV/AIDS: Action for children and young people*, UNICEF, WCRP and USAID, New York, November 2003, pp. 8, 17, 21.

[27] Ibid., p. 8.

[28] Submission from UNICEF, Regional Office for Latin America and the Caribbean, October 2005.

[29] Joint United Nations Programme on HIV/AIDS, *HIV-Related Stigma, Discrimination and Human Rights Violations: Case studies of successful programmes*, UNAIDS best practice collection, UNAIDS, Geneva, April 2005, pp. 24-25.

[30] United Nations Millennium Project, *Investing in Development*, op. cit., p. 128.

[31] Global Movement for Children and Mouvement Africain des Enfants et Jeunes Travailleurs, 'A World Fit for Us… Children: African children organisations' report of accountability on the promises governments have made to them', Executive Summary and p. 5, GMC/MAEJT, Dakar, Senegal, 2005.

[32] Caillods, Françoise and Candy Lugaz, United Nations Educational, Scientific and Cultural Organization and International Institute of Educational Planning, 'How to do the 'Missing Out' map', UNESCO/IIEP, New York, April, 2004, p. 7.

[33] Information supplied by Media Section, Department of Communication, UNICEF, New York, 2005.

[34] Jempson, Mark, 'Children and Media – A Global Concern', prepared as a contribution to 'Child Rights and the Media: Asia Regional Workshop', Bangkok, 24-25 June 2003, p. 5.

[35] Gigli, Susan and InterMedia Survey Institute for UNICEF, 'Children, Youth and Media Around the World: An overview of trends & issues', 4th World Summit on Media for Children and Adolescents, Rio de Janeiro, Brazil, April 2004, p. 11.

[36] Jempson, Mark, 'Children and the Media', MAGIC briefing, UNICEF, http://www.unicef.org/magic/briefing/child-media.html.

[37] United Nations, Joint United Nations Programme on HIV/AIDS, Kaiser Family Foundation, 'The Global Media AIDS Initiative', http://www.kff.org/hivaids/gmai.cfm.

[38] ECPAT, United Nations Children's Fund and World Tourism Organization, 'Code of Conduct for the Protection of Children from Sexual Exploitation in Travel and Tourism', http://www.thecode.org.

[39] Ibid.

CHAPTER 4 PANELS

Statistical tools for monitoring the Millennium agenda for children

Information derived from Demographic and Health Surveys; United Nations Children's Fund, Strategic Information Section.

Monitoring the effectiveness of budgets in meeting children's rights in South Africa

Information derived from the Institute for Democracy in South Africa (IDASA) website and UNICEF South Africa.

The Child Rights Index: Assessing the rights of children in Ecuador and Mexico

Information supplied by UNICEF Mexico and UNICEF Ecuador, July 2005.

UNICEF Principles and Guidelines for Ethical reporting on Children

Information supplied by Media Section, Division of Communication, UNICEF, New York, 2005.

Child labour and corporate social responsibility: The UNICEF-IKEA project to combat child labour

Information derived from Statistical Table 9, p. 130; International Labour Organization, *A future without Child Labour*, ILO, Geneva, 2002, pp. XI, 28; Submission from UNICEF India, July 2005; United Nations Children's Fund, *Child Labour Resource Guide*, 'Appendix 6 – Developing child labour policies: Examples from four major businesses', UNICEF, New

York, 2005, pp. 112-115; IKEA Services AB, 'The IKEA Way on Preventing Child Labour', IKEA, Sweden, 2002, p. 2; IKEA Services AB, 'Social and Environmental Responsibility', IKEA, Sweden, 2004, pp. 20, 22.

CHAPTER 5

[1] These include vaccines against *haemophilus influenzae* type B, hepatitis B, *streptococcus pneumoniae* and rotavirus.

[2] Real global gross domestic product (GDP) measured in US dollars at purchasing-power-parity values. Derived from the International Monetary Fund, *World Economic Outlook*, Statistical Appendix, IMF, Washington D.C., September 2005, p. 205.

[3] United Nations, 'Enhanced cooperation between the United Nations and all relevant partners, in particular the private sector', Report of the Secretary-General, A/58/227, United Nations, New York, 18 August 2003, p. 4.

[4] United Nations General Assembly, resolution 57 (I), Establishment of an International Children's Emergency Fund, United Nations, New York, December 1946.

[5] United Nations Children's Fund, *The State of the World's Children 1996*, UNICEF, New York, 1995, Chapter 2, pp. 43-46.

CHAPTER 5 PANEL

UNGEI: Making the goal of gender equality in education a reality

Information derived from United Nations Children's Fund, *Progress for Children: A report card on gender parity and primary education*, Number 2, UNICEF, New York, April 2005, p. 3; United Nations Girls' Education Initiative, UNGEI Info Sheet; and United Nations Girls' Education Initiative, 'Framework for Action at Country, Regional and Global Levels', Operation Guidelines Paper, UNGEI, July 2005.

STATISTICAL TABLES

Economic and social statistics on the countries and territories of the world, with particular reference to children's well-being.

STATISTICAL TABLES

Economic and social statistics on the countries and territories of the world, with particular reference to children's well-being.

General note on the data

The data presented in the following statistical tables are accompanied by definitions, sources and explanations of symbols. Data from the responsible United Nations organizations have been used whenever possible. Where such internationally standardized estimates do not exist, the tables draw on other sources, particularly data received from the appropriate UNICEF field office. Where possible, only comprehensive or representative national data have been used.

Data quality is likely to be adversely affected for countries that have recently suffered from man-made or natural disasters. This is particularly so where basic country infrastructure has been fragmented or major population movements have occurred.

Several of the indicators, such as the data for life expectancy, total fertility rates and crude birth and death rates, are part of the regular work on estimates and projections undertaken by the United Nations Population Division. These and other internationally produced estimates are revised periodically, which explains why some of the data will differ from those found in earlier UNICEF publications.

Several statistical tables have been revised this year. In the basic indicators table (table 1), the under-five and infant mortality rates are presented for 1990 and 2004, replacing the 1960 estimate with the 1990 estimate to better reflect the focus on monitoring progress related to the Millennium Development Goals and its baseline year of 1990. The health table (table 3) has seen the addition of data for a new immunization antigen, *Haemophilus influenzae* type b (Hib), as well as the addition of estimates for the first dose of the diphtheria, pertussis and tetanus (DPT) vaccine, which in conjunction with the DPT3 estimate permits comparison of the drop-out rate in immunizations.

Substantial changes have been made to the education data in tables 1 and 5. In table 1, the net primary school enrolment/attendance indicator has been computed based on attendance data from household surveys dated from 2000 to 2004, where available, and otherwise from administrative enrolment data reported by UNESCO/UIS (UNESCO Institute for Statistics). The net primary school attendance ratio (NAR) is an improved indicator including not only children attending primary school but also those attending secondary education. The NAR is defined as the percentage of children in the age group that officially corresponds to primary schooling who attend primary or secondary school. In addition, the adult literacy rate is now presented only for the year 2000 since comparison with previous values from 1990 is not recommended due to differences in definition and data collection. Also, secondary school participation is expanded in two new ways, first to include net ratios for enrolment and second to include secondary net attendance ratios obtained from household surveys.

The demographic indicators (table 6) have also seen some additions. These are the inclusion of estimates for the crude birth rate, the crude death rate and the life expectancy for 1990 in addition to the estimates for 1970 and the current estimate. These additions have again been made to provide data consistent with the baseline year for the MDGs.

The women's indicators (table 8) have also seen the inclusion of two new indicators – the ratio of females as a percentage of males for the net primary enrolment ratio and the net secondary enrolment ratios. These have been added to complement the ratios of gross primary enrolment and gross secondary enrolment that have been published in the past.

Finally, the rate of progress indicators (table 10) have been revised to provide data comparing change between 1970 and 1990 and 1990 and 2004. Previously this table used estimates for 1960 as the earliest point. This has been changed to 1970 to provide a more recent and more comparable time frame over which to compare change in key indicators.

Explanation of symbols

Since the aim of this statistics chapter is to provide a broad picture of the situation of children and women worldwide, detailed data qualifications and footnotes are seen as more appropriate for inclusion elsewhere. The following symbols are common across all tables; symbols specific to a particular table are included in the table's footnotes:

-   Indicates data are not available.

x   Indicates data that refer to years or periods other than those specified in the column heading, differ from the standard definition, or refer to only part of a country. Such data are not included in the regional averages or totals.

*   Data refer to the most recent year available during the period specified in the column heading.

Under-five mortality rankings

The following list ranks countries and territories in descending order of their estimated 2004 under-five mortality rate (U5MR), a critical indicator of the well-being of children. Countries and territories are listed alphabetically in the tables that follow.

	Under-5 mortality rate (2004)			Under-5 mortality rate (2004)			Under-5 mortality rate (2004)	
	Value	Rank		Value	Rank		Value	Rank
Sierra Leone	283	1	Kiribati	65	66	Bosnia and Herzegovina	15	131
Angola	260	2	Guyana	64	67	Bulgaria	15	131
Niger	259	3	Namibia	63	68	Mauritius	15	131
Afghanistan	257	4	Marshall Islands	59	69	Serbia and Montenegro	15	131
Liberia	235	5	Solomon Islands	56	70	Dominica	14	135
Somalia	225	6	Korea, Democratic People's Republic of	55	71	Saint Lucia	14	135
Mali	219	7	Mongolia	52	72	Seychelles	14	135
Congo, Democratic Republic of the	205	8	Tuvalu	51	73	Sri Lanka	14	135
Equatorial Guinea	204	9	Maldives	46	74	The former Yugoslav Republic of Macedonia	14	135
Guinea-Bissau	203	10	Georgia	45	75	Bahamas	13	140
Rwanda	203	10	Guatemala	45	75	Costa Rica	13	140
Chad	200	12	Morocco	43	77	Oman	13	140
Nigeria	197	13	Honduras	41	78	Antigua and Barbuda	12	143
Côte d'Ivoire	194	14	Algeria	40	79	Barbados	12	143
Central African Republic	193	15	Vanuatu	40	79	Kuwait	12	143
Burkina Faso	192	16	Belize	39	81	Latvia	12	143
Burundi	190	17	Suriname	39	81	Malaysia	12	143
Zambia	182	18	Indonesia	38	83	Bahrain	11	148
Malawi	175	19	Iran (Islamic Republic of)	38	83	Belarus	11	148
Ethiopia	166	20	Nicaragua	38	83	Brunei Darussalam	9	150
Swaziland	156	21	Cape Verde	36	86	Slovakia	9	150
Guinea	155	22	Egypt	36	86	Chile	8	152
Benin	152	23	Brazil	34	88	Estonia	8	152
Mozambique	152	23	Philippines	34	88	Hungary	8	152
Cameroon	149	25	Armenia	32	90	Lithuania	8	152
Cambodia	141	26	Dominican Republic	32	90	Poland	8	152
Togo	140	27	Turkey	32	90	United Arab Emirates	8	152
Uganda	138	28	China	31	93	United States	8	152
Senegal	137	29	Lebanon	31	93	Andorra	7	159
Zimbabwe	129	30	Nauru	30	95	Croatia	7	159
Djibouti	126	31	Samoa	30	95	Cuba	7	159
Tanzania, United Republic of	126	31	Peru	29	97	Australia	6	162
Iraq	125	33	El Salvador	28	98	Canada	6	162
Mauritania	125	33	Mexico	28	98	Ireland	6	162
Madagascar	123	35	Moldova, Republic of	28	98	Israel	6	162
Gambia	122	36	Jordan	27	101	Korea, Republic of	6	162
Kenya	120	37	Palau	27	101	Luxembourg	6	162
Sao Tome and Principe	118	38	Saudi Arabia	27	101	Malta	6	162
Tajikistan	118	38	Ecuador	26	104	Netherlands	6	162
Haiti	117	40	Tonga	25	105	New Zealand	6	162
Botswana	116	41	Tunisia	25	105	United Kingdom	6	162
Ghana	112	42	Occupied Palestinian Territory	24	107	Austria	5	172
Yemen	111	43	Panama	24	107	Belgium	5	172
Congo	108	44	Paraguay	24	107	Cyprus	5	172
Myanmar	106	45	Micronesia (Federated States of)	23	110	Denmark	5	172
Turkmenistan	103	46	Viet Nam	23	110	France	5	172
Pakistan	101	47	Saint Vincent and the Grenadines	22	112	Germany	5	172
Papua New Guinea	93	48	Colombia	21	113	Greece	5	172
Gabon	91	49	Cook Islands	21	113	Italy	5	172
Sudan	91	49	Grenada	21	113	Liechtenstein	5	172
Azerbaijan	90	51	Qatar	21	113	Monaco	5	172
India	85	52	Russian Federation	21	113	Portugal	5	172
Lao People's Democratic Republic	83	53	Saint Kitts and Nevis	21	113	Spain	5	172
Eritrea	82	54	Thailand	21	113	Switzerland	5	172
Lesotho	82	54	Fiji	20	120	Czech Republic	4	185
Bhutan	80	56	Jamaica	20	120	Finland	4	185
Timor-Leste	80	56	Libyan Arab Jamahiriya	20	120	Japan	4	185
Bangladesh	77	58	Romania	20	120	Norway	4	185
Nepal	76	59	Trinidad and Tobago	20	120	San Marino	4	185
Kazakhstan	73	60	Albania	19	125	Slovenia	4	185
Comoros	70	61	Venezuela	19	125	Sweden	4	185
Bolivia	69	62	Argentina	18	127	Iceland	3	192
Uzbekistan	69	62	Ukraine	18	127	Singapore	3	192
Kyrgyzstan	68	64	Uruguay	17	129	Holy See	No Data	-
South Africa	67	65	Syrian Arab Republic	16	130	Niue	No Data	-

TABLE 1. BASIC INDICATORS

Countries and territories	Under-5 mortality rank	Under-5 mortality rate		Infant mortality rate (under 1)		Total population (thousands) 2004	Annual no. of births (thousands) 2004	Annual no. of under-5 deaths (thousands) 2004	GNI per capita (US$) 2004	Life expectancy at birth (years) 2004	Total adult literacy rate 2000-2004*	Net primary school enrolment/ attendance (%) 1996-2004*	% share of household income 1993-2003*	
		1990	2004	1990	2004								lowest 40%	highest 20%
Afghanistan	4	260	257	168	165	28574	1395	359	250x	46	-	53s	-	-
Albania	125	45	19	37	17	3112	53	1	2080	74	99	95	23	37
Algeria	79	69	40	54	35	32358	671	27	2280	71	70	94s	19	43
Andorra	159	-	7	-	6	67	1	0	d	-	-	89	-	-
Angola	2	260	260	154	154	15490	749	195	1030	41	67	58s	-	-
Antigua and Barbuda	143	-	12	-	11	81	2	0	10000	-	-	-	-	-
Argentina	127	29	18	26	16	38372	685	12	3720	75	97	-	10	56
Armenia	90	60	32	52	29	3026	34	1	1120	72	99	97s	18	45
Australia	162	10	6	8	5	19942	249	1	26900	81	-	97	18	41
Austria	172	10	5	8	5	8171	75	0	32300	79	-	90	21	39
Azerbaijan	51	105	90	84	75	8355	132	12	950	67	99	91s	19	45
Bahamas	140	29	13	24	10	319	6	0	14920x	70	-	86	-	-
Bahrain	148	19	11	15	9	716	13	0	10840x	75	88	86s	-	-
Bangladesh	58	149	77	100	56	139215	3738	288	440	63	41	79s	22	41
Barbados	143	16	12	14	10	269	3	0	9270x	75	100	100	-	-
Belarus	148	17	11	13	9	9811	91	1	2120	68	100	94	21	39
Belgium	172	10	5	8	4	10400	111	1	31030	79	-	100	22	37
Belize	81	49	39	39	32	264	7	0	3940	72	77	99	-	-
Benin	23	185	152	111	90	8177	341	52	530	54	34	54s	-	-
Bhutan	56	166	80	107	67	2116	64	5	760	63	-	-	-	-
Bolivia	62	125	69	89	54	9009	265	18	960	64	87	78s	13	49
Bosnia and Herzegovina	131	22	15	18	13	3909	37	1	2040	74	95	86s	24	36
Botswana	41	58	116	45	84	1769	46	5	4340	35	79	84s	7	70
Brazil	88	60	34	50	32	183913	3728	127	3090	71	88	95s	8	63
Brunei Darussalam	150	11	9	10	8	366	8	0	24100x	77	93	-	-	-
Bulgaria	131	18	15	15	12	7780	67	1	2740	72	98	90	20	39
Burkina Faso	16	210	192	113	97	12822	601	115	360	48	13	32s	12	61
Burundi	17	190	190	114	114	7282	330	63	90	44	59	47s	15	48
Cambodia	26	115	141	80	97	13798	422	60	320	57	74	65s	18	48
Cameroon	25	139	149	85	87	16038	562	84	800	46	68	75s	15	51
Canada	162	8	6	7	5	31958	328	2	28390	80	-	100	20	40
Cape Verde	86	60	36	45	27	495	15	1	1770	71	76	99	-	-
Central African Republic	15	168	193	102	115	3986	149	29	310	39	49	43s	7	65
Chad	12	203	200	117	117	9448	456	91	260	44	26	39s	-	-
Chile	152	21	8	17	8	16124	249	2	4910	78	96	85	10	62
China	93	49	31	38	26	1307989	17372	539	1290	72	91	99	14	50
Colombia	113	36	21	30	18	44915	970	20	2000	73	94	93s	9	62
Comoros	61	120	70	88	52	777	28	2	530	64	56	31s	-	-
Congo	44	110	108	83	81	3883	172	19	770	52	83	54	-	-
Congo, Democratic Republic of the	8	205	205	129	129	55853	2788	572	120	44	65	52s	-	-
Cook Islands	113	32	21	26	18	18	0	0	-	-	-	-	-	-
Costa Rica	140	18	13	16	11	4253	79	1	4670	78	96	90	13	52
Côte d'Ivoire	14	157	194	103	117	17872	661	128	770	46	48	58s	14	51
Croatia	159	12	7	11	6	4540	41	0	6590	75	98	89	21	40
Cuba	159	13	7	11	6	11245	136	1	1170x	78	100	93	-	-
Cyprus	172	12	5	10	5	826	10	0	17580	79	97	96	-	-
Czech Republic	185	13	4	11	4	10229	91	0	9150	76	-	87	25	36
Denmark	172	9	5	8	4	5414	63	0	40650	77	-	100	23	36
Djibouti	31	163	126	122	101	779	27	3	1030	53	-	36	-	-
Dominica	135	17	14	15	13	79	2	0	3650	-	-	81	-	-
Dominican Republic	90	65	32	50	27	8768	211	7	2080	68	88	92s	14	53
Ecuador	104	57	26	43	23	13040	296	8	2180	75	91	100	11	58
Egypt	86	104	36	76	26	72642	1890	68	1310	70	56	83s	21	44
El Salvador	98	60	28	47	24	6762	166	5	2350	71	80	90	10	57
Equatorial Guinea	9	170	204	103	122	492	21	4	c	43	84	62s	-	-
Eritrea	54	147	82	88	52	4232	166	14	180	54	-	63s	-	-
Estonia	152	16	8	12	6	1335	13	0	7010	72	100	95	18	44
Ethiopia	20	204	166	131	110	75600	3064	509	110	48	42	31s	22	39
Fiji	120	31	20	25	16	841	19	0	2690	68	93	100	-	-

	Under-5 mortality rank	Under-5 mortality rate		Infant mortality rate (under 1)		Total population (thousands) 2004	Annual no. of births (thousands) 2004	Annual no. of under-5 deaths (thousands) 2004	GNI per capita (US$) 2004	Life expectancy at birth (years) 2004	Total adult literacy rate 2000-2004*	Net primary school enrolment/ attendance (%) 1996-2004*	% share of household income 1993-2003*	
		1990	2004	1990	2004								lowest 40%	highest 20%
Finland	185	7	4	6	3	5235	55	0	32790	79	-	100	24	37
France	172	9	5	7	4	60257	744	4	30090	80	-	99	20	40
Gabon	49	92	91	60	60	1362	42	4	3940	54	-	94s	-	-
Gambia	36	154	122	103	89	1478	52	6	290	56	-	53s	14	53
Georgia	75	47	45	43	41	4518	50	2	1040	71	-	89	18	44
Germany	172	9	5	7	4	82645	687	3	30120	79	-	83	22	37
Ghana	42	122	112	75	68	21664	679	76	380	57	54	61s	16	47
Greece	172	11	5	10	4	11098	102	1	16610	78	91	99	19	44
Grenada	113	37	21	30	18	102	2	0	3760	-	-	84	-	-
Guatemala	75	82	45	60	33	12295	433	19	2130	68	69	78s	9	64
Guinea	22	240	155	145	101	9202	383	59	460	54	-	57s	17	47
Guinea-Bissau	10	253	203	153	126	1540	77	16	160	45	-	41s	14	53
Guyana	67	88	64	64	48	750	16	1	990	64	-	97s	-	-
Haiti	40	150	117	102	74	8407	253	30	390	52	52	54s	-	-
Holy See	-	-	-	-	1	-	-	-	-	-	-	-	-	-
Honduras	78	59	41	44	31	7048	206	8	1030	68	80	87	9	59
Hungary	152	17	8	15	7	10124	95	1	8270	73	99	91	23	37
Iceland	192	7	3	6	2	292	4	0	38620	81	-	100	-	-
India	52	123	85	84	62	1087124	26000	2210	620	64	61	77s	21	43
Indonesia	83	91	38	60	30	220077	4513	171	1140	67	88	94s	20	43
Iran (Islamic Republic of)	83	72	38	54	32	68803	1308	50	2300	71	77	86	15	50
Iraq	33	50	125	40	102	28057	972	122	2170x	59	-	78s	-	-
Ireland	162	10	6	8	5	4080	63	0	34280	78	-	96	19	43
Israel	162	12	6	10	5	6601	134	1	17380	80	97	99	18	44
Italy	172	9	5	9	4	58033	531	3	26120	80	-	99	19	42
Jamaica	120	20	20	17	17	2639	52	1	2900	71	88	95	17	46
Japan	185	6	4	5	3	127923	1169	5	37180	82	-	100	25	36
Jordan	101	40	27	33	23	5561	150	4	2140	72	90	99s	19	44
Kazakhstan	60	63	73	53	63	14839	237	17	2260	63	100	91s	20	40
Kenya	37	97	120	64	79	33467	1322	159	460	48	74	78s	16	49
Kiribati	66	88	65	65	49	97	2	0	970	-	-	-	-	-
Korea, Democratic People's Republic of	71	55	55	42	42	22384	349	19	a	63	-	-	-	-
Korea, Republic of	162	9	6	8	5	47645	467	3	13980	77	-	100	22	38
Kuwait	143	16	12	14	10	2606	50	1	16340x	77	83	83	-	-
Kyrgyzstan	64	80	68	68	58	5204	116	8	400	67	99	89s	20	43
Lao People's Democratic Republic	53	163	83	120	65	5792	204	17	390	55	69	62s	19	45
Latvia	143	18	12	14	10	2318	21	0	5460	72	100	86	20	41
Lebanon	93	37	31	32	27	3540	66	2	4980	72	-	97s	-	-
Lesotho	54	120	82	84	61	1798	50	4	740	35	81	65s	6	67
Liberia	5	235	235	157	157	3241	164	39	110	42	56	70	-	-
Libyan Arab Jamahiriya	120	41	20	35	18	5740	133	3	4450	74	82	-	-	-
Liechtenstein	172	10	5	9	4	34	0	0	d	-	-	-	-	-
Lithuania	152	13	8	10	8	3443	31	0	5740	73	100	91	21	40
Luxembourg	162	10	6	7	5	459	6	0	56230	79	-	90	-	-
Madagascar	35	168	123	103	76	18113	704	87	300	56	71	76s	13	54
Malawi	19	241	175	146	110	12608	550	96	170	40	64	76s	13	56
Malaysia	143	22	12	16	10	24894	549	7	4650	73	89	93	13	54
Maldives	74	111	46	79	35	321	10	0	2510	67	96	92	-	-
Mali	7	250	219	140	121	13124	647	142	360	48	19	39s	13	56
Malta	162	11	6	9	5	400	4	0	12250	79	88	96	-	-
Marshall Islands	69	92	59	63	52	60	0	0	2370	-	-	84	-	-
Mauritania	33	133	125	85	78	2980	123	15	420	53	51	44s	17	46
Mauritius	131	23	15	21	14	1233	20	0	4640	72	84	97	-	-
Mexico	98	46	28	37	23	105699	2201	62	6770	75	90	99	10	59
Micronesia (Federated States of)	110	31	23	26	19	110	3	0	1990	68	-	-	-	-
Moldova, Republic of	98	40	28	30	23	4218	43	1	710	68	96	98s	18	44
Monaco	172	9	5	7	4	35	0	0	d	-	-	-	-	-

TABLE 1. BASIC INDICATORS

	Under-5 mortality rank	Under-5 mortality rate		Infant mortality rate (under 1)		Total population (thousands) 2004	Annual no. of births (thousands) 2004	Annual no. of under-5 deaths (thousands) 2004	GNI per capita (US$) 2004	Life expectancy at birth (years) 2004	Total adult literacy rate 2000-2004*	Net primary school enrolment/ attendance (%) 1996-2004*	% share of household income 1993-2003*	
		1990	2004	1990	2004								lowest 40%	highest 20%
Mongolia	72	108	52	78	41	2614	58	3	590	65	98	79s	16	51
Morocco	77	89	43	69	38	31020	713	31	1520	70	51	89s	17	47
Mozambique	23	235	152	158	104	19424	769	117	250	42	46	60s	17	47
Myanmar	45	130	106	91	76	50004	992	105	220x	61	90	80s	-	-
Namibia	68	86	63	60	47	2009	56	4	2370	47	85	78s	4	79
Nauru	95	-	30	-	25	13	0	0	-	-	-	81	-	-
Nepal	59	145	76	100	59	26591	786	60	260	62	49	74s	19	45
Netherlands	162	9	6	7	5	16226	190	1	31700	79	-	99	21	39
New Zealand	162	11	6	8	5	3989	55	0	20310	79	-	100	18	44
Nicaragua	83	68	38	52	31	5376	153	6	790	70	77	80s	15	49
Niger	3	320	259	191	152	13499	734	190	230	45	14	30s	10	53
Nigeria	13	230	197	120	101	128709	5323	1049	390	43	67	62s	13	56
Niue	-	-	-	-	-	1	0	-	-	-	-	99	-	-
Norway	185	9	4	7	4	4598	55	0	52030	80	-	100	24	37
Occupied Palestinian Territory	107	40	24	34	22	3587	136	3	1110x	73	92	91	-	-
Oman	140	32	13	25	10	2534	64	1	7830x	74	74	72	-	-
Pakistan	47	130	101	100	80	154794	4729	478	600	63	49	56s	21	42
Palau	101	34	27	28	22	20	0	0	6870	-	-	96	-	-
Panama	107	34	24	27	19	3175	70	2	4450	75	92	100	9	60
Papua New Guinea	48	101	93	74	68	5772	176	16	580	56	57	74	12	57
Paraguay	107	41	24	33	21	6017	175	4	1170	71	92	89	9	61
Peru	97	80	29	60	24	27562	627	18	2360	70	88	96s	11	53
Philippines	88	62	34	41	26	81617	2026	69	1170	71	93	88s	14	52
Poland	152	18	8	19	7	38559	365	3	6090	75	-	98	20	42
Portugal	172	14	5	11	4	10441	112	1	14350	78	-	100	17	46
Qatar	113	26	21	21	18	777	14	0	12000x	73	89	94	-	-
Romania	120	31	20	27	17	21790	213	4	2920	72	97	89	20	41
Russian Federation	113	29	21	23	17	143899	1511	32	3410	65	99	90	21	39
Rwanda	10	173	203	103	118	8882	365	74	220	44	64	75s	23x	39x
Saint Kitts and Nevis	113	36	21	30	18	42	1	0	7600	-	-	95	-	-
Saint Lucia	135	21	14	20	13	159	3	0	4310	73	90	99	-	-
Saint Vincent and the Grenadines	112	25	22	22	18	118	2	0	3650	71	-	90	-	-
Samoa	95	50	30	40	25	184	5	0	1860	71	99	98	-	-
San Marino	185	14	4	13	3	28	0	0	d	-	-	-	-	-
Sao Tome and Principe	38	118	118	75	75	153	5	1	370	63	-	78s	-	-
Saudi Arabia	101	44	27	35	21	23950	665	18	10430	72	79	54	-	-
Senegal	29	148	137	90	78	11386	419	57	670	56	39	48s	17	48
Serbia and Montenegro	131	28	15	24	13	10510	122	2	2620	74	96	96	-	-
Seychelles	135	19	14	17	12	80	3	0	8090	-	92	100	-	-
Sierra Leone	1	302	283	175	165	5336	245	69	200	41	30	41s	3x	63x
Singapore	192	9	3	7	3	4273	40	0	24220	79	93	-	14	49
Slovakia	150	14	9	12	6	5401	51	0	6480	74	100	86	24	35
Slovenia	185	10	4	8	4	1967	17	0	14810	77	100	93	23	36
Solomon Islands	70	63	56	38	34	466	15	1	550	63	-	-	-	-
Somalia	6	225	225	133	133	7964	359	81	130x	47	-	11s	-	-
South Africa	65	60	67	45	54	47208	1093	73	3630	47	82	89s	10	62
Spain	172	9	5	8	3	42646	447	2	21210	80	-	100	20x	40x
Sri Lanka	135	32	14	26	12	20570	330	5	1010	74	90	-	21	42
Sudan	49	120	91	74	63	35523	1163	106	530	57	59	53s	-	-
Suriname	81	48	39	35	30	446	9	0	2250	69	88	90s	-	-
Swaziland	21	110	156	78	108	1034	30	5	1660	31	79	72s	9	64
Sweden	185	7	4	6	3	9008	95	0	35770	80	-	100	23	37
Switzerland	172	9	5	7	5	7240	68	0	48230	81	-	99	20x	40x
Syrian Arab Republic	130	44	16	35	15	18582	526	8	1190	74	83	98	-	-
Tajikistan	38	128	118	99	91	6430	186	22	280	64	99	81s	20	41
Tanzania, United Republic of	31	161	126	102	78	37627	1403	177	330	46	69	82s	18	46
Thailand	113	37	21	31	18	63694	1015	21	2540	70	93	85	16	50

	Under-5 mortality rank	Under-5 mortality rate		Infant mortality rate (under 1)		Total population (thousands) 2004	Annual no. of births (thousands) 2004	Annual no. of under-5 deaths (thousands) 2004	GNI per capita (US$) 2004	Life expectancy at birth (years) 2004	Total adult literacy rate 2000-2004*	Net primary school enrolment/attendance (%) 1996-2004*	% share of household income 1993-2003*	
		1990	2004	1990	2004								lowest 40%	highest 20%
The former Yugoslav Republic of Macedonia	135	38	14	33	13	2030	23	0	2350	74	96	91	22	37
Timor-Leste	56	172	80	130	64	887	45	4	550	56	-	-	-	-
Togo	27	152	140	88	78	5988	233	33	380	55	53	64s	-	-
Tonga	105	32	25	26	20	102	2	0	1830	72	99	100	-	-
Trinidad and Tobago	120	33	20	28	18	1301	19	0	8580	70	98	96s	16x	46x
Tunisia	105	52	25	41	21	9995	166	4	2630	74	74	97	16	47
Turkey	90	82	32	67	28	72220	1505	48	3750	69	88	88s	17	47
Turkmenistan	46	97	103	80	80	4766	107	11	1340	63	99	85s	16	48
Tuvalu	73	56	51	40	36	10	0	0	-	-	-	-	-	-
Uganda	28	160	138	93	80	27821	1412	195	270	48	69	79s	16	50
Ukraine	127	26	18	19	14	46989	391	7	1260	66	99	84	22	38
United Arab Emirates	152	14	8	12	7	4284	67	1	18060x	78	77	83	-	-
United Kingdom	162	10	6	8	5	59479	663	4	33940	79	-	100	18	44
United States	152	12	8	9	7	295410	4134	33	41400	78	-	92	16	46
Uruguay	129	25	17	20	15	3439	57	1	3950	76	98	90	14	50
Uzbekistan	62	79	69	65	57	26209	611	42	460	67	99	80s	23	36
Vanuatu	79	62	40	48	32	207	6	0	1340	69	74	94	-	-
Venezuela	125	27	19	24	16	26282	590	11	4020	73	93	94s	11	53
Viet Nam	110	53	23	38	17	83123	1644	38	550	71	90	96s	19	45
Yemen	43	142	111	98	82	20329	826	92	570	61	49	72s	20	41
Zambia	18	180	182	101	102	11479	468	85	450	38	68	68s	11	57
Zimbabwe	30	80	129	53	79	12936	384	50	480x	37	90	79s	13	56

SUMMARY INDICATORS

Sub-Saharan Africa		188	171	112	102	697561	28263	4833	611	46	60	60	12	57
Eastern and Southern Africa		167	149	105	95	348833	13371	1992	836	46	63	65	11	59
Western and Central Africa		209	191	119	109	348728	14892	2844	399	46	58	55	13	53
Middle East and North Africa		81	56	59	44	371384	9620	539	2308	68	67	79	17	46
South Asia		129	92	89	67	1459305	37052	3409	600	63	58	74	21	43
East Asia and Pacific		58	36	43	29	1937058	29932	1078	1686	71	90	96	16	47
Latin America and Caribbean		54	31	43	26	548273	11674	362	3649	72	90	93	10	59
CEE/CIS		54	38	44	32	404154	5570	212	2667	67	97	88	20	41
Industrialized countries		10	6	9	5	956315	10839	65	32232	79	-	95	19	42
Developing countries		105	87	72	59	5166574	119663	10411	1524	65	77	80	15	50
Least developed countries		182	155	115	98	741597	27823	4313	345	52	54	60	18	46
World		95	79	65	54	6374050	132950	10503	6298	67	78	82	18	43

Countries in each category are listed on page 132.

DEFINITIONS OF THE INDICATORS

Under-five mortality rate – Probability of dying between birth and exactly five years of age expressed per 1,000 live births.

Infant mortality rate – Probability of dying between birth and exactly one year of age expressed per 1,000 live births.

GNI per capita – Gross national income (GNI) is the sum of value added by all resident producers plus any product taxes (less subsidies) not included in the valuation of output plus net receipts of primary income (compensation of employees and property income) from abroad. GNI per capita is gross national income divided by mid-year population. GNI per capita in US dollars is converted using the World Bank Atlas method.

Life expectancy at birth – The number of years newborn children would live if subject to the mortality risks prevailing for the cross-section of population at the time of their birth.

Adult literacy rate – Percentage of persons aged 15 and over who can read and write.

Net primary school enrolment/attendance – Derived from net primary school enrolment rates as reported by UNESCO/UIS (UNESCO Institute of Statistics) and from national household survey reports of attendance at primary school or higher. The net primary school attendance ratio is defined as the percentage of children in the age group that officially corresponds to primary schooling who attend primary school or higher.

Income share – Percentage of income received by the 20 per cent of households with the highest income and by the 40 per cent of households with the lowest income.

MAIN DATA SOURCES

Under-five and infant mortality rates – UNICEF, World Health Organization, United Nations Population Division and United Nations Statistics Division.

Total population – United Nations Population Division.

Births – United Nations Population Division.

Under-five deaths – UNICEF.

GNI per capita – World Bank.

Life expectancy – United Nations Population Division.

Adult literacy – United Nations Educational, Scientific and Cultural Organization (UNESCO) and UNESCO Institute of Statistics (UIS).

School enrolment/attendance – UIS, Multiple Indicator Cluster Surveys (MICS) and Demographic and Health Surveys (DHS).

Household income – World Bank.

NOTES

a: Range $825 or less.
b: Range $826 to $3255.
c: Range $3256 to $10065.
d: Range $10066 or more.

- Data not available.

s National household survey.

x Indicates data that refer to years or periods other than those specified in the column heading, differ from the standard definition, or refer to only part of a country.

* Data refer to the most recent year available during the period specified in the column heading.

TABLE 2. NUTRITION

Countries and territories	% of infants with low birthweight 1998-2004*	% of children (1996-2004*) who are: exclusively breastfed (<6 months)	breastfed with complementary food (6-9 months)	still breastfeeding (20-23 months)	% of under-fives (1996-2004*) suffering from: underweight moderate & severe	underweight severe	wasting moderate & severe	stunting moderate & severe	Vitamin A supplementation coverage rate (6-59 months) 2003	% of households consuming iodized salt 1998-2004*
Afghanistan	-	-	29	54	39	12	7	54	86t	28
Albania	3	6	24	6	14	1	11	34	-	62
Algeria	7	13	38	22	10	3	8	19	-	69
Andorra	-	-	-	-	-	-	-	-	-	-
Angola	12	11	77	37	31	8	6	45	68	35
Antigua and Barbuda	8	-	-	-	10x	4x	10x	7x	-	-
Argentina	8	-	-	-	5	1	3	12	-	90x
Armenia	7	30	51	13	3	0	2	13	-	84
Australia	7	-	-	-	-	-	-	-	-	-
Austria	7	-	-	-	-	-	-	-	-	-
Azerbaijan	11	7	39	16	7	1	2	13	-	26
Bahamas	7	-	-	-	-	-	-	-	-	-
Bahrain	8	34x,k	65x	41x	9x	2x	5x	10x	-	-
Bangladesh	36	36	69	94	48	13	13	43	87t	70
Barbados	10x	-	-	-	6x	1x	5x	7x	-	-
Belarus	5	-	-	-	-	-	-	-	-	55
Belgium	8x	-	-	-	-	-	-	-	-	-
Belize	6	24k	54	23	6x	1x	-	-	-	90x
Benin	16	38	66	62	23	5	8	31	98t	72
Bhutan	15	-	-	-	19	3	3	40	-	95
Bolivia	7	54	74	46	8	1	1	27	38	90
Bosnia and Herzegovina	4	6	-	-	4	1	6	10	-	77
Botswana	10	34	57	11	13	2	5	23	-	66
Brazil	10x	-	30	17	6	1	2	11	-	88
Brunei Darussalam	10	-	-	-	-	-	-	-	-	-
Bulgaria	10	-	-	-	-	-	-	-	-	98
Burkina Faso	19	19	38	81	38	14	19	39	95t	45
Burundi	16	62	46	85	45	13	8	57	95	96
Cambodia	11	12	72	59	45	13	15	45	47	14
Cameroon	11	21	80	29	18	4	5	32	86	61
Canada	6	-	-	-	-	-	-	-	-	-
Cape Verde	13	57k	64	13	14x	2x	6x	16x	-	0x
Central African Republic	14	17	77	53	24	6	9	39	84	86
Chad	10	2	77	66	28	9	11	29	-	58
Chile	5	63	47	-	1	-	0	2	-	100
China	4	51	32	15	8	-	-	14	-	93
Colombia	9	26	58	25	7	1	1	14	-	92x
Comoros	25	21	34	45	25	9	12	42	-	82
Congo	-	4k	94	13	14	3	4	19	89	-
Congo, Democratic Republic of the	12	24	79	52	31	9	13	38	80t	72
Cook Islands	3	19k	-	-	-	-	-	-	-	-
Costa Rica	7	35x,k	47x	12x	5	0	2	6	-	97x
Côte d'Ivoire	17	5	73	38	17	5	7	21	-	31
Croatia	6	23	-	-	1	-	1	1	-	90
Cuba	6	41	42	9	4	0	2	5	-	88
Cyprus	-	-	-	-	-	-	-	-	-	-
Czech Republic	7	-	-	-	1x	0x	2x	2x	-	-
Denmark	5	-	-	-	-	-	-	-	-	-
Djibouti	-	-	-	-	18	6	13	26	75	-
Dominica	10	-	-	-	5x	0x	2x	6x	-	-
Dominican Republic	11	10	41	16	5	1	2	9	40	18
Ecuador	16	35	70	25	12	-	-	26	-	99
Egypt	12	30	72	31	9	1	4	16	-	56
El Salvador	7	24	76	43	10	1	1	19	-	91x
Equatorial Guinea	13	24	-	-	19	4	7	39	-	20x
Eritrea	21x	52	43	62	40	12	13	38	52	68
Estonia	4	-	-	-	-	-	-	-	-	-
Ethiopia	15	55	43	77	47	16	11	52	65	28
Fiji	10	47x,k	-	-	8x	1x	8x	3x	-	31x

	% of infants with low birthweight 1998-2004*	% of children (1996-2004*) who are:			% of under-fives (1996-2004*) suffering from:				Vitamin A supplementation coverage rate (6-59 months) 2003	% of households consuming iodized salt 1998-2004*
		exclusively breastfed (<6 months)	breastfed with complementary food (6-9 months)	still breastfeeding (20-23 months)	underweight moderate & severe	underweight severe	wasting moderate & severe	stunting moderate & severe		
Finland	4	-	-	-	-	-	-	-	-	-
France	7	-	-	-	-	-	-	-	-	-
Gabon	14	6	62	9	12	2	3	21	30	36
Gambia	17	26	37	54	17	4	9	19	91	8
Georgia	7	18k	12	12	3	0	2	12	-	68
Germany	7	-	-	-	-	-	-	-	-	-
Ghana	16	53	62	67	22	5	7	30	78t	28
Greece	8	-	-	-	-	-	-	-	-	-
Grenada	9	39k	-	-	-	-	-	-	-	-
Guatemala	12	51	67	47	23	4	2	49	-	67
Guinea	16	23	43	73	21	-	11	33	98t	68
Guinea-Bissau	22	37	36	67	25	7	10	30	-	2
Guyana	12	11	42	31	14	3	11	11	-	-
Haiti	21	24	73	30	17	4	5	23	25	11
Holy See	-	-	-	-	-	-	-	-	-	-
Honduras	14	35	61	34	17	-	1	29	35	80
Hungary	9	-	-	-	2x	0x	2x	3x	-	-
Iceland	4	-	-	-	-	-	-	-	-	-
India	30	37k	44	66	47	18	16	46	45w	50
Indonesia	9	40	75	59	28	9	-	-	62	73
Iran (Islamic Republic of)	7x	44	-	0	11	2	5	15	-	94
Iraq	15	12	51	27	16	2	6	22	-	40
Ireland	6	-	-	-	-	-	-	-	-	-
Israel	8	-	-	-	-	-	-	-	-	-
Italy	6	-	-	-	-	-	-	-	-	-
Jamaica	10	-	-	-	4	-	2	5	-	100
Japan	8	-	-	-	-	-	-	-	-	-
Jordan	10x	27	70	12	4	1	2	9	-	88
Kazakhstan	8	36	73	17	4	0	2	10	-	83
Kenya	10	13	84	57	20	4	6	30	33	91
Kiribati	5	80x,k	-	-	13x	-	11x	28x	45	-
Korea, Democratic People's Republic of	7	65	31	37	23	8	7	37	95t	40
Korea, Republic of	4	-	-	-	-	-	-	-	-	-
Kuwait	7	12k	26	9	10	3	11	24	-	-
Kyrgyzstan	7x	24	77	21	11	2	3	25	-	42
Lao People's Democratic Republic	14	23	10	47	40	13	15	42	64	75
Latvia	5	-	-	-	-	-	-	-	-	-
Lebanon	6	27k	35	11	3	0	3	12	-	87
Lesotho	14	15	51	58	18	4	5	46	75t	69
Liberia	-	35	70	45	26	8	6	39	-	-
Libyan Arab Jamahiriya	7x	-	-	23x	5x	1x	3x	15x	-	90x
Liechtenstein	-	-	-	-	-	-	-	-	-	-
Lithuania	4	-	-	-	-	-	-	-	-	-
Luxembourg	8	-	-	-	-	-	-	-	-	-
Madagascar	17	67	78	64	42	11	13	48	91t	75
Malawi	16	44	93	77	22	-	5	45	92	49
Malaysia	9	29k	-	12	11	1	-	-	-	-
Maldives	22	10	85	-	30	7	13	25	-	44
Mali	23	25	32	69	33	11	11	38	61	74
Malta	6	-	-	-	-	-	-	-	-	-
Marshall Islands	12	63x,k	-	-	-	-	-	-	23	-
Mauritania	-	20	78	57	32	10	13	35	-	2
Mauritius	14	21k	-	-	15x	2x	14x	10x	-	0x
Mexico	8	38x,k	36x	21x	8	1	2	18	-	91
Micronesia (Federated States of)	18	60k	-	-	-	-	-	-	95t	-
Moldova, Republic of	5	-	-	-	3	-	3	10	-	33
Monaco	-	-	-	-	-	-	-	-	-	-
Mongolia	7	51	55	57	13	3	6	25	87t	75
Morocco	11x	31	66	15	9	2	4	24	-	41

TABLE 2. NUTRITION

	% of infants with low birthweight 1998-2004*	% of children (1996-2004*) who are:			% of under-fives (1996-2004*) suffering from:				Vitamin A supplementation coverage rate (6-59 months) 2003	% of households consuming iodized salt 1998-2004*
		exclusively breastfed (<6 months)	breastfed with complementary food (6-9 months)	still breastfeeding (20-23 months)	underweight moderate & severe	underweight severe	wasting moderate & severe	stunting moderate & severe		
Mozambique	15	30	80	65	24	6	4	41	50	54
Myanmar	15	15k	66	67	32	7	9	32	87t	60
Namibia	14	19	57	37	24	5	9	24	93	63
Nauru	-	-	-	-	-	-	-	-	-	-
Nepal	21	68	66	92	48	13	10	51	96t	63
Netherlands	-	-	-	-	-	-	-	-	-	-
New Zealand	6	-	-	-	-	-	-	-	-	83
Nicaragua	12	31	68	39	10	2	2	20	91	97
Niger	13	1	56	61	40	14	14	40	95	15
Nigeria	14	17	64	34	29	9	9	38	27	97
Niue	0	-	-	-	-	-	-	-	-	-
Norway	5	-	-	-	-	-	-	-	-	-
Occupied Palestinian Territory	9	29k	78	11	4	1	3	9	-	65
Oman	8	-	92	73	24x	4x	13x	23x	-	61
Pakistan	19x	16x,k	31x	56x	38	12	13	37	95t	17
Palau	9	59x,k	-	-	-	-	-	-	-	-
Panama	10	25x	38x	21x	7	-	1	14	-	95
Papua New Guinea	11x	59	74	66	35x	-	-	-	1	-
Paraguay	9x	22	60	-	5	-	1	14	-	88
Peru	11x	67	76	49	7	1	1	25	-	93x
Philippines	20	34	58	32	28	-	6	30	76t	56
Poland	6	-	-	-	-	-	-	-	-	-
Portugal	8	-	-	-	-	-	-	-	-	-
Qatar	10	12k	48	21	6x	-	2x	8x	-	-
Romania	9	-	-	-	6x	1x	3x	8x	-	53
Russian Federation	6	-	-	-	3x	1x	4x	13x	-	35
Rwanda	9	84	79	71	27	7	6	41	86	90
Saint Kitts and Nevis	9	56k	-	-	-	-	-	-	-	100
Saint Lucia	8	-	-	-	14x	-	6x	11x	-	-
Saint Vincent and the Grenadines	10	-	-	-	-	-	-	-	-	-
Samoa	4x	-	-	-	-	-	-	-	-	-
San Marino	-	-	-	-	-	-	-	-	-	-
Sao Tome and Principe	20	56	53	42	13	2	4	29	-	74
Saudi Arabia	11x	31k	60	30	14	3	11	20	-	-
Senegal	18	24k	64	49	23	6	8	25	-	16
Serbia and Montenegro	4	11k	33	11	2	0	4	5	-	73
Seychelles	-	-	-	-	6x	0x	2x	5x	-	-
Sierra Leone	23	4	51	53	27	9	10	34	84t	23
Singapore	8	-	-	-	14x	-	4x	11x	-	-
Slovakia	7	-	-	-	-	-	-	-	-	-
Slovenia	6	-	-	-	-	-	-	-	-	-
Solomon Islands	13x	65k	-	-	21x	4x	7x	27x	-	-
Somalia	-	9	13	8	26	7	17	23	-	-
South Africa	15	7	67	30	12	2	3	25	-	62
Spain	6x	-	-	-	-	-	-	-	-	-
Sri Lanka	22	84	-	73	29	-	14	14	-	88
Sudan	31	16	47	40	17x	7x	-	-	34	1
Suriname	13	9	25	11	13	2	7	10	-	-
Swaziland	9	24	60	25	10	2	1	30	80	59
Sweden	4	-	-	-	-	-	-	-	-	-
Switzerland	6	-	-	-	-	-	-	-	-	-
Syrian Arab Republic	6	81k	50	6	7	1	4	18	-	79
Tajikistan	15	50	-	-	-	-	5	36	-	28
Tanzania, United Republic of	13	41	91	55	22	4	3	38	91t	43
Thailand	9	4x,k	71x	27x	19x	-	6x	16x	-	63
The former Yugoslav Republic of Macedonia	6	37	8	10	6	1	4	7	-	80
Timor-Leste	12	31	82	35	46	15	12	49	95	72
Togo	18	18	65	65	25	7	12	22	84t	67
Tonga	0	62k	-	-	-	-	-	-	-	-

	% of infants with low birthweight 1998-2004*	% of children (1996-2004*) who are:			% of under-fives (1996-2004*) suffering from:					Vitamin A supplementation coverage rate (6-59 months) 2003	% of households consuming iodized salt 1998-2004*
		exclusively breastfed (<6 months)	breastfed with complementary food (6-9 months)	still breastfeeding (20-23 months)	underweight moderate & severe	underweight severe	wasting moderate & severe	stunting moderate & severe			
Trinidad and Tobago	23	2	19	10	7x	0x	4x	5x	-	1
Tunisia	7	47	-	22	4	1	2	12	-	97
Turkey	16	21	38	24	4	1	1	12	-	64
Turkmenistan	6	13	71	27	12	2	6	22	-	100
Tuvalu	5	-	-	-	-	-	-	-	-	-
Uganda	12	63	75	50	23	5	4	39	-	95
Ukraine	5	22	-	-	1	0	0	3	-	32
United Arab Emirates	15x	34x,k	52x	29x	14x	3x	15x	17x	-	-
United Kingdom	8	-	-	-	-	-	-	-	-	-
United States	8	-	-	-	1x	0x	1x	2x	-	-
Uruguay	8	-	-	-	5x	1x	1x	8x	-	-
Uzbekistan	7	19	49	45	8	2	7	21	93t	19
Vanuatu	6	50k	-	-	20x	-	-	19x	-	-
Venezuela	9	7k	50	31	4	1	3	13	-	90
Viet Nam	9	15	-	26	28	4	7	32	99t, w	83
Yemen	32x	12	76	-	46	15	12	53	36	30
Zambia	12	40	87	58	23	-	5	49	73t	77
Zimbabwe	11	33	90	35	13	2	6	27	46	93

SUMMARY INDICATORS

Sub-Saharan Africa	14	30	67	53	28	8	9	38	64	64
Eastern and Southern Africa	14	41	69	58	29	8	7	41	68	60
Western and Central Africa	15	20	65	48	28	9	10	35	60	68
Middle East and North Africa	15	29	60	23	14	3	6	21	-	58
South Asia	31	38	45	69	46	16	14	44	58	49
East Asia and Pacific	7	43	44	27	15	-	-	19	73e	85
Latin America and Caribbean	9	-	45	26	7	1	2	16	-	86
CEE/CIS	9	22	45	26	5	1	3	14	-	47
Industrialized countries	7	-	-	-	-	-	-	-	-	-
Developing countries	17	36	51	46	27	10	10	31	61e	69
Least developed countries	19	34	63	65	36	11	10	42	76	53
World	16	36	51	46	26	10	10	31	61e	68

Countries in each category are listed on page 132.

DEFINITIONS OF THE INDICATORS

Low birthweight – Infants who weigh less than 2,500 grams.

Underweight – Moderate and severe – below minus two standard deviations from median weight for age of reference population; severe – below minus three standard deviations from median weight for age of reference population.

Wasting – Moderate and severe – below minus two standard deviations from median weight for height of reference population.

Stunting – Moderate and severe – below minus two standard deviations from median height for age of reference population.

Vitamin A – Percentage of children aged 6-59 months who have received at least one high dose of vitamin A capsules in 2003.

MAIN DATA SOURCES

Low birthweight – Demographic and Health Surveys (DHS), Multiple Indicator Cluster Surveys (MICS), other national household surveys and data from routine reporting systems.

Breastfeeding – DHS, MICS and UNICEF.

Underweight, wasting and stunting – DHS, MICS, UNICEF and World Health Organization (WHO).

Vitamin A – UNICEF and WHO.

Salt iodization – MICS, DHS and UNICEF.

NOTES

-     Data not available.
- x   Indicates data that refer to years or periods other than those specified in the column heading, differ from the standard definition, or refer to only part of a country.
- k   Refers to exclusive breastfeeding for less than four months.
- *   Data refer to the most recent year available during the period specified in the column heading.
- t   Identifies countries that have achieved a second round of vitamin A coverage greater than or equal to 70 per cent.
- e   This regional figure for East Asia and Pacific does not include China.
- w   Identifies countries with vitamin A supplementation programmes that do not target children all the way up to 59 months of age.

TABLE 3. HEALTH

Countries and territories	% of population using improved drinking water sources 2002 total	urban	rural	% of population using adequate sanitation facilities 2002 total	urban	rural	% of routine EPI vaccines financed by government 2004 total	TB BCG	DPT DPT1'	DPT3'	Polio polio3	Measles measles	HepB hepB3	Hib Hib3	% newborns protected against tetanus	% under-fives with ARI 1998-2004*	% under-fives with ARI taken to health provider 1998-2004*	% under-fives with diarrhoea receiving oral rehydration and continued feeding 1996-2004*	Malaria 1999-2004 % under-fives sleeping under a mosquito net	% under-fives sleeping under a treated mosquito net	% under-fives with fever receiving anti-malarial drugs
Afghanistan	13	19	11	8	16	5	0	78	80	66	66	61	-	-	35	19	28	48	-	-	-
Albania	97	99	95	89	99	81	60	97	98	97	98	96	99	-	-	1	83	51	-	-	-
Algeria	87	92	80	92	99	82	100	98	93	86	86	81	81	-	-	9	52	-	-	-	-
Andorra	100	100	100	100	100	100	-	-	99	99	99	98	54	95	-	-	-	-	-	-	-
Angola	50	70	40	30	56	16	43	72	75	59	57	64	-	-	75	8	58	32	10	2	63
Antigua and Barbuda	91	95	89	95	98	94	100	-	91	97	97	97	97	97	-	-	-	-	-	-	-
Argentina	-	97	-	-	-	-	100	99	95	90	95	95	88	90	-	-	-	-	-	-	-
Armenia	92	99	80	84	96	61	6	96	97	91	93	92	91	-	-	11	26	48	-	-	-
Australia	100	100	100	100	100	100	100	-	97	92	92	93	95	95	-	-	-	-	-	-	-
Austria	100	100	100	100	100	100	-	-	97	83	83	74	83	83	-	-	-	-	-	-	-
Azerbaijan	77	95	59	55	73	36	100	99	98	96	97	98	97	-	-	3	36	40	12	1	1
Bahamas	97	98	86	100	100	100	100	-	99	93	92	89	93	93	-	-	-	-	-	-	-
Bahrain	-	100	-	-	100	-	100	70	97	98	98	99	98	98	-	-	-	-	-	-	-
Bangladesh	75	82	72	48	75	39	100	95	95	85	85	77	-	-	45	21	20	35	-	-	-
Barbados	100	100	100	99	99	100	94	-	97	93	93	98	93	93	-	-	-	-	-	-	-
Belarus	100	100	100	-	-	-	100	99	99	99	99	99	99	-	-	-	-	-	-	-	-
Belgium	-	100	-	-	-	-	-	-	97	96	96	82	65	95	-	-	-	-	-	-	-
Belize	91	100	82	47	71	25	100	99	99	95	95	95	96	96	-	-	66	-	-	-	-
Benin	68	79	60	32	58	12	73	99	99	83	89	85	89	-	69	12	35	42	32	7	60
Bhutan	62	86	60	70	65	70	0	92	93	89	90	87	89	-	-	-	-	-	-	-	-
Bolivia	85	95	68	45	58	23	34	93	94	81	79	64	84	81	-	22	52	54	-	-	-
Bosnia and Herzegovina	98	100	96	93	99	88	70	95	93	84	87	88	81	79	-	2	80	23	-	-	-
Botswana	95	100	90	41	57	25	100	99	98	97	97	90	79	-	-	40	14	7	-	-	-
Brazil	89	96	58	75	83	35	100	99	96	96	98	99	90	96	-	24x	46x	28	-	-	-
Brunei Darussalam	-	-	-	-	-	-	100	99	99	92	92	99	99	92	-	-	-	-	-	-	-
Bulgaria	100	100	100	100	100	100	100	98	95	95	94	95	94	-	-	-	-	-	-	-	-
Burkina Faso	51	82	44	12	45	5	100	99	99	88	83	78	-	-	65	9	36	-	20	2	50
Burundi	79	90	78	36	47	35	6	84	86	74	69	75	83	83	45	13	40	16	3	1	31
Cambodia	34	58	29	16	53	8	12	95	92	85	86	80	-	-	51	20	37	59	-	-	-
Cameroon	63	84	41	48	63	33	65	83	80	73	72	64	-	-	60	11	40	33	-	-	-
Canada	100	100	99	100	100	99	-	-	97	91	88	95	-	83	-	-	-	-	-	-	-
Cape Verde	80	86	73	42	61	19	80	79	78	75	76	69	68	-	-	-	-	-	-	-	-
Central African Republic	75	93	61	27	47	12	0	70	65	40	40	35	-	-	42	10	32	47	31	2	69
Chad	34	40	32	8	30	0	42	38	68	50	47	56	-	-	40	12	22	50	27	1	32
Chile	95	100	59	92	96	64	100	96	94	94	94	95	-	94	-	-	-	-	-	-	-
China	77	92	68	44	69	29	100	94	97	91	92	84	72	-	-	-	-	-	-	-	-
Colombia	92	99	71	86	96	54	100	92	95	89	89	92	89	89	-	13	51	44	24	1	-
Comoros	94	90	96	23	38	15	0	79	85	76	73	73	77	-	46	10	49	31	36	9	63
Congo	46	72	17	9	14	2	73	85	67	67	67	65	-	-	65	-	-	-	-	-	-
Congo, Democratic Republic of the	46	83	29	29	43	23	17	78	76	64	63	64	-	-	58	11	36	17	12	1	45
Cook Islands	95	98	88	100	100	100	11	99	99	99	99	99	99	-	-	-	-	-	-	-	-
Costa Rica	97	100	92	92	89	97	100	90	89	90	90	88	89	90	-	-	-	-	-	-	-
Côte d'Ivoire	84	98	74	40	61	23	58	51	63	50	50	49	50	-	75	4	38	34	14	4	-
Croatia	-	-	-	-	-	-	100	98	96	96	98	96	-	93	-	-	-	-	-	-	-
Cuba	91	95	78	98	99	95	99	99	89	88	88	99	99	99	-	-	-	-	-	-	-
Cyprus	100	100	100	100	100	100	25	-	99	98	98	86	88	58	-	-	-	-	-	-	-
Czech Republic	-	-	-	-	-	-	-	99	98	98	96	97	98	98	-	-	-	-	-	-	-
Denmark	100	100	100	-	-	-	-	-	95	95	95	96	-	95	-	-	-	-	-	-	-
Djibouti	80	82	67	50	55	27	85	78	81	64	64	60	-	-	-	-	-	-	-	-	-
Dominica	97	100	90	83	86	75	70	99	99	99	99	99	-	-	-	-	-	-	-	-	-
Dominican Republic	93	98	85	57	67	43	60	97	88	71	57	79	71	71	-	20	63	53	-	-	-
Ecuador	86	92	77	72	80	59	100	99	99	90	93	99	90	90	-	-	-	-	-	-	-
Egypt	98	100	97	68	84	56	100	98	98	97	97	97	97	-	71	10	70	29	-	-	-
El Salvador	82	91	68	63	78	40	100	94	90	90	90	93	83	83	-	42	62	-	-	-	-
Equatorial Guinea	44	45	42	53	60	46	100	73	65	33	39	51	-	-	40	-	-	36	15	1	49
Eritrea	57	72	54	9	34	3	0	91	91	83	83	84	83	-	62	19	44	54	12	4	4
Estonia	-	-	-	-	93	-	-	99	98	94	95	96	90	27	-	-	-	-	-	-	-
Ethiopia	22	81	11	6	19	4	18	82	93	80	80	71	-	-	45	24	16	38	-	-	3
Fiji	-	-	-	98	99	98	100	93	75	71	76	62	73	71	-	-	-	-	-	-	-

	% of population using improved drinking water sources 2002			% of population using adequate sanitation facilities 2002			% of routine EPI vaccines financed by government 2004	Immunization 2004 — 1-year-old children immunized against: TB	DPT		Polio	Measles	HepB	Hib	% new-borns protected against tetanus	% under-fives with ARI	% under-fives with ARI taken to health provider	% under-fives with diarrhoea receiving oral rehydration and continued feeding 1996-2004*	Malaria: 1999-2004 % under-fives sleeping under a mosquito net	% under-fives sleeping under a treated mosquito net	% under-fives with fever receiving anti-malarial drugs
	total	urban	rural	total	urban	rural	total	BCG	DPT1'	DPT3'	polio3	measles	hepB3	Hib3		1998-2004*	1998-2004*				
Finland	100	100	100	100	100	100	-	98	98	98	96	97	-	96	-	-	-	-	-	-	-
France	-	100	-	-	-	-	-	85	98	97	97	86	28	86	-	-	-	-	-	-	-
Gabon	87	95	47	36	37	30	100	89	69	38	31	55	-	-	45	13	48	44	-	-	-
Gambia	82	95	77	53	72	46	45	95	95	92	90	90	90	90	-	8	75	38	42	15	55
Georgia	76	90	61	83	96	69	20	91	88	78	66	86	64	-	-	4	99	-	-	-	-
Germany	100	100	100	-	-	-	-	-	98	97	94	92	81	90	-	-	-	-	-	-	-
Ghana	79	93	68	58	74	46	62	92	88	80	81	83	80	80	70	10	44	40	15	4	63
Greece	-	-	-	-	-	-	-	88	96	88	87	88	88	88	-	-	-	-	-	-	-
Grenada	95	97	93	97	96	97	100	-	87	83	84	74	83	83	-	-	-	-	-	-	-
Guatemala	95	99	92	61	72	52	100	98	94	84	84	75	-	-	-	18	64	22	6	1	-
Guinea	51	78	38	13	25	6	8	71	75	69	68	73	-	-	77	15	33	44	25	4	56
Guinea-Bissau	59	79	49	34	57	23	0	80	86	80	80	80	-	-	56	10	64	23	67	7	58
Guyana	83	83	83	70	86	60	60	94	90	91	91	88	91	91	-	5	78	40	67	6	3
Haiti	71	91	59	34	52	23	30	71	76	43	43	54	-	-	52	39	26	41	-	-	12
Holy See	-	-	-	-	-	-	-	-	-	-	-	-	-	-	-	-	-	-	-	-	-
Honduras	90	99	82	68	89	52	100	93	96	89	90	92	89	89	-	-	-	-	-	-	-
Hungary	99	100	98	95	100	85	-	99	99	99	99	99	-	99	-	-	-	-	-	-	-
Iceland	100	100	100	-	-	-	-	-	99	99	99	93	-	99	-	-	-	-	-	-	-
India	86	96	82	30	58	18	100	73	71	64	70	56	-	-	80	19	67	22	-	-	-
Indonesia	78	89	69	52	71	38	80	82	88	70	70	72	75	-	54	8	61	61	-	-	1
Iran (Islamic Republic of)	93	98	83	84	86	78	100	99	99	99	98	96	95	-	-	24	93	-	-	-	-
Iraq	81	97	50	80	95	48	100	93	93	81	87	90	70	-	70	7	76	-	-	-	-
Ireland	-	100	-	-	-	-	-	90	96	89	89	81	-	89	-	-	-	-	-	-	-
Israel	100	100	100	-	100	-	100	-	98	96	92	96	98	96	-	-	-	-	-	-	-
Italy	-	100	-	-	-	-	-	-	98	96	97	84	95	90	-	-	-	-	-	-	-
Jamaica	93	98	87	80	90	68	100	85	86	77	71	80	77	77	-	3	39	21	-	-	-
Japan	100	100	100	100	100	100	100	-	99	99	97	99	-	-	-	-	-	-	-	-	-
Jordan	91	91	91	93	94	85	100	58	96	95	95	99	95	95	-	6	78	44	-	-	-
Kazakhstan	86	96	72	72	87	52	100	65	85	82	99	99	99	-	-	3	48	22	-	-	-
Kenya	62	89	46	48	56	43	5	87	72	73	73	73	73	73	70	18	49	33	15	5	27
Kiribati	64	77	53	39	59	22	100	94	75	62	61	56	67	-	-	-	-	-	-	-	-
Korea, Democratic People's Republic of	100	100	100	59	58	60	80	95	75	72	99	95	98	-	-	12	93	-	-	-	-
Korea, Republic of	92	97	71	-	-	-	100	93	95	88	90	99	92	-	-	-	-	-	-	-	-
Kuwait	-	-	-	-	-	-	100	-	99	98	98	97	94	98	-	-	-	-	-	-	-
Kyrgyzstan	76	98	66	60	75	51	22	98	99	99	98	99	99	-	-	4x	48x	16	-	-	-
Lao People's Democratic Republic	43	66	38	24	61	14	0	60	66	45	46	36	45	-	30	1	36	37	82	18	9
Latvia	-	-	-	-	-	-	100	99	99	98	97	99	99	95	-	-	-	-	-	-	-
Lebanon	100	100	100	98	100	87	100	-	98	92	92	96	88	92	-	4	74	-	-	-	-
Lesotho	76	88	74	37	61	32	10	83	83	78	78	70	67	-	-	7	49	29	-	-	-
Liberia	62	72	52	26	49	7	0	60	48	31	33	42	-	-	35	39	70	-	-	-	-
Libyan Arab Jamahiriya	72	72	68	97	97	96	100	99	99	97	97	99	99	-	-	-	-	-	-	-	-
Liechtenstein	-	-	-	-	-	-	-	-	-	-	-	-	-	-	-	-	-	-	-	-	-
Lithuania	-	-	-	-	-	-	100	99	94	94	90	98	94	35	-	-	-	-	-	-	-
Luxembourg	100	100	100	-	-	-	-	-	98	98	98	91	49	86	-	-	-	-	-	-	-
Madagascar	45	75	34	33	49	27	0	72	71	61	63	59	61	-	55	9	48	47	-	-	34
Malawi	67	96	62	46	66	42	0	97	99	89	94	80	89	89	70	27	27	51	8	3	27
Malaysia	95	96	94	-	-	98	100	99	99	99	95	95	95	99	-	-	-	-	-	-	-
Maldives	84	99	78	58	100	42	100	98	98	96	96	97	97	-	-	22	22	-	-	-	-
Mali	48	76	35	45	59	38	100	75	99	76	72	75	73	-	50	10	36	45	72	8	38
Malta	100	100	100	-	100	-	-	-	76	55	55	87	8	55	-	-	-	-	-	-	-
Marshall Islands	85	80	95	82	93	59	-	91	71	64	68	70	72	46	-	-	-	-	-	-	-
Mauritania	56	63	45	42	64	9	100	86	83	70	68	64	-	-	33	10	41	28	-	-	-
Mauritius	100	100	100	99	100	99	100	99	99	98	98	98	98	-	-	-	-	-	-	-	-
Mexico	91	97	72	77	90	39	95	99	99	98	98	96	98	98	-	-	-	-	-	-	-
Micronesia (Federated States of)	94	95	94	28	61	14	0	62	83	78	82	85	80	65	-	-	-	-	-	-	-
Moldova, Republic of	92	97	88	68	86	52	86	96	98	98	98	96	99	-	-	1	78	52	-	-	-
Monaco	-	100	-	-	100	-	-	90	99	99	99	99	99	99	-	-	-	-	-	-	-
Mongolia	62	87	30	59	75	37	33	95	99	99	95	96	95	-	-	2	78	66	-	-	-
Morocco	80	99	56	61	83	31	100	95	99	97	97	95	95	10	-	12	38	50	-	-	-

TABLE 3. HEALTH

	% of population using improved drinking water sources 2002			% of population using adequate sanitation facilities 2002			% of routine EPI vaccines financed by government 2004	Immunization 2004 — 1-year-old children immunized against:							% newborns protected against tetanus	% under-fives with ARI	% under-fives with ARI taken to health provider	% under-fives with diarrhoea receiving oral rehydration and continued feeding 1996-2004*	Malaria: 1999-2004		
								TB	DPT		Polio	Measles	HepB	Hib			1998-2004*		% under-fives sleeping under a mosquito net	% under-fives sleeping under a treated mosquito net	% under-fives with fever receiving anti-malarial drugs
	total	urban	rural	total	urban	rural	total	BCG	DPT1'	DPT3'	polio3	measles	hepB3	Hib3							
Mozambique	42	76	24	27	51	14	47	87	88	72	70	77	72	-	60	10	55	33	10	-	15
Myanmar	80	95	74	73	96	63	0	85	86	82	82	78	54	-	85	2	66	48	-	-	-
Namibia	80	98	72	30	66	14	100	71	88	81	81	70	-	-	67	18	53	39	7	3	14
Nauru	-	-	-	-	-	-	100	95	93	80	59	40	75	-	-	-	-	-	-	-	-
Nepal	84	93	82	27	68	20	65	85	88	80	80	73	87	-	42	23	26	43	-	-	-
Netherlands	100	100	99	100	100	100	-	-	98	98	98	96	-	97	-	-	-	-	-	-	-
New Zealand	-	100	-	-	-	-	100	-	96	90	82	85	90	90	-	-	-	-	-	-	-
Nicaragua	81	93	65	66	78	51	40	88	92	79	80	84	79	79	-	31	57	49	-	-	2
Niger	46	80	36	12	43	4	100	72	75	62	62	74	-	-	43	12	27	43	17	6	48
Nigeria	60	72	49	38	48	30	100	48	43	25	39	35	-	-	51	10	33	28	6	1	34
Niue	100	100	100	100	100	100	100	96	99	99	99	99	99	99	-	-	-	-	-	-	-
Norway	100	100	100	-	-	-	-	-	91	91	91	88	-	93	-	-	-	-	-	-	-
Occupied Palestinian Territory	94	97	86	76	78	70	-	98	97	96	96	96	96	-	-	17	65	-	-	-	-
Oman	79	81	72	89	97	61	100	99	99	99	99	98	99	99	-	-	-	-	-	-	-
Pakistan	90	95	87	54	92	35	61	80	75	65	65	67	65	-	45	16x	66x	33x	-	-	-
Palau	84	79	94	83	96	52	100	-	99	98	98	99	99	98	-	-	-	-	-	-	-
Panama	91	99	79	72	89	51	100	99	99	99	99	99	99	99	-	-	-	-	-	-	-
Papua New Guinea	39	88	32	45	67	41	100	54	60	46	36	44	45	-	10	13x	75x	-	-	-	-
Paraguay	83	100	62	78	94	58	98	82	91	76	75	89	76	76	-	17x	51x	-x	-	-	-
Peru	81	87	66	62	72	33	100	91	95	87	87	89	87	91	-	20	58	46	-	-	-
Philippines	85	90	77	73	81	61	100	91	90	79	80	80	40	-	70	10	55	76	-	-	-
Poland	-	100	-	-	-	-	-	94	99	99	98	97	98	-	-	-	-	-	-	-	-
Portugal	-	-	-	-	-	-	-	83	98	95	95	95	94	95	-	-	-	-	-	-	-
Qatar	100	100	100	100	100	100	100	99	99	96	95	99	97	96	-	-	-	-	-	-	-
Romania	57	91	16	51	86	10	100	99	98	97	97	97	97	-	-	-	-	-	-	-	-
Russian Federation	96	99	88	87	93	70	100	96	98	97	98	98	96	-	-	-	-	-	-	-	-
Rwanda	73	92	69	41	56	38	50	86	94	89	89	84	89	89	76	12	20	16	6	5	13
Saint Kitts and Nevis	99	99	99	96	96	96	97	89	87	96	96	98	96	95	-	-	-	-	-	-	-
Saint Lucia	98	98	98	89	89	89	100	99	99	91	91	95	91	91	-	-	-	-	-	-	-
Saint Vincent and the Grenadines	-	-	93	-	-	96	100	99	99	99	99	99	99	99	-	-	-	-	-	-	-
Samoa	88	91	88	100	100	100	100	93	90	68	41	25	70	-	-	-	-	-	-	-	-
San Marino	-	-	-	-	-	-	-	-	95	98	98	98	97	98	-	-	-	-	-	-	-
Sao Tome and Principe	79	89	73	24	32	20	-	99	99	99	99	91	99	-	-	5	47	44	52	-	-
Saudi Arabia	-	97	-	-	100	-	100	95	96	96	96	97	96	96	-	-	-	-	-	-	-
Senegal	72	90	54	52	70	34	70	95	95	87	87	57	54	-	85	7	27	33	15	2	36
Serbia and Montenegro	93	99	86	87	97	77	25	97	96	97	96	96	89	-	-	3	97	-	-	-	-
Seychelles	87	100	75	-	-	100	100	99	99	99	99	99	99	-	-	-	-	-	-	-	-
Sierra Leone	57	75	46	39	53	30	0	83	77	61	61	64	-	-	76	9	50	39	15	2	61
Singapore	-	100	-	-	100	-	100	99	95	94	94	94	93	-	-	-	-	-	-	-	-
Slovakia	100	100	100	100	100	100	80	98	99	99	99	98	99	99	-	-	-	-	-	-	-
Slovenia	-	-	-	-	-	-	100	98	97'	97'	93	94	-	93	-	-	-	-	-	-	-
Solomon Islands	70	94	65	31	98	18	0	84	82	80	75	72	72	-	-	-	-	-	-	-	-
Somalia	29	32	27	25	47	14	0	50	50	30	30	40	-	-	60	-	-	-	1	0	19
South Africa	87	98	73	67	86	44	100	97	99	93	94	81	92	92	61	19	75	37	-	-	-
Spain	-	-	-	-	-	-	-	-	98	96	97	97	97	96	-	-	-	-	-	-	-
Sri Lanka	78	99	72	91	98	89	69	99	98	97	97	96	85	-	-	-	-	-	-	-	-
Sudan	69	78	64	34	50	24	0	51	79	55	55	59	-	-	37	5	57	38	23	0	50
Suriname	92	98	73	93	99	76	100	-	92	85	84	86	-	-	-	4	58	43	77	3	-
Swaziland	52	87	42	52	78	44	100	84	94	83	82	70	78	-	-	10	60	24	0	0	26
Sweden	100	100	100	100	100	100	-	16	99	99	99	94	1	98	-	-	-	-	-	-	-
Switzerland	100	100	100	100	100	100	-	-	98	95	95	82	-	91	-	-	-	-	-	-	-
Syrian Arab Republic	79	94	64	77	97	56	100	99	99	99	99	98	99	99	-	18	66	-	-	-	-
Tajikistan	58	93	47	53	71	47	2	97	87	82	84	89	81	-	-	1	51	29	6	2	69
Tanzania, United Republic of	73	92	62	46	54	41	23	91	99	95	95	94	95	-	90	14	68	38	36	10	58
Thailand	85	95	80	99	97	100	100	99	99	98	98	96	96	-	-	-	-	-	-	-	-
The former Yugoslav Republic of Macedonia	-	-	-	-	-	-	99	94	96	94	95	96	-	-	-	-	-	-	-	-	-
Timor-Leste	52	73	51	33	65	30	0	72	65	57	57	55	-	-	-	14	24	-	48	8	47
Togo	51	80	36	34	71	15	40	91	83	71	71	70	-	-	61	9	30	25	15	2	60
Tonga	100	100	100	97	98	96	100	99	99	99	99	99	99	-	-	-	-	-	-	-	-

	% of population using improved drinking water sources 2002			% of population using adequate sanitation facilities 2002			% of routine EPI vaccines financed by government 2004	Immunization 2004 1-year-old children immunized against:							% newborns protected against tetanus	% under-fives with ARI	% under-fives with ARI taken to health provider	% under-fives with diarrhoea receiving oral rehydration and continued feeding 1996-2004*	Malaria: 1999-2004		
								TB	DPT	DPT	Polio	Measles	HepB	Hib					% under-fives sleeping under a mosquito net	% under-fives sleeping under a treated mosquito net	% under-fives with fever receiving anti-malarial drugs
	total	urban	rural	total	urban	rural	total	BCG	DPT1'	DPT3'	polio3	measles	hepB3	Hib3		1998-2004*	1998-2004*				
Trinidad and Tobago	91	92	88	100	100	100	100	-	91	94	94	95	94	94	-	3	74	31	-	-	-
Tunisia	82	94	60	80	90	62	100	97	97	97	97	95	96	97	-	9	43	-	-	-	-
Turkey	93	96	87	83	94	62	100	88	86	85	85	81	77	-	41	29	41	19	-	-	-
Turkmenistan	71	93	54	62	77	50	67	99	98	97	98	97	96	-	-	1	51	-	-	-	-
Tuvalu	93	94	92	88	92	83	100	99	99	98	98	98	98	-	-	-	-	-	-	-	-
Uganda	56	87	52	41	53	39	7	99	99	87	86	91	87	87	53	22	67	29	7	0	-
Ukraine	98	100	94	99	100	97	100	98	96	99	99	99	98	-	-	-	-	-	-	-	-
United Arab Emirates	-	-	-	100	100	100	100	98	96	94	94	94	92	94	-	-	-	-	-	-	-
United Kingdom	-	100	-	-	-	-	-	-	96	90	91	81	-	91	-	-	-	-	-	-	-
United States	100	100	100	100	100	100	56	-	99	96	92	93	92	94	-	-	-	-	-	-	-
Uruguay	98	98	93	94	95	85	100	99	98	95	95	95	94	94	-	-	-	-	-	-	-
Uzbekistan	89	97	84	57	73	48	80	99	99	99	99	98	99	-	-	0	57	33	-	-	-
Vanuatu	60	85	52	50	78	42	100	63	73	49	53	48	56	-	-	-	-	-	-	-	-
Venezuela	83	85	70	68	71	48	100	97	99	86	83	80	82	61	-	9	72	51	-	-	-
Viet Nam	73	93	67	41	84	26	70	96	92	96	96	97	94	-	85	20	71	39	96	16	7
Yemen	69	74	68	30	76	14	100	63	92	78	78	76	49	-	21	24	47	23x	-	-	-
Zambia	55	90	36	45	68	32	10	94	94	80	80	84	-	80	83	15	69	48	16	7	52
Zimbabwe	83	100	74	57	69	51	0	95	90	85	85	80	85	-	70	16	50	80	3	-	-

SUMMARY INDICATORS

	total	urban	rural	total	urban	rural	total	BCG	DPT1'	DPT3'	polio3	measles	hepB3	Hib3							
Sub-Saharan Africa	57	82	44	36	55	26	47	76	77	65	68	66	33	-	59	14	41	34	15	3	35
Eastern and Southern Africa	56	87	43	37	60	27	24	87	89	80	79	77	54	-	62	18	47	37	14	4	26
Western and Central Africa	58	78	45	35	52	24	68	67	67	52	57	55	13	-	57	10	35	30	15	2	43
Middle East and North Africa	87	95	77	72	88	52	88	88	94	88	89	89	77	-	-	13	66	-	-	-	-
South Asia	84	94	80	35	64	23	90	77	75	67	71	61	11	-	70	19	59	26	-	-	-
East Asia and Pacific	78	92	68	50	72	35	90	92	94	86	87	83	71	-	-	10**	62**	59**	-	-	-
Latin America and Caribbean	89	95	69	75	84	44	95	96	96	91	92	92	83	91	-	-	-	36	-	-	-
CEE/CIS	91	98	79	81	92	62	89	93	94	93	94	93	90	-	-	15	50	25	-	-	-
Industrialized countries	100	100	100	100	100	100	69	-	98	96	94	92	63	92	-	-	-	-	-	-	-
Developing countries	79	92	70	49	73	31	80	84	84	76	79	74	46	-	64	16**	54**	33**	-	-	-
Least developed countries	58	80	50	35	58	27	38	82	87	75	74	72	28	-	54	16	38	36	20	3	36
World	83	95	72	58	81	37	80	84	86	78	80	76	49	-	64	16**	54**	33**	-	-	-

Countries in each category are listed on page 132.

DEFINITIONS OF THE INDICATORS

Government funding of vaccines – Percentage of vaccines routinely administered in a country to protect children that are financed by the national government (including loans).

EPI – Expanded Programme on Immunization: The immunizations in this programme include those against tuberculosis (TB), diphtheria, pertussis (whooping cough) and tetanus (DPT), polio and measles, as well as protecting babies against neonatal tetanus by vaccination of pregnant women. Other vaccines (e.g. against hepatitis B (HepB), haemophilus influenzae type B (Hib), or yellow fever) may be included in the programme in some countries.

BCG – Percentage of infants that receive Bacile Calmette-Guérin (vaccine against tuberculosis).

DPT1 – Percentage of infants that received their first dose of diphtheria, pertussis (whooping cough) vaccine and tetanus vaccine.

DPT 3 – Percentage of infants that received three doses of diphtheria, pertussis (whooping cough) and tetanus vaccine.

HepB3 – Percentage of infants that received three doses of hepatitis B vaccine.

Hib3 – Percentage of infants that received three doses of *Haemophilus influenzae* type b vaccine.

% under-fives with ARI – Percentage of children (0-4 years) with an acute respiratory infection (ARI) in the last two weeks.

% under-fives with ARI taken to health provider – Percentage of children (0-4 years) with ARI in the last two weeks taken to an appropriate health provider.

% under-fives with diarrhea receiving oral rehydration and continued feeding – Percentage of children (0-4 years) with diarrhoea (in the two weeks preceding the survey) who received either oral rehydration Therapy (Oral Rehydration Solutions or Recommended Homemade Fluids) or increased Fluids and continued feeding.

Malaria

% under-fives sleeping under a mosquito net – Percentage of children (0-4 years) who slept under a mosquito net.

% under-fives sleeping under a treated mosquito net – Percentage of children (0-4 years) who slept under an insecticide-impregnated mosquito net.

% under-fives with fever receiving anti-malarial drugs – Percentage of children (0-4 years) who were ill with fever in the last two weeks and received any appropriate (locally defined) antimalarial drugs.

MAIN DATA SOURCES

Use of improved drinking water sources and adequate sanitation facilities – UNICEF, World Health Organization (WHO), Multiple Indicator Cluster Surveys (MICS) and Demographic and Health Surveys (DHS).

Government funding of vaccines – UNICEF and WHO.

Immunization – UNICEF and WHO.

Acute respiratory infection – DHS, MICS, and other national household surveys.

Oral rehydration – DHS, MICS.

Malaria – MICS and DHS.

NOTES
-    Data not available.
- x   Indicates data that refer to years or periods other than those specified in the column heading, differ from the standard definition or refer to only part of a country.
- *   Data refer to the most recent year available during the period specified in the column heading.
- **   Excludes China.
- †   This was the first year that DPT1 coverage was estimated. Coverage for DPT1 should be at least as high as DPT3. Discrepancies where DPT1 coverage is less than DPT3 reflect deficiencies in the data collection and reporting process. UNICEF and WHO are working with national and territorial systems to eliminate these discrepancies.

TABLE 4. HIV/AIDS

Countries and territories	Adult prevalence rate (15-49 years), end-2003 estimate	Estimated number living with HIV 2003 — adults and children (0-49 years)	low estimate	high estimate	children (0-14 years)	women (15-49 years)	HIV prevalence in young pregnant women in capital city — year	median	% know condom can prevent HIV — male	female	% know healthy-looking person can have HIV — male	female	% have comprehensive knowledge of HIV — male	female	% used condom at last high-risk sex — male	female	orphaned by AIDS 2003 (thousands)	orphaned due to all causes 2003 (thousands)	Orphan school attendance ratio (1998-2004*)
Afghanistan	-	-	-	-	-	-	-	-	-	-	-	-	-	-	-	-	-	1600	-
Albania	-	-	-	-	-	-	-	-	-	42	-	40	-	0	-	-	-	-	-
Algeria	0.1	9.1	3.0	18	-	1.4	-	-	-	-	-	-	-	-	-	-	-	-	-
Andorra	-	-	-	-	-	-	-	-	-	-	-	-	-	-	-	-	-	-	-
Angola	3.9	240	97	600	23	130	-	-	-	-	-	-	-	-	-	-	110	1000	90
Antigua and Barbuda	-	-	-	-	-	-	-	-	-	-	-	-	-	-	-	-	-	-	-
Argentina	0.7	130	61	210	-	24	-	-	-	-	-	-	-	-	-	-	-	750	-
Armenia	0.1	2.6	1.2	4.3	-	0.9	-	-	56	41	48	53	8	7	44	0	-	-	-
Australia	0.1	14	6.8	22	-	1.0	-	-	-	-	-	-	-	-	-	-	-	-	-
Austria	0.3	10	5.0	16	-	2.2	-	-	-	-	-	-	-	-	-	-	-	-	-
Azerbaijan	<0.1	1.4	0.5	2.8	-	-	-	-	-	11	-	35	-	2	-	-	-	-	-
Bahamas	3.0	5.6	3.2	8.7	<0.2	2.5	-	-	-	-	-	-	-	-	-	-	-	7.6	-
Bahrain	0.2	<0.6	0.2	1.1	-	<0.5	-	-	-	-	-	-	-	-	-	-	-	-	-
Bangladesh	-	-	2.5	15	-	-	-	-	-	-	-	-	-	-	-	-	-	5300	-
Barbados	1.5	2.5	0.7	9.2	<0.2	0.8	-	-	-	-	-	-	-	-	-	-	-	3.7	-
Belarus	-	-	12	42	-	-	-	-	-	-	-	-	-	-	-	-	-	-	-
Belgium	0.2	10	5.3	17	-	3.5	-	-	-	-	-	-	-	-	-	-	-	-	-
Belize	2.4	3.6	1.2	10	<0.2	1.3	-	-	-	-	-	-	-	-	-	-	-	5.6	-
Benin	1.9	68	38	120	5.7	35	2002	2.3	53	45	69	56	14	8	34	19	34	340	-
Bhutan	-	-	-	-	-	-	-	-	-	-	-	-	-	-	-	-	-	90	-
Bolivia	0.1	4.9	1.6	11	-	1.3	-	-	74	58	67	59	-	-	37	21	-	340	82
Bosnia and Herzegovina	<0.1	0.9	0.3	1.8	-	-	-	-	-	53	-	74	-	-	-	-	-	-	-
Botswana	37.3	350	330	380	25	190	2003	32.9	90	93	79	81	33	40	88	75	120	160	99
Brazil	0.7	660	320	1100	-	240	-	-	-	-	-	-	-	-	-	-	-	4300	-
Brunei Darussalam	<0.1	<0.2	< 0.4	-	-	<0.2	-	-	-	-	-	-	-	-	-	-	-	4.2	-
Bulgaria	<0.1	<0.5	< 1.0	-	-	-	-	-	-	-	-	-	-	-	-	-	-	-	-
Burkina Faso	4.2	300	190	470	31	150	2002	2.3	61	48	61	56	23	15	67	54	260	830	109
Burundi	6.0	250	170	370	27	130	2002	13.6	-	47	-	66	-	24	-	-	200	660	70
Cambodia	2.6	170	100	290	7.3	51	-	-	-	64	-	62	-	37	-	-	-	670	71
Cameroon	6.9	560	390	810	43	290	2002	7.0	-	46	63	57	-	16m	31	16	240	930	94p
Canada	0.3	56	26	86	-	13	-	-	-	-	-	-	-	-	-	-	-	-	-
Cape Verde	-	-	-	-	-	-	-	-	-	-	60	53	-	-	-	-	-	-	-
Central African Republic	13.5	260	160	410	21	130	2002	14.0	-	20	-	46	-	5	-	-	110	290	91
Chad	4.8	200	130	300	18	100	2003	4.8	-	21	-	28	-	5	-	-	96	500	96
Chile	0.3	26	13	44	-	8.7	-	-	-	-	-	-	-	-	-	-	-	230	-
China	0.1	840	430	1500	-	190	-	-	-	-	-	-	-	-	-	-	-	20600	-
Colombia	0.7	190	90	310	-	62	-	-	-	-	-	82	-	-	-	30	-	910	-
Comoros	-	-	-	-	-	-	-	-	-	41	-	55	-	10	-	-	-	-	59
Congo	4.9	90	39	200	10	45	-	-	-	-	-	-	-	-	-	-	97	260	-
Congo, Democratic Republic of the	4.2	1100	450	2600	110	570	-	-	-	-	-	46	-	-	-	-	770	4200	72
Cook Islands	-	-	-	-	-	-	-	-	-	-	-	-	-	-	-	-	-	-	-
Costa Rica	0.6	12	6.0	21	-	4.0	-	-	-	-	-	-	-	-	-	-	-	50	-
Côte d'Ivoire	7.0	570	390	820	40	300	2002	5.2	-	53	67	64	-	16m	56	25	310	940	83
Croatia	<0.1	<0.2	< 0.4	-	-	-	-	-	-	-	-	-	-	-	-	-	-	-	-
Cuba	0.1	3.3	1.1	6.6	-	1.1	-	-	-	89	-	91	-	52	-	-	-	130	-
Cyprus	-	-	-	-	-	-	-	-	-	-	-	-	-	-	-	-	-	-	-
Czech Republic	0.1	2.5	0.8	4.9	-	0.8	-	-	-	-	-	-	-	-	-	-	-	-	-
Denmark	0.2	5.0	2.5	8.2	-	0.9	-	-	-	-	-	-	-	-	-	-	-	-	-
Djibouti	2.9	9.1	2.3	24	0.7	4.7	-	-	-	-	-	-	-	-	-	-	5	33	-
Dominica	-	-	-	-	-	-	-	-	-	-	-	-	-	-	-	-	-	-	-
Dominican Republic	1.7	88	48	160	2.2	23	-	-	88	84	89	92	-	-	52	29	-	260	96
Ecuador	0.3	21	10	38	-	6.8	-	-	-	-	-	58	-	-	-	-	-	290	-
Egypt	<0.1	12	5.0	31	-	1.6	-	-	-	-	-	-	-	-	-	-	-	-	-
El Salvador	0.7	29	14	50	-	9.6	-	-	-	-	-	68	-	-	-	-	-	180	-
Equatorial Guinea	-	-	-	-	-	-	-	-	-	26	-	46	-	4	-	-	-	24	95
Eritrea	2.7	60	21	170	5.6	31	-	-	-	62	-	79	-	37	-	-	39	230	83
Estonia	1.1	7.8	2.6	15	-	2.6	-	-	-	-	-	-	-	-	-	-	-	-	-
Ethiopia	4.4	1500	950	2300	120	770	2003	11.7	-	-	54	39	-	-	30	17	720	4000	60
Fiji	0.1	0.6	0.2	1.3	-	<0.2	-	-	-	-	-	-	-	-	-	-	-	25	-

	Adult prevalence rate (15-49 years), end-2003	Estimated number of people living with HIV, 2003 (in thousands)					HIV prevalence rate in young (15-24 years) pregnant women in capital city		% who know condom can prevent HIV		% who know healthy-looking person can have HIV		% who have compre-hensive knowledge of HIV		% who used condom at last high-risk sex		Children (0-17 years)		
		adults and children (0-49 years)	low estimate -	high estimate	children (0-14 years)	women (15-49 years)			male	female	male	female	male	female	male	female	orphaned by AIDS, 2003	orphaned due to all causes, 2003	Orphan school attendance ratio
	estimate						year	median									estimate (in thousands)	estimate (in thousands)	(1998-2004*)
Finland	0.1	1.5	0.5 -	3.0	-	<0.5	-	-	-	-	-	-	-	-	-	-	-	-	-
France	0.4	120	60 -	200	-	32	-	-	-	-	-	-	-	-	-	-	-	-	-
Gabon	8.1	48	24 -	91	2.5	26	-	-	71	64	81	72	22	24	48	33	14	57	98
Gambia	1.2	6.8	1.8 -	24	0.5	3.6	-	-	-	51	-	53	-	15	-	-	2	45	85
Georgia	0.1	3.0	2.0 -	12	-	1.0	-	-	-	56	-	51	-	-	-	-	-	-	-
Germany	0.1	43	21 -	71	-	10	-	-	-	-	-	-	-	-	-	-	-	-	-
Ghana	3.1	350	210 -	560	24	180	2003	3.9	81	77	83	78	44	38	52	33	170	1000	79p
Greece	0.2	9.1	4.5 -	15	-	1.8	-	-	-	-	-	-	-	-	-	-	-	-	-
Grenada	-	-	-		-	-	-	-	-	-	-	-	-	-	-	-	-	-	-
Guatemala	1.1	78	38 -	130	-	31	-	-	-	-	75	69	-	-	-	-	-	510	98
Guinea	3.2	140	51 -	360	9.2	72	-	-	-	-	56	60	-	-	32	17	35	420	113
Guinea-Bissau	-	-	-		-	-	-	-	-	32	-	31	-	8	-	-	-	81	103
Guyana	2.5	11	3.5 -	35	0.6	6.1	-	-	-	69	-	84	-	36	-	-	-	33	-
Haiti	5.6	280	120 -	600	19	150	-	-	72	46	78	68	28	15	30	19	-	610	87
Holy See	-	-	-		-	-	-	-	-	-	-	-	-	-	-	-	-	-	-
Honduras	1.8	63	35 -	110	3.9	33	-	-	-	-	90	81	-	-	-	-	-	180	-
Hungary	0.1	2.8	0.9 -	5.5	-	-	-	-	-	-	-	-	-	-	-	-	-	-	-
Iceland	0.2	<0.5	< 1.0		-	<0.2	-	-	-	-	-	-	-	-	-	-	-	-	-
India	-	-	2200 -	7600	-	-	-	-	-	-	-	-	17	21	59	51	-	35000	-
Indonesia	0.1	110	53 -	180	-	15	-	-	-	23	-	32	-	7	-	-	-	6100	82
Iran (Islamic Republic of)	0.1	31	10 -	61	-	3.8	-	-	-	-	-	-	-	-	-	-	-	2100	-
Iraq	<0.1	<0.5	< 1.0		-	-	-	-	-	-	-	-	-	-	-	-	-	-	-
Ireland	0.1	2.8	1.1 -	5.3	-	0.8	-	-	-	-	-	-	-	-	-	-	-	-	-
Israel	0.1	3.0	1.5 -	4.9	-	-	-	-	-	-	-	-	-	-	-	-	-	-	-
Italy	0.5	140	67 -	220	-	45	-	-	-	-	-	-	-	-	-	-	-	-	-
Jamaica	1.2	22	11 -	41	<0.5	10	-	-	-	-	-	-	-	-	-	-	-	45	-
Japan	<0.1	12	5.7 -	19	-	2.9	-	-	-	-	-	-	-	-	-	-	-	-	-
Jordan	<0.1	0.6	0.0 < 1.0		-	-	-	-	-	-	-	-	-	-	-	-	-	-	-
Kazakhstan	0.2	17	5.8 -	35	-	5.5	-	-	-	-	73	63	-	-	65	32	-	-	-
Kenya	6.7	1200	820 -	1700	100	720	-	-	68	59	86	83	47	34	47	25	650	1700	95
Kiribati	-	-	-		-	-	-	-	-	-	-	-	-	-	-	-	-	-	-
Korea, Democratic People's Republic of	-	-	-		-	-	-	-	-	-	-	-	-	-	-	-	-	710	-
Korea, Republic of	<0.1	8.3	2.7 -	16	-	0.9	-	-	-	-	-	-	-	-	-	-	-	630	-
Kuwait	-	-	-		-	-	-	-	-	-	-	-	-	-	-	-	-	-	-
Kyrgyzstan	0.1	3.9	1.5 -	8.0	-	<0.8	-	-	-	-	-	-	-	-	-	-	-	-	-
Lao People's Democratic Republic	0.1	1.7	0.6 -	3.6	-	<0.5	-	-	-	-	-	-	-	-	-	-	-	290	-
Latvia	0.6	7.6	3.7 -	12	-	2.5	-	-	-	-	-	-	-	-	-	-	-	-	-
Lebanon	0.1	2.8	0.7 -	4.1	-	<0.5	-	-	-	-	-	-	-	-	-	-	-	-	-
Lesotho	28.9	320	290 -	360	22	170	2003	27.8	-	58	-	46	-	18	-	-	100	180	87
Liberia	5.9	100	47 -	220	8.0	54	-	-	-	-	-	-	-	-	-	-	36	230	-
Libyan Arab Jamahiriya	0.3	10	3.3 -	20	-	-	-	-	-	-	-	-	-	-	-	-	-	-	-
Liechtenstein	-	-	-		-	-	-	-	-	-	-	-	-	-	-	-	-	-	-
Lithuania	0.1	1.3	0.4 -	2.6	-	<0.5	-	-	-	-	-	-	-	-	-	-	-	-	-
Luxembourg	0.2	<0.5	< 1.0		-	-	-	-	-	-	-	-	-	-	-	-	-	-	-
Madagascar	1.7	140	68 -	250	8.6	76	-	-	56	49	43	46	16	19	12	5	30	1000	76
Malawi	14.2	900	700 -	1100	83	460	2003	18.0	76	66	89	84	41	34	38	32	500	1000	93
Malaysia	0.4	52	25 -	86	-	8.5	-	-	-	-	-	-	-	-	-	-	-	480	-
Maldives	-	-	-		-	-	-	-	-	-	-	-	-	-	-	-	-	-	-
Mali	1.9	140	44 -	420	13	71	2003	2.2	56	42	59	46	15	9	30	14	75	730	72
Malta	0.2	<0.5	< 1.0		-	-	-	-	-	-	-	-	-	-	-	-	-	-	-
Marshall Islands	-	-	-		-	-	-	-	-	-	-	-	-	-	-	-	-	-	-
Mauritania	0.6	9.5	4.5 -	17	-	5.1	-	-	-	-	39	30	-	-	-	-	2	140	-
Mauritius	-	-	-		-	-	-	-	-	-	-	-	-	-	-	-	-	-	-
Mexico	0.3	160	78 -	260	-	53	-	-	-	-	-	-	-	-	-	-	-	1900	-
Micronesia (Federated States of)	-	-	-		-	-	-	-	-	-	-	-	-	-	-	-	-	-	-
Moldova, Republic of	0.2	5.5	2.7 -	9.0	-	-	-	-	-	56	-	79	-	19	-	-	-	-	-
Monaco	-	-	-		-	-	-	-	-	-	-	-	-	-	-	-	-	-	-

TABLE 4. HIV/AIDS

	Adult prevalence rate (15-49 years), end-2003	Estimated number of people living with HIV, 2003 (in thousands)					HIV prevalence rate in young (15-24 years) pregnant women in capital city		% who know condom can prevent HIV		% who know healthy-looking person can have HIV		% who have compre-hensive knowledge of HIV		% who used condom at last high-risk sex		Children (0-17 years)		Orphan school attendance ratio
	estimate	adults and children (0-49 years)	low estimate	-	high estimate	children (0-14 years)	women (15-49 years)	year	median	male	female	male	female	male	female	male	female	orphaned by AIDS, 2003 estimate (in thousands)	orphaned due to all causes, 2003 estimate (in thousands)	(1998-2004*)
Mongolia	<0.1	<0.5		<	1.0	-	<0.2	-	-	-	77	-	57	-	32	-	-	-	78	-
Morocco	0.1	15	5.0	-	30	-	-	-	-	-	-	-	-	-	-	-	-	-	-	-
Mozambique	12.2	1300	980	-	1700	99	670	2002	14.7	74	56	82	65	33	20	33	29	470	1500	80
Myanmar	1.2	330	170	-	620	7.6	97	-	-	-	-	-	-	-	-	-	-	-	1900	-
Namibia	21.3	210	180	-	250	15	110	-	-	86	73	87	82	41	31	69	48	57	120	92
Nauru	-	-		-		-	-	-	-	-	-	-	-	-	-	-	-	-	-	-
Nepal	0.5	61	29	-	110	-	16	-	-	-	-	-	-	-	-	-	-	-	1000	-
Netherlands	0.2	19	9.5	-	31	-	3.8	-	-	-	-	-	-	-	-	-	-	-	-	-
New Zealand	0.1	1.4	0.5	-	2.8	-	<0.2	-	-	-	-	-	-	-	-	-	-	-	-	-
Nicaragua	0.2	6.4	3.1	-	12	-	2.1	-	-	-	-	-	73	-	-	-	17	-	150	-
Niger	1.2	70	36	-	130	5.9	36	-	-	-	30	41	37	-	5m	30	7	24	680	-
Nigeria	5.4	3600	2400	-	5400	290	1900	2003	4.2	63	43	65	52	21	18	46	24	1800	7000	64p
Niue	-	-		-		-	-	-	-	-	-	-	-	-	-	-	-	-	-	-
Norway	0.1	2.1	0.7	-	4.0	-	<0.5	-	-	-	-	-	-	-	-	-	-	-	-	-
Occupied Palestinian Territory	-	-		-		-	-	-	-	59	44	-	49	-	-	-	-	-	-	-
Oman	0.1	1.3	0.5	-	3.0	-	<0.5	-	-	-	-	-	-	-	-	-	-	-	-	-
Pakistan	0.1	74	24	-	150	-	8.9	-	-	-	-	-	-	-	-	-	-	-	4800	-
Palau	-	-		-		-	-	-	-	-	-	-	-	-	-	-	-	-	-	-
Panama	0.9	16	7.7	-	26	-	6.2	-	-	-	-	-	-	-	-	-	-	-	48	-
Papua New Guinea	0.6	16	7.8	-	28	-	4.8	-	-	-	-	-	-	-	-	-	-	-	220	-
Paraguay	0.5	15	7.3	-	25	-	3.9	-	-	-	-	-	-	-	-	-	-	-	150	-
Peru	0.5	82	40	-	140	-	27	-	-	-	-	-	72	-	-	-	19	-	720	85p
Philippines	<0.1	9.0	3.0	-	18	-	2.0	-	-	59	44	-	67	-	-	-	-	-	2100	-
Poland	0.1	14	6.9	-	23	-	-	-	-	-	-	-	-	-	-	-	-	-	-	-
Portugal	0.4	22	11	-	36	-	4.3	-	-	-	-	-	-	-	-	-	-	-	-	-
Qatar	-	-		-		-	-	-	-	-	-	-	-	-	-	-	-	-	-	-
Romania	<0.1	6.5	4.8	-	8.9	-	-	-	-	-	-	77	70	-	-	-	-	-	-	-
Russian Federation	1.1	860	420	-	1400	-	290	-	-	-	-	-	-	-	-	-	-	-	-	-
Rwanda	5.1	250	170	-	380	22	130	2002	11.6	76	63	69	64	20	23	55	23	160	810	80
Saint Kitts and Nevis	-	-		-		-	-	-	-	-	-	-	-	-	-	-	-	-	-	-
Saint Lucia	-	-		-		-	-	-	-	-	-	-	-	-	-	-	-	-	-	-
Saint Vincent and the Grenadines	-	-		-		-	-	-	-	-	-	-	-	-	-	-	-	-	-	-
Samoa	-	-		-		-	-	-	-	-	-	-	-	-	-	-	-	-	-	-
San Marino	-	-		-		-	-	-	-	-	-	-	-	-	-	-	-	-	-	-
Sao Tome and Principe	-	-		-		-	-	-	-	-	32	-	65	-	11	-	-	-	-	-
Saudi Arabia	-	-		-		-	-	-	-	-	-	-	-	-	-	-	-	-	-	-
Senegal	0.8	44	22	-	89	3.1	23	2002	1.1	-	49	-	46	-	13	-	-	17	460	74p
Serbia and Montenegro	0.2	10	3.4	-	20	-	2.0	-	-	-	-	-	-	-	-	-	-	-	-	-
Seychelles	-	-		-		-	-	-	-	-	-	-	-	-	-	-	-	-	-	-
Sierra Leone	-	-		-		-	-	-	-	-	30	-	35	-	16	-	-	-	350	71
Singapore	0.2	4.1	1.3	-	8.0	-	1.0	-	-	-	-	-	-	-	-	-	-	-	-	-
Slovakia	<0.1	<0.2		<	0.4	-	-	-	-	-	-	-	-	-	-	-	-	-	-	-
Slovenia	<0.1	<0.5		<	1.0	-	-	-	-	-	-	-	-	-	-	-	-	-	-	-
Solomon Islands	-	-		-		-	-	-	-	-	-	-	-	-	-	-	-	-	-	-
Somalia	-	-		-		-	-	-	-	-	2	-	13	-	0	-	-	-	770	65
South Africa	21.5	5300	4500	-	6200	230	2900	2002	24.0	-	83	-	54	-	20	-	20	1100	2200	95
Spain	0.7	140	67	-	220	-	27	-	-	-	-	-	-	-	-	-	-	-	-	-
Sri Lanka	<0.1	3.5	1.2	-	6.9	-	0.6	-	-	-	-	-	-	-	-	-	-	-	340	-
Sudan	2.3	400	120	-	1300	21	220	-	-	-	-	-	-	-	-	-	-	-	1300	96
Suriname	1.7	5.2	1.4	-	18	<0.2	1.7	-	-	-	58	-	70	-	27	-	-	-	13	89
Swaziland	38.8	220	210	-	230	16	110	2002	39.0	-	63	-	81	-	27	-	-	65	100	91
Sweden	0.1	3.6	1.2	-	6.9	-	0.9	-	-	-	-	-	-	-	-	-	-	-	-	-
Switzerland	0.4	13	6.5	-	21	-	3.9	-	-	-	-	-	-	-	-	-	-	-	-	-
Syrian Arab Republic	<0.1	<0.5	0.3	-	2.1	-	<0.2	-	-	-	-	-	-	-	-	-	-	-	-	-
Tajikistan	<0.1	<0.2		<	0.4	-	-	-	-	-	5	-	8	-	-	-	-	-	-	-
Tanzania, United Republic of	8.8	1600	1200	-	2300	140	840	2002	7.0	72	66	78	74	49	44	47	42	980	2500	82
The former Yugoslav Republic of Macedonia	<0.1	<0.2		<	0.4	-	-	-	-	-	-	-	-	-	-	-	-	-	-	-
Thailand	1.5	570	310	-	1000	12	200	-	-	-	-	-	-	-	-	-	-	-	1400	-
Timor-Leste	-	-		-		-	-	-	-	-	6	-	8	-	-	-	-	-	-	-

	HIV Prevalence							Knowledge and behaviour (1998-2004)* (15-24 years)								Orphans		
	Adult prevalence rate (15-49 years), end-2003	Estimated number of people living with HIV, 2003 (in thousands)					HIV prevalence rate in young (15-24 years) pregnant women in capital city		% who know condom can prevent HIV		% who know healthy-looking person can have HIV		% who have comprehensive knowledge of HIV		% who used condom at last high-risk sex		Children (0-17 years)		Orphan school attendance ratio
		adults and children (0-49 years)	low estimate -	high estimate	children (0-14 years)	women (15-49 years)	year	median	male	female	male	female	male	female	male	female	orphaned by AIDS, 2003	orphaned due to all causes, 2003	
	estimate																estimate (in thousands)	estimate (in thousands)	(1998-2004*)
Togo	4.1	110	67 -	170	9.3	54	2003	9.1	-	63	73	66	-	20m	41	22	54	240	96
Tonga	-	-	-		-	-	-	-	-	-	-	-	-	-	-	-	-	-	-
Trinidad and Tobago	3.2	29	11 -	74	0.7	14	-	-	-	54	-	95	-	33	-	-	-	28	-
Tunisia	<0.1	1.0	0.4 -	2.4	-	<0.5	-	-	-	-	-	-	-	-	-	-	-	-	-
Turkey	-	-	-		-	-	-	-	-	-	-	-	-	-	-	-	-	-	-
Turkmenistan	<0.1	<0.2	<	0.4	-	-	-	-	-	19	-	42	-	3	-	-	-	-	-
Tuvalu	-	-	-		-	-	-	-	-	-	-	-	-	-	-	-	-	-	-
Uganda	4.1	530	350 -	880	84	270	2001	10.0	81	68	83	76	40	28	62	44	940	2000	95
Ukraine	1.4	360	180 -	590	-	120	-	-	-	57	-	78	-	-	-	-	-	-	-
United Arab Emirates	-	-	-		-	-	-	-	-	-	-	-	-	-	-	-	-	-	-
United Kingdom	0.1	32	16 -	52	-	7.0	-	-	-	-	-	-	-	-	-	-	-	-	-
United States	0.6	950	470 -	1600	-	240	-	-	-	-	-	-	-	-	-	-	-	-	-
Uruguay	0.3	6.0	2.8 -	9.7	-	1.9	-	-	-	-	-	-	-	-	-	-	-	62	-
Uzbekistan	0.1	11	4.9 -	30	-	3.7	-	-	50	28	58	55	7	8	50	-	-	-	-
Vanuatu	-	-	-		-	-	-	-	-	-	-	-	-	-	-	-	-	-	-
Venezuela	0.7	110	47 -	170	-	32	-	-	-	28	-	78	-	-	-	-	-	460	-
Viet Nam	0.4	220	110 -	360	-	65	-	-	-	60	-	61	-	25	-	-	-	2100	-
Yemen	0.1	12	4.0 -	24	-	-	-	-	-	-	-	-	-	-	-	-	-	-	-
Zambia	16.5	920	730 -	1100	85	470	2002	22.1	68	67	73	74	33	31	42	33	630	1100	92
Zimbabwe	24.6	1800	1500 -	2000	120	930	-	-	81	73	83	74	-	-	69	42	980	1300	98

SUMMARY INDICATORS

Sub-Saharan Africa	7.5	25000	23000 -	27900	1900	13100	-		68	54	68	58	31	23	43	27	12100	42000	83
Eastern and Southern Africa	10.2	17100	15900 -	18800	1200	9100	-		73	64	71	61	39	28	42	27	7900	22200	82
Western and Central Africa	4.8	7800	6400 -	10300	650	4100	-		64	46	65	53	23	18	45	26	4200	19800	-
Middle East and North Africa	0.3	510	230 -	1400	22	230	-		-	-	-	-	-	-	-	-	-	-	-
South Asia	0.7	5000	2400 -	7700	130	1500	-		-	-	-	-	17	21	59	51	-	48100	-
East Asia and Pacific	0.2	2400	1800 -	3200	39	640	-		-	-	-	-	-	-	-	-	-	37400	-
Latin America and Caribbean	0.7	2000	1600 -	2600	48	760	-		-	-	-	-	-	-	-	-	-	12400	-
CEE/CIS	0.6	1300	840 -	1900	8.1	440	-		-	-	-	-	-	-	-	-	-	-	-
Industrialized countries	0.4	1600	1100 -	2300	17	410	-		-	-	-	-	-	-	-	-	-	-	-
Developing countries	1.2	34900	31600 -	39600	2100	16300	-		-	-	-	-	-	-	-	-	-	-	-
Least developed countries	3.2	12000	10800 -	14300	1000	6100	-		-	-	-	-	-	-	-	-	-	-	-
World	1.1	37800	34600 -	42300	2100	17000	-		-	-	-	-	-	-	-	-	-	143400	-

Countries in each category are listed on page 132.

DEFINITIONS OF THE INDICATORS

Adult prevalence rate – Percentage of adults (15-49 years) living with HIV/AIDS as of end-2003.

Estimated number of people living with HIV/AIDS – Estimated number of adults and children living with HIV/AIDS as of end-2003.

HIV prevalence among pregnant women – Percentage of blood samples taken from pregnant women (15-24 years) that test positive for HIV during 'unlinked anonymous' sentinel surveillance at selected antenatal clinics.

Know condom can prevent HIV – Percentage of young men and women (15-24 years) who report through prompted questions that condom use can prevent HIV transmission.

Know healthy-looking person can have HIV – Percentage of young men and women (15-24 years) who know that a healthy-looking person can have the AIDS virus.

Comprehensive knowledge of HIV – Percentage of young men and women (15-24 years) who correctly identify the two major ways of preventing the sexual transmission of HIV (using condoms and limiting sex to one faithful, uninfected partner), who reject the two most common local misconceptions about HIV transmission, and who know that a healthy-looking person can have the AIDS virus.

Condom use at last high-risk sex – Percentage of young men and women (15-24 years) who say they used a condom the last time they had sex with a non-marital, non-cohabiting partner, of those who have had sex with such a partner in the last 12 months.

Children orphaned by AIDS – Estimated number of children (0-17 years) as of end-2003, who have lost one or both parents to AIDS.

Orphan school attendance ratio – Percentage of children (10-14 years) who lost both biological parents and who are currently attending school as a percentage of non-orphaned children of the same age who live with at least one parent and who are attending school.

MAIN DATA SOURCES

Adult prevalence rate – Joint United Nations Programme on HIV/AIDS (UNAIDS), *Report on the Global HIV/AIDS Epidemic*, 2004.

Estimated number of people living with HIV/AIDS – UNAIDS, *Report on the Global HIV/AIDS Epidemic*, 2004.

HIV prevalence among pregnant women – UNAIDS, *Report on the Global HIV/AIDS Epidemic*, 2004.

Know condom can prevent HIV – Demographic and Health Surveys (DHS), Multiple Indicator Cluster Surveys (MICS), behavioural surveillance surveys (BSS) and Reproductive Health Surveys (RHS) (1998-2003) and www.measuredhs.com/hivdata.

Know healthy-looking person can have HIV – DHS, BSS, RHS and MICS (1998-2003) and www.measuredhs.com/hivdata.

Comprehensive knowledge of HIV – DHS, BSS, RHS and MICS (1998-2003) and www.measuredhs.com/hivdata.

Condom use at last high-risk sex – DHS, MICS, BSS and RHS (1998-2003) and www.measuredhs.com/hivdata.

Children orphaned by AIDS – UNAIDS, UNICEF and USAID, *Children on the Brink 2004*.

Orphan school attendance ratio – MICS and DHS (1998-2003) and www.measuredhs.com/hivdata.

NOTES
-   Data not available.
- m   Data for the three knowledge indicators come from different sources.
- p   Proportion of orphans (10-14 years) attending school is based on 25-49 cases.
- *   Data refer to the most recent year available during the period specified in the column heading.

TABLE 5. EDUCATION

Countries and territories	Adult literacy rate 2000-2004* male	female	Number per 100 population 2002-2003* phones	Internet users	Primary school enrolment ratio (2000-2004*) gross male	female	net male	female	Primary school attendance ratio (1996-2004*) net male	female	% of primary school entrants reaching grade 5 Admin. data 2000-2004*	Survey data 1997-2004*	Secondary school enrolment ratio (2000-2004*) gross male	female	net male	female	Secondary school attendance ratio (1996-2004*) net male	female
Afghanistan	-	-	1	0	120	63	-	-	66	40	-	92	24	-	-	-	18	6
Albania	99	98	44	1	105	102	96	94	-	-	90y	-	81	81	76	78	39	39
Algeria	79	60	11	2	113	104	96	94	94	93	97	95	77	83	65	69	-	-
Andorra	-	-	115	12	101	101	88	90	-	-	-	-	80	84	69	74	-	-
Angola	82	54	2	0	80	69	66x	57x	57	59	-	76	21	17	-	-	22	20
Antigua and Barbuda	-	-	98	13	-	-	-	-	-	-	-	-	-	-	-	-	-	-
Argentina	97	97	40	11	120	119	-	-	-	-	92	78	97	103	79	84	-	-
Armenia	100	99	18	4	100	97	95	93	97	97	96	100	86	88	82	85	66	71
Australia	-	-	126	57	104	104	96	97	-	-	-	-	156	152	87	89	-	-
Austria	-	-	136	46	103	103	89	91	-	-	-	-	102	97	89	89	-	-
Azerbaijan	99	98	24	4	94	91	81	79	91	91	97y	99	84	81	77	75	76	75
Bahamas	-	-	78	26	92	93	85	88	-	-	73y	-	90	93	74	77	-	-
Bahrain	92	83	91	22	97	97	89	91	86	87	99	99	93	99	84	90	-	-
Bangladesh	50	31	2	0	94	98	82	86	78	80	54	86	45	50	42	47	35	36
Barbados	100	100	102	37	109	108	100	100	-	-	99	-	105	107	90	90	-	-
Belarus	100	99	42	14	103	101	95	94	-	-	99y	-	90	92	83	86	-	-
Belgium	-	-	128	39	106	105	100	100	-	-	-	-	153	169	97	98	-	-
Belize	77	77	32	11	123	121	98	100	-	-	81	-	76	80	67	71	-	-
Benin	46	23	4	1	127	92	69	47	61	47	68	92	38	17	27	13	19	12
Bhutan	-	-	5	2	-	-	-	-	-	-	91	-	-	-	-	-	-	-
Bolivia	93	80	22	3	116	115	95	95	78	77	84	50	88	85	72	71	57	56
Bosnia and Herzegovina	98	91	52	3	-	-	-	-	87	85	-	99	-	-	-	-	79	79
Botswana	76	82	37	3	103	103	79	83	83	86	88	96	70	75	50	57	-	-
Brazil	88	89	49	8	151	143	90	91	96	96	80y	84x	105	115	72	78	42	50
Brunei Darussalam	95	90	66x	10x	106	106	-	-	-	-	93	-	87	92	-	-	-	-
Bulgaria	99	98	85	21	101	99	91	90	-	-	94y	-	100	97	88	86	-	-
Burkina Faso	19	8	2	0	53	39	42	31	35	29	78	93	14	9	11	7	12	10
Burundi	67	52	1	0	86	69	62	52	50	44	68	80	13	9	10	8	6	6
Cambodia	85	64	4	0	130	117	96	91	66	65	61	93	31	20	30	19	21	13
Cameroon	77	60	5	0	116	99	-	-	76	73	64	93	34	28	-	-	24	22
Canada	-	-	107	48	101	102	100	100	-	-	-	-	106	105	97	98	-	-
Cape Verde	85	68	27	4	124	118	100	98	-	-	88	-	67	73	55	61	-	-
Central African Republic	65	33	1	0	78	53	-	-	47	39	-	70	-	-	-	-	10	7
Chad	41	13	1	0	95	61	75	51	46	33	44	96	22	7	12	4	9	5
Chile	96	96	73	27	99	97	85	84	-	-	99	-	91	92	80	81	-	-
China	95	87	42	6	115	115	99	99	-	-	99	-	71	69	-	-	-	-
Colombia	94	95	32	5	111	110	88	87	92	93	69	86	67	74	53	58	61	66
Comoros	63	49	2	1	98	81	59	50	31	31	-	24	34	28	-	-	10	11
Congo	89	77	10	0	83	77	55	53	-	-	66	-	37	27	-	-	-	-
Congo, Democratic Republic of the	80	52	1	0	52x	47x	-	-	55	49	-	54	24	13	-	-	18	15
Cook Islands	-	-	43	20	-	-	-	-	-	-	51x	-	-	-	-	-	-	-
Costa Rica	96	96	46	29	108	107	90	91	-	-	92	-	64	69	50	55	-	-
Côte d'Ivoire	60	38	9	1	86	69	67	54	62	53	88	94	33	18	27	15	15	11
Croatia	99	97	95	23	97	96	90	89	-	-	100y	-	89	91	86	87	-	-
Cuba	100	100	7	1	100	96	94	93	-	-	98	99	94	92	86	86	-	-
Cyprus	99	95	132	34	97	98	96	96	-	-	99	-	98	99	91	94	-	-
Czech Republic	-	-	132	31	103	101	87	87	-	-	98	-	96	98	89	92	-	-
Denmark	-	-	155	54	104	104	100	100	-	-	100	-	126	132	94	98	-	-
Djibouti	-	-	5	1	47	37	40	32	-	-	88	-	29	20	25	17	-	-
Dominica	-	-	42	16	91	85	83	79	-	-	84	-	108	120	86	98	-	-
Dominican Republic	88	87	39	10	123	125	99	94	92	93	65	93	53	65	30	41	19	26
Ecuador	92	90	31	5	117	117	99	100	-	-	74	-	59	60	50	51	-	-
Egypt	67	44	21	4	100	95	93	90	84	82	98	99	88	82	83	79	73	68
El Salvador	82	77	29	8	116	109	90	90	-	-	69	-	59	59	48	49	-	-
Equatorial Guinea	92	76	9	0	132	120	91	78	61	62	33	75	38	22	33	19	19	18
Eritrea	-	-	1	1	70	57	49	42	65	62	86	82	34	22	25	18	38	35
Estonia	100	100	112	44	103	99	95	94	-	-	98	-	95	98	87	90	-	-
Ethiopia	49	34	1	0	79	61	55	47	33	28	62	65	28	16	23	13	-	-
Fiji	94	91	26	7	109	109	100	100	-	-	88	-	78	83	73	79	-	-

	Adult literacy rate 2000-2004*		Number per 100 population 2002-2003*		Primary school enrolment ratio (2000-2004*)				Primary school attendance ratio (1996-2004*) net		% of primary school entrants reaching grade 5		Secondary school enrolment ratio (2000-2004*)				Secondary school attendance ratio (1996-2004*) net	
					gross		net				Admin. data 2000-2004*	Survey data 1997-2004*	gross		net			
	male	female	phones	Internet users	male	female	male	female	male	female			male	female	male	female	male	female
Finland	-	-	140	53	102	102	100	100	-	-	100	-	122	135	94	95	-	-
France	-	-	126	37	105	104	99	99	-	-	98x	-	108	109	93	95	-	-
Gabon	-	-	25	3	133	132	79	78	94	94	69	91	49	42	-	-	34	36
Gambia	-	-	10	2	86	84	79	78	55	50	-	98	41	28	39	27	23	20
Georgia	-	-	28	2	91	90	89	88	99y	100y	98y	-	80	80	62	61	-	-
Germany	-	-	144	47	100	99	82	84	-	-	99y	-	101	99	88	88	-	-
Ghana	63	46	5	1	87	79	65	53	62	60	63	98	47	38	39	33	34	35
Greece	94	88	136	15	101	101	99	99	-	-	-	-	98	97	85	87	-	-
Grenada	-	-	67	17	121	119	89	80	-	-	79	-	152	146	95	97	-	-
Guatemala	75	63	20	3	110	102	89	86	80	76	65	72	44	41	30	29	23	23
Guinea	-	-	2	1	92	71	73	58	59	54	-	94	33	15	28	13	17	8
Guinea-Bissau	-	-	1	1	84	56	53	37	44	38	-	85	23	13	11	6	10	7
Guyana	-	-	19	14	126	123	100	98	96	97	77	97	93	97	75	81	70	75
Haiti	54	50	6	2	-	-	-	-	52	57	-	88	-	-	-	-	14	18
Holy See	-	-	-	-	-	-	-	-	-	-	-	-	-	-	-	-	-	-
Honduras	80	80	10	4	105	107	87	88	-	-	-	-	-	-	-	-	-	-
Hungary	99	99	112	23	101	100	91	90	-	-	98y	-	106	106	94	94	-	-
Iceland	-	-	163	67	100	99	100	99	-	-	100	-	110	119	84	88	-	-
India	73	48	7	2	111	104	90	85	80	73	61	95	58	47	-	-	45	36
Indonesia	92	83	13	4	113	111	93	92	94	95	89	97	61	60	54	54	54	56
Iran (Islamic Republic of)	84	70	27	7	93	90	88	85	94y	91y	94	-	80	75	-	-	-	-
Iraq	-	-	3	0	120	100	98	83	84	72	66x	88	50	35	40	26	32	22
Ireland	-	-	137	32	106	106	95	97	-	-	99	-	102	112	80	87	-	-
Israel	98	96	142	30	112	112	99	99	-	-	85	-	94	92	89	89	-	-
Italy	-	-	150	34	102	101	100	99	-	-	96	-	100	99	91	92	-	-
Jamaica	84	91	70	23	100	99	94	95	-	-	90	92	83	85	74	77	-	-
Japan	-	-	115	48	100	100	100	100	-	-	-	-	102	102	99	100	-	-
Jordan	95	85	36	8	99	99	91	93	99	99	97	99	85	87	79	81	-	-
Kazakhstan	100	99	19	2	102	101	92	91	98	99	98y	99	92	92	87	87	73	76
Kenya	78	70	6	1	95	90	66	66	77	78	59	98	34	32	25	24	10	11
Kiribati	-	-	6	2	103	120	-	-	-	-	-	-	98	111	-	-	-	-
Korea, Democratic People's Republic of	-	-	4	0x	-	-	-	-	-	-	-	-	-	-	-	-	-	-
Korea, Republic of	-	-	124	61	106	105	100	100	-	-	100	-	90	91	88	88	-	-
Kuwait	85	81	77	23	93	94	82	84	-	-	97y	-	87	92	75	79	-	-
Kyrgyzstan	99	98	10	4	102	100	91	88	95	95	93y	100	91	92	-	-	58	60
Lao People's Democratic Republic	77	61	3	0	124	108	88	82	65	60	64	93	50	37	38	32	27	21
Latvia	100	100	81	40	95	93	86	85	-	-	98y	-	95	95	88	88	-	-
Lebanon	-	-	43	14	105	102	91	90	97	97	92	95	76	83	-	-	-	-
Lesotho	74	90	6	1	125	127	83	89	62	69	73	89	30	39	18	27	12	17
Liberia	72	39	0x	0x	122	89	79	61	59x,y	53x,y	-	-	40	28	23	13	-	-
Libyan Arab Jamahiriya	92	71	16	3	114	114	-	-	-	-	-	-	102	108	-	-	-	-
Liechtenstein	-	-	93	59	-	-	-	-	-	-	-	-	-	-	-	-	-	-
Lithuania	100	100	87	20	99	98	91	91	-	-	98y	-	103	102	94	94	-	-
Luxembourg	-	-	199	38	99	99	90	91	-	-	99	-	93	99	77	83	-	-
Madagascar	76	65	2	0	122	117	78	79	74	77	53	51	15x	14x	11x	12x	17	21
Malawi	75	54	2	0	143	137	-	-	74	77	44	80	37	29	32	26	7	9
Malaysia	92	85	62	34	93	93	93	93	-	-	87	-	67	74	66	74	-	-
Maldives	96	96	25	5	119	117	92	93	-	-	99y	-	62	71	48	55	-	-
Mali	27	12	1	0	66	50	50	39	45	34	75	93	25	14	-	-	15	11
Malta	86	89	125	30	105	104	96	96	-	-	99	-	95	95	86	88	-	-
Marshall Islands	-	-	9	3	110	103	85	84	-	-	-	-	75	76	64	66	-	-
Mauritania	60	43	14	0	89	87	68	67	46	42	61	83	25	20	18	14	14	9
Mauritius	88	81	55	12	103	104	96	98	-	-	99	-	81	81	74	74	-	-
Mexico	92	89	45	12	111	110	99	100	-	-	93	-	76	83	61	64	-	-
Micronesia (Federated States of)	-	-	16	9	-	-	-	-	-	-	-	-	-	-	-	-	-	-
Moldova, Republic of	97	95	35	8	86	86	79	79	98	99	91y	99	72	75	68	70	75	80
Monaco	-	-	149	49	-	-	-	-	-	-	-	-	-	-	-	-	-	-

TABLE 5. EDUCATION

	Adult literacy rate 2000-2004*		Number per 100 population 2002-2003*		Primary school enrolment ratio (2000-2004*) gross		net		Primary school attendance ratio (1996-2004*) net		% of primary school entrants reaching grade 5		Secondary school enrolment ratio (2000-2004*) gross		net		Secondary school attendance ratio (1996-2004*) net	
	male	female	phones	Internet users	male	female	male	female	male	female	Admin. data 2000-2004*	Survey data 1997-2004*	male	female	male	female	male	female
Mongolia	98	98	19	6	100	102	78	80	79	80	92y	95	78	90	72	83	58	69
Morocco	63	38	28	3	115	104	92	87	91	87	81	86	49	41	38	33	39	36
Mozambique	62	31	2	0	114	93	58	53	63	57	49	55	19	13	14	10	6	4
Myanmar	94	86	1	0	91	92	84	85	79	80	65	78	40	38	36	34	36	38
Namibia	87	83	18	3	105	106	76	81	78	78	92	95	59	66	39	50	29	40
Nauru	-	-	29x	3x	80x	82x	80	82x	-	-	-	-	52x	56x	-	-	-	-
Nepal	63	35	2	0	126	112	75	66	80	67	65	92	50	39	-	-	35	27
Netherlands	-	-	138	52	109	107	100	99	-	-	100		123	121	88	89	-	-
New Zealand	-	-	110	53	102	101	100	99	-	-	-	-	109	116	91	93	-	-
Nicaragua	77	77	12	2	109	108	86	85	77	84	65	63	56	66	36	42	35	47
Niger	20	9	0	0	51	36	45	31	36	25	69	89	8	6	7	5	8	5
Nigeria	74	59	3	1	132	107	74	60	66	58	-	97	40	32	32	26	38	33
Niue	-	-	84	48	121	114	99	98	-	-	76x		95	93	95	93	-	-
Norway	-	-	162	35	101	101	100	100	-	-	-	-	113	116	96	97	-	-
Occupied Palestinian Territory	96	87	22	4	99	99	91	91	91y	92y	98y	99	85	90	82	86	80	83
Oman	82	65	32	7	81	80	72	72	-	-	98		82	79	69	70	-	-
Pakistan	62	35	4	1	80	57	68	50	62	51	-	90	26	19	-	-	-	-
Palau	-	-	-	-	115	111	98	94	-	-	84x		89	89	-	-	-	-
Panama	93	91	39	6	114	110	100	99	-	-	90		68	73	60	66	-	-
Papua New Guinea	63	51	1	1	79	70	79	69	-	-	69		28	22	27	21	-	-
Paraguay	93	90	34	2	112	108	89	89	87x,y	87x,y	70	90x	64	66	50	53	-	-
Peru	93	82	17	10	119	118	100	100	96	95	84	97	93	86	70	68	48	48
Philippines	93	93	31	4	113	112	93	95	88	89	76	93	80	88	54	65	55	70
Poland	-	-	77	23	100	99	98	98	-	-	99		107	102	90	93	-	-
Portugal	-	-	131	19	118	112	100	99	-	-	-	-	108	118	81	89	-	-
Qatar	-	-	79	20	107	104	95	94	-	-	-	-	92	96	80	85	-	-
Romania	98	96	52	18	100	98	89	88	-	-	95y		84	85	79	82	-	-
Russian Federation	100	99	50	4	118	118	89	90	-	-	99y		-	-	-	-	-	-
Rwanda	70	59	2	0	122	122	85	88	75	75	47	78	18	15	-	-	5	5
Saint Kitts and Nevis	-	-	61	21	109	115	90	100	-	-	88y		92	121	94	100	-	-
Saint Lucia	90	91	41	8x	112	111	99	100	-	-	84x		77	96	68	85	-	-
Saint Vincent and the Grenadines	-	-	80	6	109	106	90	90	-	-	82		66	73	56	61	-	-
Samoa	99	98	13	2	107	104	99	96	-	-	94		73	79	59	65	-	-
San Marino	-	-	139	54	-	-	-	-	-	-	-	-	-	-	-	-	-	-
Sao Tome and Principe	-	-	8	10	130	122	100	94	77	78	61	71	42	36	32	26	39	39
Saudi Arabia	87	69	48	7	68	65	55	54	-	-	91		70	63	54	52	-	-
Senegal	51	29	8	2	83	77	61	54	52	45	80	93	23	16	-	-	16	10
Serbia and Montenegro	99	94	58	8	98	98	96	96	98y	96y	96y	94	88	89	-	-	-	-
Seychelles	91	92	85	14	115	114	100	99	-	-	99		111	111	100	100	-	-
Sierra Leone	40	21	2	0	93	65	-	-	43	39	-	94	31	22	-	-	14	12
Singapore	97	89	130	51	-	-	-	-	-	-	-	-	-	-	-	-	-	-
Slovakia	100	100	92	26	101	100	85	86	-	-	98y		91	92	88	88	-	-
Slovenia	100	100	128	40	108	107	94	93	-	-	99y		110	109	93	94	-	-
Solomon Islands	-	-	2	1	-	-	-	-	-	-	-	-	-	-	-	-	-	-
Somalia	-	-	5	1	-	-	-	-	12	10	-	79	-	-	-	-	-	-
South Africa	84	81	41	7	108	104	89	89	93	94	65	99	84	91	63	68	41	48
Spain	-	-	135	24	109	107	100	99	-	-	-	-	114	121	94	98	-	-
Sri Lanka	92	89	12	2	111	110	-	-	-	-	98		84	89	-	-	-	-
Sudan	69	50	5	1	64	56	50	42	54	52	84	71	38	32	-	-	11	12
Suriname	92	84	47	4	127	125	96	98	88	91	-	84	63	85	54	74	40	47
Swaziland	80	78	13	3	102	94	75	75	72	71	73	94	45	46	29	36	24	32
Sweden	-	-	162	57	109	112	100	99	-	-	-	-	127	151	99	100	-	-
Switzerland	-	-	157	40	108	107	99	99	-	-	-	-	101	95	89	84	-	-
Syrian Arab Republic	91	74	15	1	118	112	100	96	-	-	91		50	46	44	41	-	-
Tajikistan	100	99	4	0	113	108	97	91x	80	82	99y	94	94	78	90	76	80	73
Tanzania, United Republic of	78	62	3	1	98	95	83	81	47	51	88	97	6	5	5x	4x	2	3
Thailand	95	91	50	11	99	95	87	84	-	-	-	-	77	77	-	-	-	-
The former Yugoslav Republic of Macedonia	98	94	45	5	96	97	91	91	-	-	96y		86	84	82	80	-	-
Timor-Leste	-	-	-	-	-	-	-	-	76y	74y	-	-	-	-	-	-	-	-

	Adult literacy rate 2000-2004*		Number per 100 population 2002-2003*		Primary school enrolment ratio (2000-2004*)				Primary school attendance ratio (1996-2004*) net		% of primary school entrants reaching grade 5		Secondary school enrolment ratio (2000-2004*)				Secondary school attendance ratio (1996-2004*) net	
					gross		net				Admin. data 2000-2004*	Survey data 1997-2004*	gross		net			
	male	female	phones	Internet users	male	female	male	female	male	female			male	female	male	female	male	female
Togo	68	38	6	4	132	110	99	83	68	59	69	88	51	22	36	17	21	11
Tonga	99	99	15	3	114	111	100	100	-	-	84x,y	-	96	111	67	77	-	-
Trinidad and Tobago	99	98	53	11	101	99	91	90	95	96	71	100	79	86	69	75	69	75
Tunisia	83	65	31	6	113	109	97	97	95y	93y	96	92	75	81	61	68	-	-
Turkey	96	81	66	8	95	88	89	84	89	88	-	97	90	67	-	-	49	36
Turkmenistan	99	98	8	0x	-	-	-	-	86	84	-	100	-	-	-	-	50	61
Tuvalu	-	-	7	19	96	109	-	-	-	-	-	-	87	81	-	-	-	-
Uganda	79	59	3	0	142	139	-	-	78	79	64	89	22	18	17	16	14	15
Ukraine	100	99	37	2	93	93	84	84	-	-	99y	-	97	96	84	85	-	-
United Arab Emirates	76	81	102	27	98	95	84	82	-	-	93	-	77	80	70	72	-	-
United Kingdom	-	-	143	42	100	100	100	100	-	-	-	-	159	199	94	97	-	-
United States	-	-	117	56	98	98	92	93	-	-	-	-	94	94	88	89	-	-
Uruguay	97	98	47	12x	110	108	90	91	-	-	93	-	99	112	70	77	-	-
Uzbekistan	100	99	8	2	103	102	-	-	81	80	96y	89	97	94	-	-	70	73
Vanuatu	-	-	7	4	113	113	93	95	-	-	72	-	27	29	27	28	-	-
Venezuela	93	93	38	6	105	103	90	91	93	95	84	96	65	75	55	64	8	10
Viet Nam	94	87	9	4	105	97	98	92	97	96	87	96	75	70	-	-	59	57
Yemen	69	29	5	1	98	68	84	59	68	41	76	88	65	29	47	21	35	13
Zambia	76	60	3	1	85	79	69	68	68	68	77	88	30	25	25	21	21	23
Zimbabwe	94	86	6	4	94	92	79	80	85	86	70	94	38	35	35	33	44	42

SUMMARY INDICATORS

	male	female	phones	Internet users	male	female	male	female	male	female	Admin.	Survey	male	female	male	female	male	female
Sub-Saharan Africa	68	52	6	1	104	90	70	62	60	57	66	84	33	26	29	24	22	20
Eastern and Southern Africa	70	56	8	2	101	92	71	68	62	62	65	81	32	28	29	25	17	19
Western and Central Africa	69	48	4	1	105	85	68	55	59	51	-	87	39	29	35	28	25	21
Middle East and North Africa	77	57	22	4	98	89	84	78	82	77	91	90	70	63	60	55	46	39
South Asia	70	45	6	1	106	97	86	80	77	70	61	93	52	44	-	-	43	35
East Asia and Pacific	94	86	38	8	112	111	96	96	-	-	93	-	69	68	54**	55**	52**	55**
Latin America and Caribbean	91	89	40	9	121	118	95	94	91	91	83	-	85	91	64	68	40	46
CEE/CIS	99	96	46	6	101	98	89	87	89	88	98	96	91	83	-	-	-	-
Industrialized countries	-	-	125	45	101	101	95	96	-	-	-	-	106	109	91	92	-	-
Developing countries	83	70	24	5	108	101	88	83	76	72	78	90	61	57	50**	49**	40**	37**
Least developed countries	63	45	2	0	97	85	71	65	60	55	65	80	32	26	30	26	21	19
World	84	72	40	11	108	101	88	85	76	72	79	90	66	63	60**	60**	40**	37**

Countries in each category are listed on page 132.

DEFINITIONS OF THE INDICATORS

Adult literacy rate – Percentage of persons aged 15 and over who can read and write.

Gross primary school enrolment ratio – The number of children enrolled in a primary level, regardless of age, divided by the population of the age group that officially corresponds to the same level.

Gross secondary school enrolment ratio – The number of children enrolled in a secondary level, regardless of age, divided by the population of the age group that officially corresponds to the same level.

Net primary school enrolment ratio – The number of children enrolled in primary school who belong to the age group that officially corresponds to primary schooling, divided by the total population of the same age group.

Net secondary school enrolment ratio – The number of children enrolled in secondary school who belong to the age group that officially corresponds to secondary schooling, divided by the total population of the same age group.

Net primary school attendance – Percentage of children in the age group that officially corresponds to primary schooling who attend primary school or higher. These data come from national household surveys.

Net secondary school attendance – Percentage of children in the age group that officially corresponds to secondary schooling who attend secondary school or higher. These data come from national household surveys.

Primary school entrants reaching grade five – Percentage of children entering the first grade of primary school who eventually reach grade five.

MAIN DATA SOURCES

Adult literacy – UNESCO Institute for Statistics.

Phone and Internet use – International Telecommunications Union (Geneva).

Primary and secondary school enrolment – UNESCO Institute for Statistics.

Primary and secondary school attendance – Demographic and Health Surveys (DHS) and Multiple Indicator Cluster Surveys (MICS).

Reaching grade five – Administrative data: UNESCO Institute for Statistics. Survey data: DHS and MICS.

NOTES

-   Data not available.
x   Indicates data that refer to years or periods other than those specified in the column heading, differ from the standard definition or refer to only part of a country.
y   Indicates data that differ from the standard definition or refer to only part of a country, but are included in the calculation of regional and global averages.
*   Data refer to the most recent year available during the period specified in the column heading.
**   Excludes China.

TABLE 6. DEMOGRAPHIC INDICATORS

Countries and territories	Population (thousands) 2004		Population annual growth rate (%)		Crude death rate			Crude birth rate			Life expectancy			Total fertility rate 2004	% of population urbanized 2004	Average annual growth rate of urban population (%)	
	under 18	under 5	1970-1990	1990-2004	1970	1990	2004	1970	1990	2004	1970	1990	2004			1970-1990	1990-2004
Afghanistan	15183	5329	0.7	4.8	26	21	19	51	51	49	39	45	46	7.4	24	3.3	6.7
Albania	1048	256	2.2	-0.4	8	6	7	33	24	17	67	72	74	2.2	44	2.8	1.1
Algeria	12103	3099	3.0	1.8	16	7	5	49	32	21	53	67	71	2.5	59	4.4	2.8
Andorra	12	3	3.8	1.8	-	-	-	-	-	-	-	-	-	-	91	3.8	1.5
Angola	8277	2887	2.7	2.8	28	25	22	52	53	48	37	40	41	6.7	36	5.5	5.1
Antigua and Barbuda	27	8	-0.2	1.7	-	-	-	-	-	-	-	-	-	-	38	0.0	2.2
Argentina	12277	3350	1.5	1.2	9	8	8	23	22	18	66	71	75	2.3	90	2.0	1.4
Armenia	852	164	1.7	-1.1	5	8	9	23	21	11	70	68	72	1.3	64	2.3	-1.4
Australia	4816	1257	1.4	1.2	9	7	7	20	15	13	71	77	81	1.7	92	1.4	1.8
Austria	1571	387	0.2	0.4	13	11	10	15	12	9	70	76	79	1.4	66	0.2	0.4
Azerbaijan	2802	607	1.7	1.1	7	7	7	29	27	16	65	66	67	1.8	50	2.0	0.5
Bahamas	108	30	2.0	1.6	7	7	7	31	24	19	66	68	70	2.3	90	2.8	2.1
Bahrain	231	65	4.0	2.7	9	4	3	40	29	18	62	71	75	2.4	90	4.2	2.8
Bangladesh	58970	17284	2.4	2.1	21	12	8	45	35	27	44	55	63	3.2	25	7.1	3.6
Barbados	64	16	0.4	0.3	9	9	9	22	15	12	69	75	75	1.5	52	0.8	1.4
Belarus	2048	444	0.6	-0.3	7	11	15	16	14	9	71	71	68	1.2	71	2.7	0.2
Belgium	2131	565	0.2	0.3	12	11	10	14	12	11	71	76	79	1.7	97	0.3	0.4
Belize	116	34	2.1	2.5	8	5	5	40	35	27	66	72	72	3.1	48	1.8	2.6
Benin	4192	1406	3.0	3.3	22	15	13	47	47	42	46	53	54	5.7	45	6.7	5.2
Bhutan	973	289	2.2	1.8	23	14	8	43	39	30	41	54	63	4.2	9	5.1	5.2
Bolivia	4043	1231	2.3	2.1	20	11	8	46	36	29	46	59	64	3.8	64	4.0	3.1
Bosnia and Herzegovina	827	194	0.9	-0.7	7	7	7	23	15	9	66	72	74	1.3	45	2.8	0.3
Botswana	806	221	3.2	1.5	13	6	27	48	34	26	55	66	35	3.1	52	11.5	3.0
Brazil	62194	17946	2.2	1.5	11	7	7	35	24	20	59	66	71	2.3	84	3.7	2.3
Brunei Darussalam	128	40	3.4	2.5	7	3	3	36	28	23	67	74	77	2.4	77	3.7	3.6
Bulgaria	1406	332	0.1	-0.8	9	12	14	16	12	9	71	71	72	1.2	70	1.4	-0.4
Burkina Faso	6982	2393	2.4	2.9	23	18	17	50	50	47	43	48	48	6.6	18	6.6	5.0
Burundi	3875	1270	2.4	1.8	20	20	19	44	47	45	44	45	44	6.8	10	7.2	5.3
Cambodia	6250	1801	1.7	2.5	20	13	11	42	44	31	44	55	57	4.0	19	2.1	5.5
Cameroon	7801	2434	2.8	2.3	21	14	17	45	42	35	44	53	46	4.5	52	6.2	4.1
Canada	7007	1705	1.2	1.0	7	7	7	17	14	10	73	78	80	1.5	81	1.3	1.4
Cape Verde	236	70	1.4	2.4	12	8	5	40	39	30	57	65	71	3.6	57	5.5	4.2
Central African Republic	1997	636	2.4	2.0	22	17	22	43	42	37	42	49	39	4.9	43	3.4	3.0
Chad	5087	1804	2.4	3.2	25	19	20	48	48	48	40	46	44	6.7	25	5.3	4.5
Chile	4989	1246	1.6	1.4	10	6	5	29	23	15	62	73	78	2.0	87	2.1	1.8
China	358887	86055	1.6	0.9	8	7	7	33	21	13	62	68	72	1.7	40	3.9	3.5
Colombia	16685	4734	2.2	1.8	9	7	5	38	27	22	61	68	73	2.6	77	3.2	2.6
Comoros	380	125	3.3	2.8	18	11	8	50	41	36	48	56	64	4.7	36	5.1	4.5
Congo	2085	727	3.2	3.2	14	12	13	44	44	44	54	55	52	6.3	54	5.1	4.0
Congo, Democratic Republic of the	30127	10829	3.0	2.8	20	19	20	48	49	50	45	46	44	6.7	32	2.6	3.8
Cook Islands	7	2	-0.8	-0.1	-	-	-	-	-	-	-	-	-	-	72	-0.4	1.4
Costa Rica	1500	393	2.6	2.3	7	4	4	33	27	19	67	75	78	2.2	61	4.2	3.3
Côte d'Ivoire	8829	2751	4.3	2.5	18	14	14	51	45	37	49	52	46	4.9	45	6.2	3.4
Croatia	886	210	0.4	0.0	10	11	12	15	12	9	69	72	75	1.3	59	1.9	0.7
Cuba	2706	689	1.1	0.5	7	7	7	30	17	12	70	74	78	1.6	76	2.1	0.7
Cyprus	207	49	0.5	1.4	10	8	7	19	19	12	71	77	79	1.6	69	2.8	1.8
Czech Republic	1917	449	0.2	-0.1	13	12	11	16	12	9	70	72	76	1.2	74	2.1	-0.1
Denmark	1203	329	0.2	0.4	10	12	12	16	12	12	73	75	77	1.8	85	0.5	0.4
Djibouti	378	120	6.2	2.4	21	15	13	49	43	35	43	51	53	4.9	84	7.6	3.2
Dominica	27	7	0.1	0.6	-	-	-	-	-	-	-	-	-	-	72	1.9	1.1
Dominican Republic	3476	997	2.4	1.5	11	7	7	42	30	24	58	65	68	2.7	60	3.9	2.1
Ecuador	5090	1449	2.7	1.7	12	6	5	42	29	23	58	68	75	2.7	62	4.4	2.6
Egypt	29491	8795	2.3	1.9	17	9	6	40	32	26	51	63	70	3.2	42	2.4	1.7
El Salvador	2727	804	1.8	2.0	12	7	6	44	30	25	57	65	71	2.8	60	2.9	3.4
Equatorial Guinea	250	86	0.9	2.4	25	20	20	42	44	43	40	46	43	5.9	49	2.2	4.9
Eritrea	2183	733	2.5	2.4	21	16	11	47	42	39	43	48	54	5.4	20	4.0	4.2
Estonia	273	63	0.7	-1.2	11	13	14	15	14	10	71	69	72	1.4	70	1.2	-1.4
Ethiopia	39005	12861	2.7	2.8	21	18	16	49	47	41	43	47	48	5.7	16	4.6	4.4
Fiji	318	93	1.6	1.1	8	6	6	34	29	23	60	67	68	2.9	52	2.5	2.7

	Population (thousands) 2004		Population annual growth rate (%)		Crude death rate			Crude birth rate			Life expectancy			Total fertility rate 2004	% of population urbanized 2004	Average annual growth rate of urban population (%)	
	under 18	under 5	1970-1990	1990-2004	1970	1990	2004	1970	1990	2004	1970	1990	2004			1970-1990	1990-2004
Finland	1108	281	0.4	0.3	10	10	10	14	13	11	70	75	79	1.7	61	1.4	0.3
France	13290	3722	0.6	0.4	11	9	9	17	13	12	72	77	80	1.9	76	0.8	0.7
Gabon	646	193	3.0	2.5	21	11	13	35	39	31	47	60	54	3.9	85	6.9	4.1
Gambia	689	228	3.5	3.3	28	16	12	50	43	35	36	50	56	4.6	26	6.0	3.6
Georgia	1115	245	0.7	-1.4	9	9	11	19	16	11	68	71	71	1.4	52	1.5	-1.8
Germany	14933	3615	0.1	0.3	12	11	10	14	11	8	71	76	79	1.3	88	0.4	0.5
Ghana	10057	3069	2.7	2.4	17	12	11	46	40	31	49	56	57	4.2	46	3.9	4.0
Greece	1968	517	0.7	0.6	8	9	10	17	10	9	72	77	78	1.2	61	1.3	0.9
Grenada	35	10	0.1	0.4	-	-	-	-	-	-	-	-	-	-	41	0.1	2.2
Guatemala	6175	1988	2.5	2.3	15	9	7	44	39	35	52	61	68	4.5	47	3.2	3.2
Guinea	4625	1562	2.2	2.8	27	18	14	50	45	42	38	47	54	5.8	36	5.2	5.2
Guinea-Bissau	828	300	2.8	3.0	29	23	20	49	50	50	36	42	45	7.1	35	5.0	5.7
Guyana	264	76	0.1	0.2	11	10	9	38	25	21	60	60	64	2.2	38	0.7	1.2
Haiti	3842	1137	2.1	1.4	19	16	13	39	38	30	47	49	52	3.9	38	4.1	3.3
Holy See	-	-	-	-	-	-	-	-	-	-	-	-	-	-	100	-	-
Honduras	3284	975	3.2	2.6	15	7	6	48	38	29	52	65	68	3.6	46	4.8	3.6
Hungary	1993	481	0.0	-0.2	11	14	13	15	12	9	69	69	73	1.3	66	1.2	0.2
Iceland	78	21	1.1	1.0	7	7	6	21	18	14	74	78	81	2.0	93	1.4	1.2
India	419442	120155	2.1	1.8	17	11	9	40	31	24	49	58	64	3.0	28	3.4	2.5
Indonesia	75682	21477	2.1	1.4	17	9	7	41	26	21	48	62	67	2.3	47	5.0	4.4
Iran (Islamic Republic of)	25915	5890	3.4	1.4	14	7	5	43	35	19	54	65	71	2.1	67	4.9	2.7
Iraq	13499	4274	3.0	3.0	12	8	10	46	39	35	56	63	59	4.7	67	4.1	2.7
Ireland	1004	296	0.9	1.1	11	9	8	22	15	16	71	75	78	1.9	60	1.3	1.5
Israel	2169	660	2.2	2.7	7	6	6	27	22	20	71	76	80	2.8	92	2.6	2.8
Italy	9861	2661	0.3	0.2	10	10	10	17	10	9	72	77	80	1.3	67	0.4	0.2
Jamaica	998	262	1.2	0.8	8	7	8	35	25	20	68	72	71	2.4	52	2.3	0.9
Japan	21949	5912	0.8	0.2	7	7	8	19	10	9	72	79	82	1.3	66	1.7	0.5
Jordan	2442	734	3.5	3.8	16	6	4	52	37	27	54	67	72	3.4	79	4.7	4.5
Kazakhstan	4515	1079	1.1	-0.8	9	8	11	26	22	16	62	67	63	1.9	56	1.8	-0.9
Kenya	16898	5557	3.7	2.5	15	10	15	51	42	39	52	59	48	5.0	41	8.0	6.1
Kiribati	38	12	2.5	2.2	-	-	-	-	-	-	-	-	-	-	49	4.0	4.6
Korea, Democratic People's Republic of	6810	1763	1.6	0.9	9	8	11	33	21	16	61	65	63	2.0	61	1.9	1.3
Korea, Republic of	11031	2521	1.5	0.8	9	6	6	31	16	10	60	71	77	1.2	81	4.5	1.4
Kuwait	748	235	5.3	1.4	6	2	2	48	24	19	66	75	77	2.3	96	6.3	1.5
Kyrgyzstan	2027	539	2.0	1.2	11	8	7	31	31	22	60	66	67	2.6	34	2.0	0.4
Lao People's Democratic Republic	2788	884	2.1	2.4	23	17	12	44	43	35	40	50	55	4.7	21	4.5	4.7
Latvia	465	99	0.7	-1.1	11	14	13	14	14	9	70	69	72	1.3	66	1.3	-1.6
Lebanon	1230	327	0.7	1.8	8	8	7	33	26	19	65	69	72	2.3	88	2.4	2.2
Lesotho	848	232	2.2	0.9	17	11	25	42	36	28	49	58	35	3.5	18	5.6	1.2
Liberia	1744	621	2.2	3.0	22	21	21	50	50	50	42	43	42	6.8	47	4.6	3.8
Libyan Arab Jamahiriya	2119	623	3.9	2.0	16	5	4	49	28	23	51	68	74	2.9	87	6.7	2.6
Liechtenstein	7	2	1.5	1.2	-	-	-	-	-	-	-	-	-	-	22	1.6	1.5
Lithuania	769	154	0.8	-0.5	9	11	12	17	15	9	71	71	73	1.3	67	2.4	-0.6
Luxembourg	103	29	0.5	1.4	12	10	8	13	13	13	70	75	79	1.7	92	1.7	1.9
Madagascar	9193	3064	2.8	2.9	21	15	12	47	44	39	44	51	56	5.3	27	5.3	3.8
Malawi	6775	2319	3.7	2.1	24	19	21	56	51	44	41	46	40	6.0	17	7.0	4.6
Malaysia	9529	2738	2.5	2.4	10	5	5	37	31	22	61	70	73	2.8	64	4.5	4.2
Maldives	156	46	2.9	2.8	17	10	6	40	41	31	50	60	67	4.1	29	6.1	3.7
Mali	7231	2540	2.5	2.8	28	20	17	55	50	49	37	46	48	6.8	33	5.0	5.1
Malta	89	20	0.9	0.7	9	8	8	17	15	10	70	76	79	1.5	92	1.5	1.1
Marshall Islands	24	7	4.2	1.7	-	-	-	-	-	-	-	-	-	-	67	4.3	1.9
Mauritania	1471	513	2.4	2.7	21	17	14	46	43	41	42	49	53	5.7	63	8.2	5.3
Mauritius	364	98	1.2	1.1	7	6	7	28	20	16	62	69	72	2.0	44	1.0	1.6
Mexico	39787	10962	2.6	1.6	10	5	4	45	29	21	61	71	75	2.3	76	3.6	1.9
Micronesia (Federated States of)	51	16	2.2	0.9	9	7	6	41	34	31	62	66	68	4.3	30	2.7	1.8
Moldova, Republic of	1052	211	1.0	-0.2	10	10	11	18	19	10	65	68	68	1.2	46	2.9	-0.4
Monaco	7	2	1.2	1.0	-	-	-	-	-	-	-	-	-	-	100	1.2	1.0
Mongolia	1009	268	2.8	1.2	14	9	7	42	32	22	53	61	65	2.4	57	4.0	1.2
Morocco	11734	3343	2.4	1.6	17	8	6	47	29	23	52	64	70	2.7	58	4.1	2.9

TABLE 6. DEMOGRAPHIC INDICATORS

	Population (thousands) 2004		Population annual growth rate (%)		Crude death rate			Crude birth rate			Life expectancy			Total fertility rate 2004	% of population urbanized 2004	Average annual growth rate of urban population (%)	
	under 18	under 5	1970-1990	1990-2004	1970	1990	2004	1970	1990	2004	1970	1990	2004			1970-1990	1990-2004
Mozambique	9869	3254	1.8	2.6	24	21	20	48	44	40	40	43	42	5.4	37	8.3	6.6
Myanmar	18111	4716	2.1	1.5	18	12	10	41	31	20	48	56	61	2.3	30	2.5	2.8
Namibia	990	273	3.0	2.6	15	9	15	43	42	28	53	62	47	3.8	33	4.8	4.1
Nauru	5	2	1.9	2.5	-	-	-	-	-	-	-	-	-	-	100	1.9	2.5
Nepal	12260	3638	2.3	2.4	21	13	8	42	39	30	43	54	62	3.6	15	6.4	6.3
Netherlands	3556	979	0.7	0.6	8	9	9	17	13	12	74	77	79	1.7	66	1.0	1.3
New Zealand	1050	276	1.0	1.1	9	8	7	22	17	14	71	75	79	2.0	86	1.2	1.2
Nicaragua	2512	730	2.9	2.2	14	7	5	48	38	28	54	64	70	3.2	58	3.5	2.8
Niger	7511	2775	3.1	3.3	28	26	21	58	57	54	38	40	45	7.8	23	6.3	5.8
Nigeria	66211	21943	2.8	2.5	22	18	19	47	47	41	42	47	43	5.7	48	5.5	4.7
Niue	1	0	-	-	-	-	-	-	-	-	-	-	-	-	36	-	-
Norway	1082	286	0.4	0.6	10	11	10	17	14	12	74	77	80	1.8	80	0.9	1.3
Occupied Palestinian Territory	1885	637	3.4	3.6	19	7	4	50	46	38	54	69	73	5.4	72	4.4	4.2
Oman	1050	302	4.5	2.3	17	4	3	50	38	25	50	70	74	3.6	78	13.0	3.9
Pakistan	71297	20922	3.1	2.3	16	11	8	43	41	31	51	60	63	4.1	34	4.2	3.2
Palau	8	2	1.5	1.9	-	-	-	-	-	-	-	-	-	-	68	2.4	1.8
Panama	1153	341	2.4	2.0	8	5	5	38	26	22	65	72	75	2.7	57	3.0	2.4
Papua New Guinea	2717	820	2.4	2.4	19	13	10	42	38	30	44	52	56	3.9	13	3.9	2.4
Paraguay	2688	814	2.9	2.5	9	6	5	37	35	29	65	68	71	3.8	58	4.3	3.8
Peru	10701	3007	2.5	1.7	14	7	6	42	30	23	53	65	70	2.8	74	3.4	2.2
Philippines	34448	9873	2.6	2.1	11	7	5	40	33	25	57	65	71	3.1	62	4.5	3.8
Poland	8243	1830	0.8	0.1	8	10	10	17	15	10	70	71	75	1.2	62	1.5	0.2
Portugal	2010	562	0.7	0.3	11	10	11	21	12	11	67	74	78	1.5	55	3.6	1.5
Qatar	199	65	7.2	3.6	13	3	3	34	23	19	61	69	73	2.9	92	7.5	3.9
Romania	4490	1063	0.7	-0.4	9	11	12	21	14	10	68	69	72	1.3	55	2.1	-0.3
Russian Federation	29809	7052	0.6	-0.2	9	12	16	15	13	11	70	69	65	1.3	73	1.5	-0.2
Rwanda	4640	1477	3.2	1.6	21	33	18	53	48	41	44	32	44	5.6	20	5.7	11.0
Saint Kitts and Nevis	14	4	-0.5	0.3	-	-	-	-	-	-	-	-	-	-	32	-0.4	-0.3
Saint Lucia	57	14	1.4	1.0	8	7	7	41	26	19	64	71	73	2.2	31	2.2	2.1
Saint Vincent and the Grenadines	43	12	0.9	0.6	11	7	7	40	25	20	61	69	71	2.2	59	3.0	3.3
Samoa	87	26	0.6	0.9	10	7	6	39	34	28	55	65	71	4.3	22	0.9	1.2
San Marino	5	1	1.2	1.0	-	-	-	-	-	-	-	-	-	-	89	3.1	0.9
Sao Tome and Principe	72	23	2.3	1.9	13	10	9	47	37	34	56	62	63	3.9	38	4.4	2.2
Saudi Arabia	10517	3178	5.2	2.7	18	5	4	48	36	28	52	68	72	3.9	88	7.6	3.6
Senegal	5718	1820	2.8	2.5	25	14	11	49	44	37	39	53	56	4.9	50	3.7	4.2
Serbia and Montenegro	2416	611	0.8	0.2	9	10	11	19	15	12	68	72	74	1.6	52	2.1	0.4
Seychelles	41	14	1.4	0.7	-	-	-	-	-	-	-	-	-	-	50	4.6	0.8
Sierra Leone	2627	925	2.1	1.9	29	26	23	48	48	47	35	39	41	6.5	40	4.8	3.9
Singapore	1033	226	1.9	2.5	5	5	5	23	18	9	69	75	79	1.3	100	1.9	2.5
Slovakia	1174	259	0.7	0.2	10	10	10	19	15	9	70	72	74	1.2	58	2.3	0.3
Slovenia	352	87	0.7	0.1	10	10	10	17	11	9	69	73	77	1.2	51	2.3	0.2
Solomon Islands	223	71	3.4	2.8	10	9	7	46	38	33	54	61	63	4.2	17	5.5	4.2
Somalia	4016	1446	3.1	1.3	25	22	18	51	46	45	40	42	47	6.3	35	4.4	2.6
South Africa	18417	5248	2.4	1.8	14	8	18	38	29	23	53	62	47	2.8	57	2.5	2.9
Spain	7407	2160	0.8	0.6	9	9	9	20	10	11	72	77	80	1.3	77	1.4	0.7
Sri Lanka	6108	1631	1.7	1.0	9	6	6	31	21	16	62	71	74	1.9	21	1.5	0.9
Sudan	16328	5180	2.9	2.2	21	14	11	47	39	33	44	53	57	4.3	40	5.3	5.1
Suriname	163	46	0.4	0.8	8	7	7	37	24	21	63	68	69	2.6	77	2.1	1.9
Swaziland	519	138	3.2	1.3	18	10	29	50	41	29	48	58	31	3.8	24	7.5	1.5
Sweden	1949	479	0.3	0.4	10	11	10	14	14	11	74	78	80	1.7	83	0.4	0.4
Switzerland	1473	361	0.5	0.4	9	9	9	16	12	9	73	78	81	1.4	68	1.6	0.3
Syrian Arab Republic	8309	2488	3.5	2.6	13	5	4	47	36	28	55	68	74	3.3	50	4.1	2.8
Tajikistan	3062	839	2.9	1.4	10	8	8	40	39	29	60	63	64	3.7	24	2.2	-0.5
Tanzania, United Republic of	18833	5998	3.3	2.6	17	13	17	48	44	37	48	54	46	4.9	36	9.2	6.3
Thailand	18617	5020	2.1	1.1	9	6	7	37	21	16	60	68	70	1.9	32	3.8	1.7
The former Yugoslav Republic of Macedonia	504	119	1.0	0.4	8	8	9	24	17	12	66	71	74	1.5	60	2.0	0.7
Timor-Leste	442	160	1.0	1.3	22	18	12	46	40	50	40	45	56	7.8	8	0.1	1.2
Togo	3030	996	3.1	3.0	18	12	12	48	44	39	48	58	55	5.2	36	7.0	4.6
Tonga	44	12	-0.2	0.6	6	6	6	37	30	24	65	70	72	3.4	34	1.6	1.1

	Population (thousands) 2004		Population annual growth rate (%)		Crude death rate			Crude birth rate			Life expectancy			Total fertility rate 2004	% of population urbanized 2004	Average annual growth rate of urban population (%)	
	under 18	under 5	1970-1990	1990-2004	1970	1990	2004	1970	1990	2004	1970	1990	2004			1970-1990	1990-2004
Trinidad and Tobago	365	89	1.1	0.5	7	7	8	27	20	14	66	72	70	1.6	76	1.6	1.2
Tunisia	3312	806	2.4	1.4	14	6	5	39	27	17	54	69	74	1.9	64	3.7	2.1
Turkey	25283	7236	2.3	1.7	12	8	7	39	25	21	56	65	69	2.4	67	4.5	2.5
Turkmenistan	1896	484	2.6	1.9	11	8	8	37	35	22	58	63	63	2.7	46	2.3	1.9
Tuvalu	4	1	1.3	0.7	-	-	-	-	-	-	-	-	-	-	56	4.6	3.0
Uganda	15964	5744	3.2	3.2	16	18	15	50	50	51	50	46	48	7.1	12	4.9	3.9
Ukraine	9467	1930	0.5	-0.7	9	13	17	15	13	8	71	69	66	1.1	67	1.5	-0.7
United Arab Emirates	1150	325	10.6	5.9	11	3	1	36	27	16	61	73	78	2.5	85	10.7	6.1
United Kingdom	13208	3398	0.2	0.3	12	11	10	16	14	11	72	76	79	1.7	89	0.9	0.4
United States	74694	20243	1.0	1.0	9	9	8	17	16	14	71	75	78	2.0	80	1.1	1.5
Uruguay	997	283	0.5	0.7	10	10	9	21	18	17	69	72	76	2.3	93	0.9	1.0
Uzbekistan	10797	2815	2.7	1.7	10	7	7	37	35	23	63	67	67	2.7	36	3.1	1.1
Vanuatu	98	30	2.8	2.3	14	7	6	43	37	31	53	64	69	4.0	23	4.5	4.0
Venezuela	9947	2842	3.1	2.0	7	5	5	37	29	22	65	71	73	2.7	88	3.9	2.4
Viet Nam	30741	7900	2.2	1.6	18	8	6	41	31	20	49	65	71	2.3	26	2.7	3.5
Yemen	10986	3581	3.2	3.7	26	13	8	54	51	40	38	54	61	6.0	26	5.6	5.1
Zambia	6127	1987	3.3	2.3	17	17	23	51	46	41	49	47	38	5.5	36	4.7	1.6
Zimbabwe	6289	1756	3.5	1.4	13	9	23	49	38	30	55	60	37	3.4	35	6.1	2.9

SUMMARY INDICATORS

	under 18	under 5	1970-1990	1990-2004	1970	1990	2004	1970	1990	2004	1970	1990	2004	2004	2004	1970-1990	1990-2004
Sub-Saharan Africa	354355	117346	2.9	2.5	20	16	18	48	45	40	45	50	46	5.4	36	4.8	4.3
Eastern and Southern Africa	174309	56702	2.9	2.4	19	15	17	47	43	38	47	51	46	5.1	31	4.7	4.3
Western and Central Africa	180046	60644	2.8	2.6	22	18	18	48	47	43	43	48	46	5.8	41	4.9	4.4
Middle East and North Africa	153626	44067	3.0	2.1	16	8	6	45	35	26	52	63	68	3.2	58	4.4	2.9
South Asia	584389	169294	2.2	1.9	17	11	9	40	33	25	49	58	63	3.2	28	3.7	2.8
East Asia and Pacific	579131	146536	1.8	1.1	10	7	7	35	22	15	59	66	71	1.9	42	3.9	3.4
Latin America and Caribbean	199054	56526	2.2	1.6	11	7	6	37	27	21	60	68	72	2.5	77	3.3	2.2
CEE/CIS	106302	26430	1.0	0.2	9	11	12	21	18	14	67	68	67	1.7	63	2.0	0.2
Industrialized countries	205133	54200	0.7	0.6	10	9	9	17	13	11	71	76	79	1.6	77	1.1	0.9
Developing countries	1925281	548486	2.1	1.6	13	9	9	38	29	23	55	62	65	2.9	43	3.8	3.0
Least developed countries	361520	117229	2.5	2.5	21	16	14	47	43	37	44	50	52	4.9	27	4.9	4.4
World	2181991	614399	1.8	1.4	12	10	9	32	26	21	59	65	67	2.6	49	2.7	2.2

Countries in each category are listed on page 132.

DEFINITIONS OF THE INDICATORS

Life expectancy at birth – The number of years newborn children would live if subject to the mortality risks prevailing for the cross-section of population at the time of their birth.

Crude death rate – Annual number of deaths per 1,000 population.

Crude birth rate – Annual number of births per 1,000 population.

Total fertility rate – Number of children that would be born per woman if she were to live to the end of her childbearing years and bear children at each age in accordance with prevailing age-specific fertility rates.

Urban population – Percentage of population living in urban areas as defined according to the national definition used in the most recent population census.

MAIN DATA SOURCES

Child population – United Nations Population Division.

Crude death and birth rates – United Nations Population Division.

Life expectancy – United Nations Population Division.

Fertility – United Nations Population Division.

Urban population – United Nations Population Division.

NOTES - Data not available.

TABLE 7. ECONOMIC INDICATORS

Countries and territories	GNI per capita (US$) 2004	GDP per capita average annual growth rate (%) 1970-1990	GDP per capita average annual growth rate (%) 1990-2004	Average annual rate of inflation (%) 1990-2004	% of population below $1 a day 1993-2003*	% of central government expenditure allocated to: (1993-2004*) health	% of central government expenditure allocated to: (1993-2004*) education	% of central government expenditure allocated to: (1993-2004*) defence	ODA inflow in millions US$ 2003	ODA inflow as a % of recipient GNI 2003	Debt service as a % of exports of goods and services 1990	Debt service as a % of exports of goods and services 2003
Afghanistan	250x	0.7x	-	-	-	-	-	-	1533	-	-	-
Albania	2080	-0.6x	5.2	24	<2	4	2	4	342	6	4x	2
Algeria	2280	1.7	0.8	14	<2	4	24	17	232	0	62	19
Andorra	d	-	-	-	-	-	-	-	-	-	-	-
Angola	1030	0.4x	0.7	460	-	6x	15x	34x	499	5	7	15
Antigua and Barbuda	10000	6.3x	1.6	2	-	-	-	-	5	1	-	-
Argentina	3720	-0.7	1.0	5	3	5	4	3	109	0	30	20
Armenia	1120	-	3.6	103	13	-	-	-	247	8	-	6
Australia	26900	1.5	2.5	2	-	14	9	7	-	-	-	-
Austria	32300	2.5	1.8	2	-	13	10	2	-	-	-	-
Azerbaijan	950	-	-1.3	101	4	1	3	11	297	4	-	5
Bahamas	14920x	1.9	0.3x	3x	-	16	20	3	-	-	-	-
Bahrain	10840x	-1.9x	1.9x	1x	-	7	13	14	38	-	-	-
Bangladesh	440	0.5	3.1	4	36	7	18	10	1393	3	17	5
Barbados	9270x	1.8	1.4x	3x	-	-	-	-	20	1	14	5
Belarus	2120	-	1.6	225	<2	4	4	5	-	-	-	1
Belgium	31030	2.2	1.8	2	-	15	3	3	-	-	-	-
Belize	3940	2.9	2.2	1	-	8	20	5	12	-	6	24
Benin	530	0.3	2.1	7	-	6x	31x	17x	294	10	7	6
Bhutan	760	5.4x	3.6	8	-	11	17	0	77	13	5	5
Bolivia	960	-1.1	1.3	7	14	10	23	6	930	12	31	20
Bosnia and Herzegovina	2040	-	11.7x	3x	-	-	-	-	539	8	-	4
Botswana	4340	8.1	2.9	8	31	5	26	8	30	1	4	1
Brazil	3090	2.3	1.2	103	8	6	6	3	296	0	19	48
Brunei Darussalam	24100x	-	-	-	-	-	-	-	-	-	-	-
Bulgaria	2740	3.4x	1.0	68	5	12	5	7	-	-	5x	9
Burkina Faso	360	1.3	1.8	5	45	7x	17x	14x	451	13	6	10
Burundi	90	1.4	-3.1	12	55	2	15	23	224	32	41	63
Cambodia	320	-	4.1x	3x	34	-	-	-	508	12	-	0
Cameroon	800	3.4	0.4	4	17	3	12	10	884	9	18	11
Canada	28390	2.0	2.3	2	-	3	2	6	-	-	-	-
Cape Verde	1770	-	3.3	4	-	-	-	-	144	21	5	5
Central African Republic	310	-1.2	-0.5	4	67	-	-	-	50	5	8	12
Chad	260	-0.9	0.9	7	-	8x	8x	-	247	12	2	7
Chile	4910	1.5	3.9	7	<2	14	18	6	76	0	20	31
China	1290	6.6	8.4	5	17	0	2	12	1325	0	10	7
Colombia	2000	2.0	0.4	17	8	9	20	13	802	1	39	43
Comoros	530	0.2x	-0.9	4	-	-	-	-	24	9	2	3x
Congo	770	3.0	-1.2	7	-	-	-	-	70	3	32	3
Congo, Democratic Republic of the	120	-2.3	-5.8	523	-	0	0	18	5381	100	5x	0
Cook Islands	-	-	-	-	-	-	-	-	6	-	-	-
Costa Rica	4670	0.5	2.6	14	2	21	22	0	28	0	21	9
Côte d'Ivoire	770	-1.3	-0.6	7	11	4x	21x	4x	252	2	26	7
Croatia	6590	-	2.3	46	<2	16	8	5	121	1	-	20
Cuba	1170x	-	3.5x	-	-	23x	10x	-	70	-	-	-
Cyprus	17580	6.2x	3.1	4	-	6	12	4	-	-	-	-
Czech Republic	9150	-	1.7	9	<2	17	9	5	-	-	-	9
Denmark	40650	1.5	1.9	2	-	1	13	5	-	-	-	-
Djibouti	1030	-	-3.0	3	-	-	-	-	78	12	-	4
Dominica	3650	4.7x	1.1	2	-	-	-	-	11	5	4	13
Dominican Republic	2080	2.0	4.0	10	<2	13	17	6	69	0	7	7
Ecuador	2180	1.3	0.3	4	18	11x	18x	13x	176	1	27	25
Egypt	1310	4.2	2.4	7	3	3	15	9	894	1	18	11
El Salvador	2350	-1.8	1.9	6	31	13	15	3	192	1	14	8
Equatorial Guinea	c	-	16.3	17	-	-	-	-	21	-	3	0
Eritrea	180	-	0.8x	11x	-	-	-	-	307	36	-	13
Estonia	7010	1.5x	3.7	32	<2	16	7	5	-	-	-	16
Ethiopia	110	-	2.0	5	23	6	16	9	1504	24	33	6
Fiji	2690	0.6	1.7	3	-	9	18	6	51	3	12	6

	GNI per capita (US$) 2004	GDP per capita average annual growth rate (%)		Average annual rate of inflation (%) 1990-2004	% of population below $1 a day 1993-2003*	% of central government expenditure allocated to: (1993-2004*)			ODA inflow in millions US$ 2003	ODA inflow as a % of recipient GNI 2003	Debt service as a % of exports of goods and services	
		1970-1990	1990-2004			health	education	defence			1990	2003
Finland	32790	2.9	2.5	2	-	3	10	4	-	-	-	-
France	30090	2.1	1.6	1	-	16x	7x	6x	-	-	-	-
Gabon	3940	-0.1	-0.4	5	-	-	-	-	-11	0	4	11
Gambia	290	0.9	0.2	7	54x	7x	12x	4x	60	14	18	3
Georgia	1040	3.2	-0.7	156	3	5	5	5	220	6	-	9
Germany	30120	2.2x	1.2	2	-	19	0	4	-	-	-	-
Ghana	380	-2.2	1.9	26	45	7	22	5	907	14	21	14
Greece	16610	1.3	2.2	7	-	7	11	8	-	-	-	-
Grenada	3760	4.9x	2.3	2	-	10	17	0	12	3	2	18
Guatemala	2130	0.2	1.0	9	16	11	17	11	247	1	11	7
Guinea	460	-	1.6	6	-	3x	11x	29x	238	7	18	13
Guinea-Bissau	160	-0.2	-2.5	20	-	1x	3x	4x	145	72	21	11
Guyana	990	-1.5	3.3	9	<2	-	-	-	87	13	-	6
Haiti	390	0.0	-2.8	19	-	-	-	-	200	6	4	3
Holy See	-	-	-	-	-	-	-	-	-	-	-	-
Honduras	1030	0.6	0.3	15	21	10x	19x	7x	389	6	30	10
Hungary	8270	2.9	2.7	16	<2	6	5	3	-	-	30	29
Iceland	38620	3.2	2.2	4	-	26	10	0	-	-	-	-
India	620	2.2	4.1	7	35	2	2	14	942	0	25	18
Indonesia	1140	4.7	2.1	16	8	1	4	3	1743	1	31	23
Iran (Islamic Republic of)	2300	-3.5x	2.3	24	<2	7	7	10	133	0	1	4
Iraq	2170x	-4.3	-	-	-	-	-	-	2265	-	-	-
Ireland	34280	2.8	6.5	4	-	16	14	3	-	-	-	-
Israel	17380	1.9	1.5	8	-	13	15	20	-	-	-	-
Italy	26120	2.6	1.4	3	-	11x	8x	4x	-	-	-	-
Jamaica	2900	-1.3	0.0	17	<2	7	15	2	3	0	20	16
Japan	37180	3.0	1.0	-1	-	2	6	4	-	-	-	-
Jordan	2140	2.5x	1.1	2	<2	10	16	19	1234	13	18	15
Kazakhstan	2260	-	1.3	104	<2	3	3	6	268	1	-	34
Kenya	460	1.3	-0.6	12	23	7	26	6	483	4	26	15
Kiribati	970	-5.3	2.5	2	-	-	-	-	18	21	-	22
Korea, Democratic People's Republic of	a	-	-	-	-	-	-	-	167	-	-	-
Korea, Republic of	13980	6.2	4.5	5	<2	0	18	13	-55x	0x	10x	10
Kuwait	16340x	-6.8x	-2.3x	3x	-	7	15	17	-	-	-	-
Kyrgyzstan	400	-	-1.7	64	<2	11	20	10	198	12	-	12
Lao People's Democratic Republic	390	-	3.7	28	26	-	-	-	299	16	8	8
Latvia	5460	3.3	2.9	28	<2	11	7	4	-	-	-	17
Lebanon	4980	-	2.9	11	-	2	7	11	228	1	1	63
Lesotho	740	4.2	2.3	9	36	9	27	7	79	8	4	8
Liberia	110	-4.6	3.7	50	36	5x	11x	9x	107	24	-	0
Libyan Arab Jamahiriya	4450	-4.8x	-	-	-	-	-	-	7x	-	-	-
Liechtenstein	d	-	-	-	-	-	-	-	-	-	-	-
Lithuania	5740	-	1.2	40	<2	12	7	5	-	-	-	66
Luxembourg	56230	2.7	3.5	3	-	13	10	1	-	-	-	-
Madagascar	300	-2.2	-0.8	15	61	8	21	0	539	11	32	6
Malawi	170	0.3	0.9	30	42	7x	12x	5x	498	27	23	6
Malaysia	4650	4.0	3.3	3	<2	6	23	11	109	0	12	8
Maldives	2510	-	4.6x	1x	-	11	18	9	18	3	4	3
Mali	360	-0.3	2.5	6	72	2x	9x	8x	528	15	8	5
Malta	12250	6.5	3.0	3	-	11	12	2	-9	-	0x	3
Marshall Islands	2370	-	-	4	-	-	-	-	56	39	-	-
Mauritania	420	-0.6	1.7	6	26	4x	23x	-	243	21	24	20
Mauritius	4640	5.1x	3.9	6	-	8	16	1	-15	0	6	5
Mexico	6770	1.7	1.4	16	10	5	25	3	103	0	16	21
Micronesia (Federated States of)	1990	-	-1.4	2	-	-	-	-	115	44	-	-
Moldova, Republic of	710	1.9x	-4.6	70	22	6	9	2	117	5	-	8
Monaco	d	-	-	-	-	-	-	-	-	-	-	-
Mongolia	590	-	-1.8	40	27	6	9	9	247	21	-	31
Morocco	1520	2.1	1.1	2	<2	3	18	13	523	1	18	23

TABLE 7. ECONOMIC INDICATORS

	GNI per capita (US$) 2004	GDP per capita average annual growth rate (%)		Average annual rate of inflation (%) 1990-2004	% of population below $1 a day 1993-2003*	% of central government expenditure allocated to: (1993-2004*)			ODA inflow in millions US$ 2003	ODA inflow as a % of recipient GNI 2003	Debt service as a % of exports of goods and services	
		1970-1990	1990-2004			health	education	defence			1990	2003
Mozambique	250	-1.6x	4.8	23	38	5x	10x	35x	1033	27	21	6
Myanmar	220x	1.6	5.7x	25x	-	3	8	29	126	-	17	4
Namibia	2370	-2.0x	0.9	10	35	10x	22x	7x	146	4	-	-
Nauru	-	-	-	-	-	-	-	-	16	-	-	-
Nepal	260	1.3	2.0	7	39	5	18	10	467	8	12	6
Netherlands	31700	1.5	2.0	2	-	10	11	4	-	-	-	-
New Zealand	20310	0.8	2.1	2	-	17	21	3	-	-	-	-
Nicaragua	790	-3.9	0.9	26	45	13	15	6	833	21	2	11
Niger	230	-2.2	-0.6	5	61	-	-	-	453	19	12	6
Nigeria	390	-1.6	0.2	23	70	1x	3x	3x	318	1	22	8
Niue	-	-	-	-	-	-	-	-	9	-	-	-
Norway	52030	3.4	2.8	3	-	16	6	5	-	-	-	-
Occupied Palestinian Territory	1110x	-	-6.0x	9x	-	-	-	-	972	26	-	-
Oman	7830x	3.6	0.9	2x	-	7	15	33	45	-	12	10
Pakistan	600	3.0	1.1	10	13	1	2	18	1068	2	16	12
Palau	6870	-	0.0x	2x	-	-	-	-	26	17	-	-
Panama	4450	0.3	2.5	3	7	18	16	0	30	0	3	11
Papua New Guinea	580	-0.8	0.0	8	-	7	22	4	221	8	37	12
Paraguay	1170	2.9	-0.7	11	16	7	22	11	51	1	12	10
Peru	2360	-0.6	2.1	16	18	13	7	-	500	1	6	20
Philippines	1170	0.8	1.3	8	16	2	19	5	737	1	23	20
Poland	6090	-	4.2	17	<2	2	5	4	-	-	4	25
Portugal	14350	2.6	2.1	5	<2	9x	11x	6x	-	-	-	-
Qatar	12000x	-	-	-	-	-	-	-	-	-	-	-
Romania	2920	0.9x	1.0	72	<2	15	6	5	-	-	0	17
Russian Federation	3410	-	-0.7	95	<2	1	3	11	-	-	-	10
Rwanda	220	1.4	0.9	10	52	5x	26x	-	332	18	10	13
Saint Kitts and Nevis	7600	6.3x	2.9	3	-	-	-	-	29x	10x	3	34
Saint Lucia	4310	5.3x	0.3	2	-	-	-	-	34x	5x	2	7
Saint Vincent and the Grenadines	3650	3.2	1.9	3	-	12	16	0	5x	1x	3	7
Samoa	1860	0.0x	2.2	4	-	-	-	-	33	12	5	5
San Marino	d	-	-	-	-	-	-	-	-	-	-	-
Sao Tome and Principe	370	-	0.0	37	-	-	-	-	38	76	28	31
Saudi Arabia	10430	-1.2	-0.5	2	-	6x	14x	36x	22	-	-	-
Senegal	670	-0.4	1.4	4	22	3	14	7	450	8	14	9
Serbia and Montenegro	2620	-	4.1x	51x	-	-	-	-	1317	8	-	13
Seychelles	8090	2.9	1.7	2	-	6	10	4	9	1	8	14
Sierra Leone	200	-0.4	-2.5	22	57x	10x	13x	10x	297	37	8	11
Singapore	24220	5.7	3.5	1	-	6	23	29	-	-	-	-
Slovakia	6480	-	2.6	9	<2	20	3	5	-	-	-	13
Slovenia	14810	-	3.1	19	<2	15	14	3	-10	0	10	16
Solomon Islands	550	3.4	-2.6	8	-	-	-	-	60	22	10x	7
Somalia	130x	-1.0	-	-	-	1x	2x	38x	175	-	25x	-
South Africa	3630	0.1	0.4	9	11	-	-	-	625	0	-	9
Spain	21210	1.9	2.4	4	-	15	2	4	-	-	-	-
Sri Lanka	1010	3.2	3.3	9	8	6	10	18	672	4	10	7
Sudan	530	0.3	3.3	44	-	1	8	28	621	4	4	0
Suriname	2250	-2.2x	0.9	64	-	-	-	-	11	-	-	-
Swaziland	1660	2.1	0.2	12	8	8	20	8	27	2	6	2
Sweden	35770	1.8	2.1	2	-	3	6	6	-	-	-	-
Switzerland	48230	1.1	0.6	1	-	0	3	6	-	-	-	-
Syrian Arab Republic	1190	2.2	1.3	6	-	2	9	24	160	1	20	3
Tajikistan	280	-	-5.1	136	7	2	4	9	144	12	-	7
Tanzania, United Republic of	330	-	1.3	16	49x	6x	8x	16x	1669	16	25	4
Thailand	2540	4.7	2.9	3	<2	11	23	7	-966	-1	14	15
The former Yugoslav Republic of Macedonia	2350	-	-0.5	43	<2	-	-	-	234	6	-	12
Timor-Leste	550	-	-	-	-	-	-	-	151	43	-	-
Togo	380	-0.2	0.3	5	-	5x	20x	11x	45	3	8	0
Tonga	1830	-	2.0	4	-	7x	13x	-	27	18	2	2

	GNI per capita (US$) 2004	GDP per capita average annual growth rate (%)		Average annual rate of inflation (%) 1990-2004	% of population below $1 a day 1993-2003*	% of central government expenditure allocated to: (1993-2004*)			ODA inflow in millions US$ 2003	ODA inflow as a % of recipient GNI 2003	Debt service as a % of exports of goods and services	
		1970-1990	1990-2004			health	education	defence			1990	2003
Trinidad and Tobago	8580	0.5	3.5	5	4x	9	15	2	-2	0	18	4
Tunisia	2630	2.5	3.2	4	<2	6	20	5	306	1	22	13
Turkey	3750	1.9	1.4	65	<2	3	10	8	166	0	27	34
Turkmenistan	1340	-	0.2	191	12	-	-	-	27	0	-	30
Tuvalu	-	-	-	-	-	-	-	-	6	-	-	-
Uganda	270	-	3.8	8	85	2x	15x	26x	959	16	47	5
Ukraine	1260	-	-3.5	134	3	3	7	5	-	-	-	12
United Arab Emirates	18060x	-4.8x	-2.1x	3x	-	8	18	31	-	-	-	-
United Kingdom	33940	2.0	2.5	3	-	15	4	7	-	-	-	-
United States	41400	2.2	2.1	2	-	23	3	19	-	-	-	-
Uruguay	3950	0.9	0.8	22	<2	7	8	4	17	0	31	21
Uzbekistan	460	-	-0.1	144	17	-	-	-	194	2	-	21
Vanuatu	1340	-0.6x	-0.8	3	-	-	-	-	32	13	2	1
Venezuela	4020	-1.6	-1.3	38	14	6	20	7	82	0	22	30
Viet Nam	550	-	5.8	11	<2	4	14	-	1769	5	7x	3
Yemen	570	-	2.1	18	16	4	22	19	243	2	4	3
Zambia	450	-2.2	-0.6	39	64	13	14	4	560	14	13	22
Zimbabwe	480x	-0.3	-0.8x	32x	56	8	24	7	186	-	20	6

SUMMARY INDICATORS

	GNI per capita	1970-1990	1990-2004	inflation	below $1 a day	health	education	defence	ODA millions	ODA % GNI	1990	2003
Sub-Saharan Africa	611	0.0	0.6	36	45	-	-	-	21505	7	17	9
Eastern and Southern Africa	836	-	0.7	35	38	-	-	-	9893	5	14	9
Western and Central Africa	399	-0.5	0.2	38	55	-	-	-	11612	10	19	-
Middle East and North Africa	2308	0.4	1.2	10	3	5	14	13	7994	2	20	11
South Asia	600	2.1	3.7	7	33	2	4	14	6170	1	21	16
East Asia and Pacific	1686	5.6	6.2	6	14	1	9	12	6891	0	16	10
Latin America and Caribbean	3649	1.4	1.3	40	10	7	16	4	5359	0	20	26
CEE/CIS	2667	-	0.1	90	4	4	5	9	-	-	-	17
Industrialized countries	32232	2.3	1.9	2	-	16	4	11	-	-	-	-
Developing countries	1524	2.6	3.5	20	22	4	11	10	49680	1	19	16
Least developed countries	345	-0.1	1.8	59	41	6	16	13	23457	13	12	7
World	6298	2.4	2.1	7	21	13	5	11	52331	0	18	16

Countries in each category are listed on page 132.

DEFINITIONS OF THE INDICATORS

GNI per capita – Gross national income (GNI) is the sum of value added by all resident producers plus any product taxes (less subsidies) not included in the valuation of output plus net receipts of primary income (compensation of employees and property income) from abroad. GNI per capita is gross national income divided by mid-year population. GNI per capita in US dollars is converted using the World Bank Atlas method.

GDP per capita – Gross domestic product (GDP) is the sum of value added by all resident producers plus any product taxes (less subsidies) not included in the valuation of output. GDP per capita is gross domestic product divided by mid-year population. Growth is calculated from constant price GDP data in local currency.

% of population below $1 a day – Percentage of population living on less than $1.08 a day at 1993 international prices (equivalent to $1 a day in 1985 prices, adjusted for purchasing power parity). As a result of revisions in purchasing power parity exchange rates, poverty rates for individual countries cannot be compared with poverty rates reported in previous editions.

ODA – Net official development assistance.

Debt service – The sum of interest payments and repayments of principal on external public and publicly guaranteed long-term debts.

MAIN DATA SOURCES

GNI per capita – World Bank.

GDP per capita – World Bank.

Rate of inflation – World Bank.

% of population below $1 a day – World Bank.

Expenditure on health, education and defence – International Monetary Fund (IMF).

ODA – Organisation for Economic Co-operation and Development (OECD).

Debt service – World Bank.

NOTES

a: Range $825 or less.
b: Range $826 to $3255.
c: Range $3256 to $10065.
d: Range $10066 or more.

- Data not available.
x Indicates data that refer to years or periods other than those specified in the column heading, differ from the standard definition or refer to only part of a country.
* Data refer to the most recent year available during the period specified in the column heading.

TABLE 8. WOMEN

Countries and territories	Life expectancy: females as a % of males 2004	Adult literacy rate: females as a % of males 2000-2004*	Gross enrolment ratios: females as a % of males				Contraceptive prevalence (%) 1996-2004*	Antenatal care coverage (%) 1996-2004*	Skilled attendant at delivery (%) 1996-2004*	Maternal mortality ratio†		
			primary school 2000-2004*		secondary school 2000-2004*					1990-2004* reported	2000	
			gross	net	gross	net					adjusted	Lifetime risk of maternal death. 1 in:
Afghanistan	101	-	53	-	-	-	10	16	14	1600	1900	6
Albania	108	99	97	98	100	103	75	91	98	23	55	610
Algeria	104	76	92	98	108	106	57	81	96	120	140	190
Andorra	-	-	100	102	105	107	-	-	-	-	-	-
Angola	107	66	86	86x	81	-	6	66	45	-	1700	7
Antigua and Barbuda	-	-	-	-	-	-	53	100	100	65	-	-
Argentina	111	100	99	-	106	106	74x	98	99	44	82	410
Armenia	110	99	97	98	102	104	61	92	97	9	55	1200
Australia	107	-	100	101	97	102	76x	100x	100	-	8	5800
Austria	108	-	100	102	95	100	51	100x	100x	-	4	16000
Azerbaijan	112	99	97	98	96	97	55	66	84	25	94	520
Bahamas	109	-	101	104	103	104	62x	-	99	-	60	580
Bahrain	104	90	100	102	106	107	62x	97x	98x	46	28	1200
Bangladesh	103	62	104	105	111	112	59	49	13	380	380	59
Barbados	110	100	99	100	102	100	55	89	98	0	95	590
Belarus	119	99	98	99	102	104	50x	100	100	18	35	1800
Belgium	108	-	99	100	110	101	78x	-	100x	-	10	5600
Belize	107	100	98	102	105	106	56	96	83	140	140	190
Benin	103	50	72	68	45	48	19	81	66	500	850	17
Bhutan	104	-	-	-	-	-	31	-	37	260	420	37
Bolivia	107	86	99	100	97	99	58	79	67	230	420	47
Bosnia and Herzegovina	108	93	-	-	-	-	48	99	100	10	31	1900
Botswana	100	108	100	105	107	114	48	97	94	330	100	200
Brazil	112	101	95	93	110	108	77	86	96	64	260	140
Brunei Darussalam	106	95	100	-	106	-	-	100x	99	0	37	830
Bulgaria	110	99	98	99	97	98	42	-	99	15	32	2400
Burkina Faso	103	42	74	74	64	64	14	73	38	480	1000	12
Burundi	104	78	80	84	69	80	16	78	25	-	1000	12
Cambodia	114	75	90	95	65	63	24	38	32	440	450	36
Cameroon	102	78	85	-	82	-	26	83	62	430	730	23
Canada	106	-	101	100	99	101	75x	-	98	-	6	8700
Cape Verde	109	80	95	98	109	111	53	99	89	76	150	160
Central African Republic	104	51	68	-	-	-	28	62	44	1100	1100	15
Chad	105	32	64	68	32	33	8	42	16	830	1100	11
Chile	108	100	98	99	101	101	56x	95x	100	17	31	1100
China	105	92	100	100	97	-	87	89	96	51	56	830
Colombia	109	101	99	99	110	109	77	91	86	78	130	240
Comoros	107	78	83	85	82	-	26	74	62	520x	480	33
Congo	105	87	93	96	73	-	-	-	-	-	510	26
Congo, Democratic Republic of the	105	65	90x	-	54	-	31	68	61	1300	990	13
Cook Islands	-	-	-	-	-	-	44	-	98	6	-	-
Costa Rica	106	100	99	101	108	110	80	70	98	33	43	690
Côte d'Ivoire	103	63	80	81	55	56	15	88	68	600	690	25
Croatia	110	98	99	99	102	101	-	-	100	2	8	6100
Cuba	105	100	96	99	98	100	73	100	100	34	33	1600
Cyprus	107	96	101	100	101	103	-	-	100x	0	47	890
Czech Republic	109	-	98	100	102	103	72	99x	100	3	9	7700
Denmark	106	-	100	100	105	104	78x	-	100x	10	5	9800
Djibouti	104	-	79	80	69	68	-	67	61	74	730	19
Dominica	-	-	93	95	111	114	50	100	100	67	-	-
Dominican Republic	111	99	102	95	123	137	70	99	99	180	150	200
Ecuador	108	98	100	101	102	102	66	69	69	80	130	210
Egypt	106	66	95	97	93	95	60	69	69	84	84	310
El Salvador	109	94	94	100	100	102	67	86	92	170	150	180
Equatorial Guinea	102	83	91	86	58	58	-	86	65	-	880	16
Eritrea	107	-	81	86	65	72	8	70	28	1000	630	24
Estonia	117	100	96	99	103	103	70x	-	100	46	63	1100
Ethiopia	104	69	77	85	57	57	8	27	6	870	850	14
Fiji	107	97	100	100	106	108	44	-	99	38	75	360

	Life expectancy: females as a % of males 2004	Adult literacy rate: females as a % of males 2000-2004*	Gross enrolment ratios: females as a % of males				Contraceptive prevalence (%) 1996-2004*	Antenatal care coverage (%) 1996-2004*	Skilled attendant at delivery (%) 1996-2004*	Maternal mortality ratio[†]		
			primary school 2000-2004*		secondary school 2000-2004*					1990-2004* reported	2000	
			gross	net	gross	net					adjusted	Lifetime risk of maternal death. 1 in:
Finland	109	-	100	100	111	101	77x	100x	100	6	6	8200
France	109	-	99	100	101	102	75x	99x	99x	10	17	2700
Gabon	102	-	99	99	86	-	33	94	86	520	420	37
Gambia	105	-	98	99	68	69	18	91	55	730	540	31
Georgia	112	-	99	99	100	98	41	95	96	52	32	1700
Germany	108	-	99	102	98	100	75x	-	100x	8	8	8000
Ghana	102	73	91	82	81	85	25	92	47	210x	540	35
Greece	107	94	100	100	99	102	-	-	-	1	9	7100
Grenada	-	-	98	90	96	102	54	98	100	1	-	-
Guatemala	112	84	93	97	93	97	43	84	41	150	240	74
Guinea	101	-	77	79	45	46	7	84	56	530	740	18
Guinea-Bissau	106	-	67	70	57	55	8	62	35	910	1100	13
Guyana	110	-	98	98	104	108	37	81	86	190	170	200
Haiti	103	93	-	-	-	-	27	79	24	520	680	29
Holy See	-	-	-	-	-	-	-	-	-	-	-	-
Honduras	106	100	102	101	-	-	62	83	56	110	110	190
Hungary	112	100	99	99	100	100	77x	-	100	5	16	4000
Iceland	105	-	99	99	108	105	-	-	-	-	0	0
India	105	66	94	94	81	-	47	60	43	540	540	48
Indonesia	106	90	98	99	98	100	57	92	72	310	230	150
Iran (Islamic Republic of)	104	83	97	97	94	-	74	77	90	37	76	370
Iraq	105	-	83	85	70	65	44	77	72	290	250	65
Ireland	107	-	100	102	110	109	-	-	100	6	5	8300
Israel	105	98	100	100	98	100	68x	-	99x	5	17	1800
Italy	108	-	99	99	99	101	60	-	-	7	5	13900
Jamaica	105	108	99	101	102	104	66	99	97	110	87	380
Japan	109	-	100	100	100	101	59x	-	100	8	10	6000
Jordan	104	89	100	102	102	103	56	99	100	41	41	450
Kazakhstan	119	99	99	99	100	100	66	91	99	50	210	190
Kenya	96	90	95	100	94	96	39	88	42	410	1000	19
Kiribati	-	-	117	-	113	-	21	88x	85	56	-	-
Korea, Democratic People's Republic of	110	-	-	-	-	-	62x	-	97	110	67	590
Korea, Republic of	110	-	99	100	101	100	81	-	100	20	20	2800
Kuwait	106	95	101	102	106	105	50	95	98	5	5	6000
Kyrgyzstan	113	99	98	97	101	-	60	97	98	44	110	290
Lao People's Democratic Republic	105	79	87	93	74	84	32	27	19	530	650	25
Latvia	117	100	98	99	100	100	48x	-	100	25	42	1800
Lebanon	106	-	97	99	109	-	63	87x	89	100x	150	240
Lesotho	106	122	102	107	130	150	30	85	60	-	550	32
Liberia	105	54	73	77	70	57	10	85	51	580x	760	16
Libyan Arab Jamahiriya	106	77	100	-	106	-	45x	81x	94x	77	97	240
Liechtenstein	-	-	-	-	-	-	-	-	-	-	-	-
Lithuania	117	100	99	100	99	100	47x	-	100	13	13	4900
Luxembourg	108	-	100	101	106	108	-	-	100	0	28	1700
Madagascar	105	86	96	101	93x	109x	27	80	51	470	550	26
Malawi	99	72	96	-	78	81	31	94	61	1100	1800	7
Malaysia	107	92	100	100	110	112	55x	74	97	30	41	660
Maldives	99	100	98	101	115	115	39	81	70	140	110	140
Mali	103	44	76	78	56	-	8	57	41	580	1200	10
Malta	106	103	99	100	100	102	-	-	98x	-	0	0
Marshall Islands	-	-	94	99	101	103	34	-	95	-	-	-
Mauritania	106	72	98	99	80	78	8	64	57	750	1000	14
Mauritius	110	92	101	102	100	100	76	-	98	22	24	1700
Mexico	107	97	99	101	109	105	73	86x	95	65	83	370
Micronesia (Federated States of)	102	-	-	-	-	-	45	-	88	120	-	-
Moldova, Republic of	111	98	100	100	104	103	62	99	99	44	36	1500
Monaco	-	-	-	-	-	-	-	-	-	-	-	-
Mongolia	106	100	102	103	115	115	69	94	97	99	110	300
Morocco	106	60	90	95	84	87	63	68	63	230	220	120

TABLE 8. WOMEN

	Life expectancy: females as a % of males 2004	Adult literacy rate: females as a % of males 2000-2004*	Gross enrolment ratios: females as a % of males				Contraceptive prevalence (%) 1996-2004*	Antenatal care coverage (%) 1996-2004*	Skilled attendant at delivery (%) 1996-2004*	Maternal mortality ratio†		
			primary school 2000-2004*		secondary school 2000-2004*						2000	
			gross	net	gross	net				1990-2004* reported	adjusted	Lifetime risk of maternal death. 1 in:
Mozambique	103	50	82	91	68	71	17	85	48	410	1000	14
Myanmar	110	91	101	101	95	94	34	76	57	230	360	75
Namibia	101	95	101	107	112	128	44	91	76	270	300	54
Nauru	-	-	103x	103x	108x	-	-	-	-	-	-	-
Nepal	101	56	89	88	78	-	38	28	15	540	740	24
Netherlands	107	-	98	99	98	101	79x	-	100	7	16	3500
New Zealand	106	-	99	99	106	102	75x	95x	100x	15	7	6000
Nicaragua	107	100	99	99	118	117	69	86	67	83	230	88
Niger	100	45	71	69	75	71	14	41	16	590	1600	7
Nigeria	101	80	81	81	80	81	13	58	35	-	800	18
Niue	-	-	94	99	98	98	-	-	100	-	-	-
Norway	106	-	100	100	103	101	74x	-	100x	6	16	2900
Occupied Palestinian Territory	104	91	100	100	106	105	51	96	97	-	100	140
Oman	104	79	99	100	96	101	32	100	95	23	87	170
Pakistan	101	56	71	74	73	-	28	43	23	530	500	31
Palau	-	-	97	96	100	-	17	-	100	0x	-	-
Panama	107	98	96	99	107	110	58x	72	93	70	160	210
Papua New Guinea	102	81	89	87	79	78	26	78	41	370x	300	62
Paraguay	107	97	96	100	103	106	57	94	77	180	170	120
Peru	108	88	99	100	92	97	69	84	59	190	410	73
Philippines	106	100	99	102	110	120	49	88	60	170	200	120
Poland	111	-	99	100	95	103	49x	-	100	4	13	4600
Portugal	109	-	95	99	109	110	66x	-	100	8	5	11100
Qatar	107	-	97	99	104	106	43	94x	99	10	140	170
Romania	111	98	98	99	101	104	64	-	99	31	49	1300
Russian Federation	122	99	100	101	-	-	-	-	99	32	67	1000
Rwanda	108	84	100	104	83	-	13	92	31	1100	1400	10
Saint Kitts and Nevis	-	-	106	111	132	106	41	100x	99	250	-	-
Saint Lucia	104	101	99	101	125	125	47	100x	100	35	-	-
Saint Vincent and the Grenadines	108	-	97	100	111	109	58	99	100	93	-	-
Samoa	109	99	97	97	108	110	30x	-	100	-	130	150
San Marino	-	-	-	-	-	-	-	-	-	-	-	-
Sao Tome and Principe	103	-	94	94	86	81	29	91	76	100	-	-
Saudi Arabia	106	79	96	98	90	96	32	90	91	-	23	610
Senegal	104	57	93	89	70	-	11	79	58	560	690	22
Serbia and Montenegro	107	95	100	100	101	-	58	-	93	7	11	4500
Seychelles	-	101	99	99	100	100	-	-	-	57	-	-
Sierra Leone	107	53	70	-	71	-	4	68	42	1800	2000	6
Singapore	105	92	-	-	-	-	74x	-	100	6	30	1700
Slovakia	111	100	99	101	101	100	74x	-	99	16	3	19800
Slovenia	110	100	99	99	99	101	74x	98x	100	17	17	4100
Solomon Islands	102	-	-	-	-	-	11	-	85	550x	130	120
Somalia	105	-	-	-	-	-	1x	32	25	-	1100	10
South Africa	105	96	96	100	108	108	56	94	84	150	230	120
Spain	110	-	98	99	106	104	81x	-	-	6	4	17400
Sri Lanka	107	97	99	-	106	-	70	95	96	92	92	430
Sudan	105	72	88	84	84	-	7	60	87	550	590	30
Suriname	110	91	98	102	135	137	42	91	85	150	110	340
Swaziland	100	98	92	100	102	124	48	90	74	230	370	49
Sweden	106	-	103	99	119	101	78x	-	100x	5	2	29800
Switzerland	107	-	99	100	94	94	82x	-	-	5	7	7900
Syrian Arab Republic	105	81	95	96	92	93	48	71	77x	65	160	130
Tajikistan	108	99	96	94x	83	84	34	71	71	45	100	250
Tanzania, United Republic of	101	79	97	98	83	80x	26	94	46	580	1500	10
Thailand	111	96	96	97	100	-	79	92	99	24	44	900
The former Yugoslav Republic of Macedonia	107	96	101	100	98	98	-	81	99	7	23	2100
Timor-Leste	104	-	-	-	-	-	10	61	18	-	660	30

	Life expectancy: females as a % of males 2004	Adult literacy rate: females as a % of males 2000-2004*	Gross enrolment ratios: females as a % of males				Contraceptive prevalence (%) 1996-2004*	Antenatal care coverage (%) 1996-2004*	Skilled attendant at delivery (%) 1996-2004*	Maternal mortality ratio†		
			primary school 2000-2004*		secondary school 2000-2004*					1990-2004* reported	2000	
			gross	net	gross	net					adjusted	Lifetime risk of maternal death. 1 in:
Togo	107	56	83	84	43	47	26	85	61	480	570	26
Tonga	104	100	97	100	116	115	33	-	95	-	-	-
Trinidad and Tobago	109	99	98	99	109	109	38	92	96	45	160	330
Tunisia	106	78	96	100	108	111	66	92	90	69	120	320
Turkey	107	84	93	94	74	-	71	81	83	130x	70	480
Turkmenistan	115	99	-	-	-	-	62	98	97	14	31	790
Tuvalu	-	-	114	-	93	-	32	-	100	-	-	-
Uganda	102	75	98	-	82	94	23	92	39	510	880	13
Ukraine	120	99	100	100	99	101	89	-	100	13	35	2000
United Arab Emirates	106	107	97	98	104	103	28x	97x	99x	3	54	500
United Kingdom	106	-	100	100	125	103	82x	-	99	7	13	3800
United States	107	-	100	101	100	101	76x	99x	99	8	17	2500
Uruguay	110	101	98	101	113	110	84	94	100	26	27	1300
Uzbekistan	110	99	99	-	97	-	68	97	96	34	24	1300
Vanuatu	106	-	100	102	107	104	28	-	88	68	130	140
Venezuela	108	100	98	101	115	116	77	94	94	68	96	300
Viet Nam	106	93	92	94	93	-	79	86	85	170	130	270
Yemen	105	42	69	70	45	45	23	41	27	370	570	19
Zambia	97	79	93	99	83	84	34	93	43	730	750	19
Zimbabwe	97	91	98	101	92	94	54	93	73	700	1100	16

SUMMARY INDICATORS

Sub-Saharan Africa	103	76	87	90	79	83	23	69	42	-	940	16
Eastern and Southern Africa	103	80	91	96	88	86	28	72	39	-	980	15
Western and Central Africa	103	70	81	83	74	80	17	66	45	-	900	16
Middle East and North Africa	105	74	91	93	90	92	52	71	76	-	220	100
South Asia	104	64	92	93	85	-	46	54	36	-	560	43
East Asia and Pacific	106	91	99	100	99	102**	79	87	86	-	110	360
Latin America and Caribbean	109	98	98	99	107	106	72	87	87	-	190	160
CEE/CIS	115	97	97	98	91	-	69	86	93	-	64	770
Industrialized countries	108	-	100	101	103	101	-	-	99	-	13	4000
Developing countries	106	84	94	94	93	98**	60	71	59	-	440	61
Least developed countries	104	71	88	92	81	87	28	59	35	-	890	17
World	106	86	94	97	95	100**	60	71	63	-	400	74

Countries in each category are listed on page 132.

DEFINITIONS OF THE INDICATORS

Life expectancy at birth – The number of years newborn children would live if subject to the mortality risks prevailing for the cross-section of population at the time of their birth.

Adult literacy rate – Percentage of persons aged 15 and over who can read and write.

Net enrolment ratios: females as a % of males – Girls' net enrolment ratio divided by that of boys, as a percentage. The net enrolment ratio is the number of children enrolled in a primary or secondary school that belong to the age group that officially corresponds to primary or secondary schooling, divided by the total population of the same age group.

Contraceptive prevalence – Percentage of women in union aged 15-49 years currently using contraception.

Antenatal care – Percentage of women aged 15-49 years attended at least once during pregnancy by skilled health personnel (doctors, nurses or midwives).

Skilled attendant at delivery – Percentage of births attended by skilled health personnel (doctors, nurses or midwives).

Maternal mortality ratio – Annual number of deaths of women from pregnancy-related causes per 100,000 live births. This 'reported' column shows country reported figures that are not adjusted for underreporting and misclassification.

Lifetime risk of maternal death – The lifetime risk of maternal death takes into account both the probability of becoming pregnant and the probability of dying as a result of that pregnancy accumulated across a woman's reproductive years.

MAIN DATA SOURCES

Life expectancy – United Nations Population Division.

Adult literacy – United Nations Educational, Scientific and Cultural Organization (UNESCO).

School enrolment – UIS (UNESCO Institute of Statistics) and UNESCO.

Contraceptive prevalence – Demographic and Health Surveys (DHS), Multiple Indicator Cluster Surveys (MICS), United Nations Population Division and UNICEF.

Antenatal care – DHS, MICS, World Health Organization (WHO) and UNICEF.

Skilled attendant at delivery – DHS, MICS, WHO and UNICEF.

Maternal mortality – WHO and UNICEF.

Lifetime risk – WHO and UNICEF.

† The maternal mortality data in the column headed 'reported' are those reported by national authorities. Periodically, UNICEF, WHO and UNFPA evaluate these data and make adjustments to account for the well-documented problems of underreporting and misclassification of maternal deaths and to develop estimates for countries with no data. The column with 'adjusted' estimates for the year 2000 reflects the most recent of these reviews.

NOTES
- - Data not available.
- x Indicates data that refer to years or periods other than those specified in the column heading, differ from the standard definition or refer to only part of a country.
- * Data refer to the most recent year available during the period specified in the column heading.
- ** Excludes China.

TABLE 9. CHILD PROTECTION

| Countries and territories | Child labour (5-14 years) 1999-2004* | | | Child marriage 1986-2004* | | | Birth registration 1999-2004* | | | Female genital mutilation/cutting 1998-2004* | | | |
| | | | | | | | | | | women[a] (15-49 years) | | | daughters[b] |
	total	male	female	total	urban	rural	total	urban	rural	total	urban	rural	total
Afghanistan	34y	31y	38y	43	-	-	6	12	4	-	-	-	-
Albania	23	26	19	-	-	-	99	99	99	-	-	-	-
Angola	22	21	23	-	-	-	29	34	19	-	-	-	-
Armenia	-	-	-	19	12	31	97	100	94	-	-	-	-
Azerbaijan	8	9	7	-	-	-	97	98	96	-	-	-	-
Bahrain	5	6	3	-	-	-	-	-	-	-	-	-	-
Bangladesh	7	10	4	65	44	72	7	9	7	-	-	-	-
Benin	26y	23y	29y	37	25	45	70	78	66	17	13	20	6
Bolivia	21	22	20	26	22	37	82	83	79	-	-	-	-
Bosnia and Herzegovina	11	12	10	-	-	-	98	98	99	-	-	-	-
Botswana	-	-	-	10	13	9	58	66	52	-	-	-	-
Brazil	7y	9y	4y	24	22	30	76	-	-	-	-	-	-
Burkina Faso	57y	-	-	52	22	62	-	-	-	77	75	77	32
Burundi	24	26	23	17y	36y	17y	75	71	75	-	-	-	-
Cambodia	-	-	-	25	19	26	22	30	21	-	-	-	-
Cameroon	51	52	50	43	30	51	79	94	73	1.4	1	2	-
Central African Republic	56	54	57	57	54	59	73	88	63	36	29	41	-
Chad	57	60	55	71	65	74	25	53	18	45	43	46	-
Colombia	5	7	4	21	18	34	91	95	84	-	-	-	-
Comoros	28	27	29	30	23	33	83	87	83	-	-	-	-
Congo, Democratic Republic of the	28y	26y	29y	-	-	-	34	30	36	-	-	-	-
Costa Rica	50y	71y	29y	-	-	-	-	-	-	-	-	-	-
Côte d'Ivoire	35	34	36	33	24	43	72	88	60	45	39	48	24
Cuba	-	-	-	-	-	-	100	100	100	-	-	-	-
Dominican Republic	9	11	6	41	37	51	75	82	66	-	-	-	-
Ecuador	6y	9y	4y	26y	21y	34y	-	-	-	-	-	-	-
Egypt	6	6	5	19	11	24	-	-	-	97	95	99	47
El Salvador	-	-	-	27	-	-	-	-	-	-	-	-	-
Equatorial Guinea	27	27	27	-	-	-	32	43	24	-	-	-	-
Eritrea	-	-	-	47	31	60	-	-	-	89	86	91	63
Ethiopia	43y	47y	37y	49	32	53	-	-	-	80	80	80	48
Gabon	-	-	-	34	30	49	89	90	87	-	-	-	-
Gambia	22	23	22	-	-	-	32	37	29	-	-	-	-
Georgia	-	-	-	-	-	-	95	97	92	-	-	-	-
Ghana	57y	57y	58y	28	18	39	21	-	-	5	4	7	-
Guatemala	24y	-	-	34	25	44	-	-	-	-	-	-	-
Guinea	-	-	-	65	46	75	67	88	56	99	98	99	54
Guinea-Bissau	54	54	54	-	-	-	42	32	47	-	-	-	-
Guyana	19	21	17	-	-	-	97	99	96	-	-	-	-
Haiti	-	-	-	24	18	31	70	78	66	-	-	-	-
India	14	14	15	46	26	55	35	54	29	-	-	-	-
Indonesia	4y	5y	4y	24	15	33	55	69	43	-	-	-	-
Iraq	8	11	5	-	-	-	98	99	97	-	-	-	-
Jamaica	2	3	1	-	-	-	96	95	96	-	-	-	-
Jordan	-	-	-	11	11	12	-	-	-	-	-	-	-
Kazakhstan	-	-	-	14	12	17	-	-	-	-	-	-	-
Kenya	26	27	25	25	19	27	48y	64y	44y	32	21	36	21
Korea, Democratic People's Republic of	-	-	-	-	-	-	99	99	99	-	-	-	-
Kyrgyzstan	-	-	-	21	19	22	-	-	-	-	-	-	-
Lao People's Democratic Republic	24	23	25	-	-	-	59	71	56	-	-	-	-
Lebanon	6	8	4	11	-	-	-	-	-	-	-	-	-
Lesotho	17	19	14	-	-	-	51	41	53	-	-	-	-
Liberia	-	-	-	48y	38y	58y	-	-	-	-	-	-	-
Madagascar	30	35	26	39	29	42	75	87	72	-	-	-	-
Malawi	17	18	16	47	32	50	-	-	-	-	-	-	-
Maldives	-	-	-	-	-	-	73	-	-	-	-	-	-
Mali	30	33	28	65	46	74	48	71	41	92	90	93	73
Mauritania	10y	-	-	37	32	42	55	72	42	71	65	77	66
Mexico	16y	15y	16y	28y	31y	21y	-	-	-	-	-	-	-
Moldova, Republic of	28	29	28	-	-	-	98	98	98	-	-	-	-
Mongolia	30	30	30	-	-	-	98	98	97	-	-	-	-
Morocco	11y	-	-	16	12	21	85	92	80	-	-	-	-
Mozambique	-	-	-	56	41	66	-	-	-	-	-	-	-
Myanmar	-	-	-	-	-	-	65y	66y	64y	-	-	-	-
Namibia	-	-	-	10	9	10	71	82	64	-	-	-	-
Nepal	31	30	33	56	34	60	34	37	34	-	-	-	-
Nicaragua	10y	-	-	43	36	55	81	90	73	-	-	-	-
Niger	66	69	64	77	46	86	46	85	40	5	2	5	4
Nigeria	39y	-	-	43	27	52	30	53	20	19	28	14	10
Occupied Palestinian Territory	-	-	-	-	-	-	98	98	97	-	-	-	-
Pakistan	-	-	-	32	21	37	-	-	-	-	-	-	-

| | Child labour (5-14 years) 1999-2004* | | | Child marriage 1986-2004* | | | Birth registration 1999-2004* | | | Female genital mutilation/cutting 1998-2004* | | | |
| | | | | | | | | | | women[a] (15-49 years) | | | daughters[b] |
	total	male	female	total	urban	rural	total	urban	rural	total	urban	rural	total
Paraguay	8y	10y	6y	24	18	32	-	-	-	-	-	-	-
Peru	-	-	-	19	12	35	93	93	92	-	-	-	-
Philippines	11	12	10	14	10	22	83	87	78	-	-	-	-
Romania	1y	-	-	-	-	-	-	-	-	-	-	-	-
Rwanda	31	31	30	20	21	19	65	61	66	-	-	-	-
Sao Tome and Principe	14	15	13	-	-	-	70	73	67	-	-	-	-
Senegal	33	36	30	36	15	53	62	82	51	-	-	-	-
Sierra Leone	57	57	57	-	-	-	46	66	40	-	-	-	-
Somalia	32	29	36	-	-	-	-	-	-	-	-	-	-
South Africa	-	-	-	8	5	12	-	-	-	-	-	-	-
Sri Lanka	-	-	-	14y	10y	15y	-	-	-	-	-	-	-
Sudan	13	14	12	27y	19y	34y	64	82	46	90	92	88	58
Suriname	-	-	-	-	-	-	95	94	94	-	-	-	-
Swaziland	8	8	8	-	-	-	53	72	50	-	-	-	-
Syrian Arab Republic	8y	10y	6y	-	-	-	-	-	-	-	-	-	-
Tajikistan	18	19	17	-	-	-	75	77	74	-	-	-	-
Tanzania, United Republic of	32	34	30	39	23	48	6	22	3	18	10	20	7
Thailand	-	-	-	21y	13y	23y	-	-	-	-	-	-	-
Timor-Leste	4y	4y	4y	-	-	-	22	32	20	-	-	-	-
Togo	60	62	59	31	17	41	82	93	78	-	-	-	-
Trinidad and Tobago	2	3	2	34y	37y	32y	95	-	-	-	-	-	-
Tunisia	-	-	-	10y	7y	14y	-	-	-	-	-	-	-
Turkey	-	-	-	23	19	30	-	-	-	-	-	-	-
Turkmenistan	-	-	-	9	12	7	-	-	-	-	-	-	-
Uganda	34	34	33	54	34	59	4	11	3	-	-	-	-
Uzbekistan	15	18	12	13	16	11	100	100	100	-	-	-	-
Venezuela	7	9	5	-	-	-	92	-	-	-	-	-	-
Viet Nam	23	23	22	11	5	13	72	92	68	-	-	-	-
Yemen	-	-	-	48	39	53	-	-	-	23	26	22	20
Zambia	11	10	11	42	32	49	10	16	6	-	-	-	-
Zimbabwe	26y	-	-	29	21	36	42	56	35	-	-	-	-

SUMMARY INDICATORS

	total	male	female	total	urban	rural	total	urban	rural	total	urban	rural	total
Sub-Saharan Africa	36	37	34	40	25	48	38	55	33	38	31	42	24
Eastern and Southern Africa	32	34	29	36	21	43	32	44	28	-	-	-	-
Western and Central Africa	41	41	41	45	28	56	41	59	35	29	29	29	19
Middle East and North Africa	9	9	7	-	-	-	-	-	-	-	-	-	-
South Asia	14	14	15	46	27	54	30	47	25	-	-	-	-
East Asia and Pacific	10**	11**	10**	20**	12**	25**	65**	77**	56**	-	-	-	-
Latin America and Caribbean	11	11	8	25	24	31	82	92	80	-	-	-	-
CEE/CIS	-	-	-	-	-	-	-	-	-	-	-	-	-
Industrialized countries	-	-	-	-	-	-	-	-	-	-	-	-	-
Developing countries	18**	18**	17**	36**	22**	45**	45**	62**	35**	-	-	-	-
Least developed countries	28	29	26	50	33	57	32	44	28	-	-	-	-
World	18**	18**	17**	36**	22**	45**	45**	62**	35**	-	-	-	-

Countries in each category are listed on page 132.

DEFINITIONS OF THE INDICATORS

Child labour – Percentage of children aged 5 to 14 years of age involved in child labour activities at the moment of the survey. A child is considered to be involved in child labour activities under the following classification: (a) children 5 to 11 years of age that during the week preceding the survey did at least one hour of economic activity or at least 28 hours of domestic work, and (b) children 12 to 14 years of age that during the week preceding the survey did at least 14 hours of economic activity or at least 42 hours of economic activity and domestic work combined.

Child labour background variables – Sex of the child; urban or rural place of residence; poorest 20% or richest 20% of the population constructed from household assets (a more detailed description of the household wealth estimation procedure can be found at www.childinfo.org); mother's education, reflecting mothers with and without some level of education.

Birth registration – Percentage of children less than five years of age that were registered at the moment of the survey. The numerator of this indicator includes children whose birth certificate was seen by the interviewer or whose mother or caretaker says the birth has been registered. MICS data refer to children alive at the time of the survey.

Child marriage – Percentage of women 20-24 years of age that were married or in union before they were 18 years old.

Female genital mutilation/cutting – (a) Women – the percentage of women aged 15 to 49 years of age who have been mutilated/cut. (b) Daughters – the percentage of women aged 15 to 49 with at least one mutilated/cut daughter. Female genital mutilation/cutting (FGM/C) involves the cutting or alteration of the female genitalia for social reasons. Generally, there are three recognized types of FGM/C: clitoridectomy, excision and infibulation. Clitoridectomy is the removal of the prepuce with or without excision of all or part of the clitoris. Excision is the removal of the prepuce and clitoris along with all or part of the labia minora. Infibulation is the most severe form and consists of removal of all or part of the external genitalia, followed by joining together of the two sides of the labia minora using threads, thorns or other materials to narrow the vaginal opening. A more detailed analysis of this data can be found at www.measuredhs.com and www.prb.org.

MAIN DATA SOURCES

Child labour – Multiple Indicator Cluster Survey (MICS) and Demographic and Health Surveys (DHS).

Child marriage – MICS, DHS and other national surveys.

Birth registration – MICS, DHS and other national surveys.

Female genital mutilation/cutting – DHS conducted during the period 1998-2004 and MICS conducted during the period 1999-2001.

NOTES

-     Data not available.
- y   Indicates data that differ from the standard definition or refer to only part of a country but are included in the calculation of regional and global averages.
- *   Data refer to the most recent year available during the period specified in the column heading.
- **   Excludes China.

Summary indicators

Averages given at the end of each table are calculated using data from the countries and territories as grouped below.

Sub-Saharan Africa

Angola; Benin; Botswana; Burkina Faso; Burundi; Cameroon; Cape Verde; Central African Republic; Chad; Comoros; Congo; Congo, Democratic Republic of the; Côte d'Ivoire; Equatorial Guinea; Eritrea; Ethiopia; Gabon; Gambia; Ghana; Guinea; Guinea-Bissau; Kenya; Lesotho; Liberia; Madagascar; Malawi; Mali; Mauritania; Mauritius; Mozambique; Namibia; Niger; Nigeria; Rwanda; Sao Tome and Principe; Senegal; Seychelles; Sierra Leone; Somalia; South Africa; Swaziland; Tanzania, United Republic of; Togo; Uganda; Zambia; Zimbabwe

Middle East and North Africa

Algeria; Bahrain; Djibouti; Egypt; Iran (Islamic Republic of); Iraq; Jordan; Kuwait; Lebanon; Libyan Arab Jamahiriya; Morocco; Occupied Palestinian Territory; Oman; Qatar; Saudi Arabia; Sudan; Syrian Arab Republic; Tunisia; United Arab Emirates; Yemen

South Asia

Afghanistan; Bangladesh; Bhutan; India; Maldives; Nepal; Pakistan; Sri Lanka

East Asia and Pacific

Brunei Darussalam; Cambodia; China; Cook Islands; Fiji; Indonesia; Kiribati; Korea, Democratic People's Republic of; Korea, Republic of; Lao People's Democratic Republic; Malaysia; Marshall Islands; Micronesia (Federated States of); Mongolia; Myanmar; Nauru; Niue; Palau; Papua New Guinea; Philippines; Samoa; Singapore; Solomon Islands; Thailand; Timor-Leste; Tonga; Tuvalu; Vanuatu; Viet Nam

Latin America and Caribbean

Antigua and Barbuda; Argentina; Bahamas; Barbados; Belize; Bolivia; Brazil; Chile; Colombia; Costa Rica; Cuba; Dominica; Dominican Republic; Ecuador; El Salvador; Grenada; Guatemala; Guyana; Haiti; Honduras; Jamaica; Mexico; Nicaragua; Panama; Paraguay; Peru; Saint Kitts and Nevis; Saint Lucia; Saint Vincent and the Grenadines; Suriname; Trinidad and Tobago; Uruguay; Venezuela

CEE/CIS

Albania; Armenia; Azerbaijan; Belarus; Bosnia and Herzegovina; Bulgaria; Croatia; Georgia; Kazakhstan; Kyrgyzstan; Moldova, Republic of; Romania; Russian Federation; Serbia and Montenegro; Tajikistan; the former Yugoslav Republic of Macedonia; Turkey; Turkmenistan; Ukraine; Uzbekistan

Industrialized countries

Andorra; Australia; Austria; Belgium; Canada; Cyprus; Czech Republic; Denmark; Estonia; Finland; France; Germany; Greece; Holy See; Hungary; Iceland; Ireland; Israel; Italy; Japan; Latvia; Liechtenstein; Lithuania; Luxembourg; Malta; Monaco; Netherlands; New Zealand; Norway; Poland; Portugal; San Marino; Slovakia; Slovenia; Spain; Sweden; Switzerland; United Kingdom; United States

Developing countries

Afghanistan; Algeria; Angola; Antigua and Barbuda; Argentina; Armenia; Azerbaijan; Bahamas; Bahrain; Bangladesh; Barbados; Belize; Benin; Bhutan; Bolivia; Botswana; Brazil; Brunei Darussalam; Burkina Faso; Burundi; Cambodia; Cameroon; Cape Verde; Central African Republic; Chad; Chile; China; Colombia; Comoros; Congo; Congo, Democratic Republic of the; Cook Islands; Costa Rica; Côte d'Ivoire; Cuba; Cyprus; Djibouti; Dominica; Dominican Republic; Ecuador; Egypt; El Salvador; Equatorial Guinea; Eritrea; Ethiopia; Fiji; Gabon; Gambia; Georgia; Ghana; Grenada; Guatemala; Guinea; Guinea-Bissau; Guyana; Haiti; Honduras; India; Indonesia; Iran (Islamic Republic of); Iraq; Israel; Jamaica; Jordan; Kazakhstan; Kenya; Kiribati; Korea, Democratic People's Republic of; Korea, Republic of; Kuwait; Kyrgyzstan; Lao People's Democratic Republic; Lebanon; Lesotho; Liberia; Libyan Arab Jamahiriya; Madagascar; Malawi; Malaysia; Maldives; Mali; Marshall Islands; Mauritania; Mauritius; Mexico; Micronesia (Federated States of); Mongolia; Morocco; Mozambique; Myanmar; Namibia; Nauru; Nepal; Nicaragua; Niger; Nigeria; Niue; Occupied Palestinian Territory; Oman; Pakistan; Palau; Panama; Papua New Guinea; Paraguay; Peru; Philippines; Qatar; Rwanda; Saint Kitts and Nevis; Saint Lucia; Saint Vincent/Grenadines; Samoa; Sao Tome and Principe; Saudi Arabia; Senegal; Seychelles; Sierra Leone; Singapore; Solomon Islands; Somalia; South Africa; Sri Lanka; Sudan; Suriname; Swaziland; Syrian Arab Republic; Tajikistan; Tanzania, United Republic of; Thailand; Timor-Leste; Togo; Tonga; Trinidad and Tobago; Tunisia; Turkey; Turkmenistan; Tuvalu; Uganda; United Arab Emirates; Uruguay; Uzbekistan; Vanuatu; Venezuela; Viet Nam; Yemen; Zambia; Zimbabwe

Least developed countries

Afghanistan; Angola; Bangladesh; Benin; Bhutan; Burkina Faso; Burundi; Cambodia; Cape Verde; Central African Republic; Chad; Comoros; Congo, Democratic Republic of the; Djibouti; Equatorial Guinea; Eritrea; Ethiopia; Gambia; Guinea; Guinea-Bissau; Haiti; Kiribati; Lao People's Democratic Republic; Lesotho; Liberia; Madagascar; Malawi; Maldives; Mali; Mauritania; Mozambique; Myanmar; Nepal; Niger; Rwanda; Samoa; Sao Tome and Principe; Senegal; Sierra Leone; Solomon Islands; Somalia; Sudan; Tanzania, United Republic of; Timor-Leste; Togo; Tuvalu; Uganda; Vanuatu; Yemen; Zambia

Measuring human development
An introduction to table 10

If development is to assume a more human face, then there arises a corresponding need for a means of measuring human as well as economic progress. From UNICEF's point of view, in particular, there is a need for an agreed method of measuring the level of child well-being and its rate of change.

The under-five mortality rate (U5MR) is used in table 10 (next page) as the principal indicator of such progress.

The U5MR has several advantages. First, it measures an end result of the development process rather than an 'input' such as school enrolment level, per capita calorie availability, or the number of doctors per thousand population — all of which are means to an end.

Second, the U5MR is known to be the result of a wide variety of inputs: the nutritional health and the health knowledge of mothers; the level of immunization and ORT use; the availability of maternal and child health services (including prenatal care); income and food availability in the family; the availability of clean water and safe sanitation; and the overall safety of the child's environment.

Third, the U5MR is less susceptible than, say, per capita GNI to the fallacy of the average. This is because the natural scale does not allow the children of the rich to be one thousand times as likely to survive, even if the man-made scale does permit them to have one thousand times as much income. In other words, it is much more difficult for a wealthy minority to affect a nation's U5MR, and it therefore presents a more accurate, if far from perfect, picture of the health status of the majority of children (and of society as a whole).

For these reasons, the U5MR is chosen by UNICEF as its single most important indicator of the state of a nation's children.

The speed of progress in reducing the U5MR can be measured by calculating its average annual reduction rate (AARR). Unlike the comparison of absolute changes, the AARR reflects the fact that the lower limits to U5MR are approached only with increasing difficulty. As lower levels of under-five mortality are reached, for example, the same absolute reduction obviously represents a greater percentage of reduction. The AARR therefore shows a higher rate of progress for, say, a 10-point reduction if that reduction happens at a lower level of under-five mortality. (A fall in U5MR of 10 points from 100 to 90 represents a reduction of 10 per cent, whereas the same 10-point fall from 20 to 10 represents a reduction of 50 per cent).

When used in conjunction with GDP growth rates, the U5MR and its reduction rate can therefore give a picture of the progress being made by any country or region, and over any period of time, towards the satisfaction of some of the most essential of human needs.

As table 10 shows, there is no fixed relationship between the annual reduction rate of the U5MR and the annual rate of growth in per capita GDP. Such comparisons help to throw the emphasis on the policies, priorities, and other factors which determine the ratio between economic and social progress.

Finally, the table gives the total fertility rate for each country and territory and the average annual rate of reduction. It will be seen that many of the nations that have achieved significant reductions in their U5MR have also achieved significant reductions in fertility.

TABLE 10. THE RATE OF PROGRESS

Countries and territories	Under-5 mortality rank	Under-5 mortality rate			Average annual rate of reduction (%)		Reduction since 1990 (%)	GDP per capita average annual growth rate (%)		Total fertility rate			Average annual rate of reduction (%)	
		1970	1990	2004	1970-90	1990-2004		1970-90	1990-2004	1970	1990	2004	1970-90	1990-2004
Afghanistan	4	320	260	257	1.0	0.1	1	0.7x	-	7.7	8.0	7.4	-0.2	0.6
Albania	125	109	45	19	4.4	6.2	58	-0.6x	5.2	4.9	2.9	2.2	2.6	2.0
Algeria	79	220	69	40	5.8	3.9	42	1.7	0.8	7.4	4.7	2.5	2.3	4.5
Andorra	159	-	-	7	-	-	-	-	-	-	-	-	-	-
Angola	2	300	260	260	0.7	0.0	0	0.4x	0.7	7.3	7.2	6.7	0.1	0.5
Antigua and Barbuda	143	-	-	12	-	-	-	6.3x	1.6	-	-	-	-	-
Argentina	127	71	29	18	4.5	3.4	38	-0.7	1.0	3.1	3.0	2.3	0.2	1.9
Armenia	90	-	60	32	-	4.5	47	-	3.6	3.2	2.5	1.3	1.2	4.7
Australia	162	20	10	6	3.5	3.6	40	1.5	2.5	2.7	1.9	1.7	1.8	0.8
Austria	172	33	10	5	6.0	5.0	50	2.5	1.8	2.3	1.5	1.4	2.1	0.5
Azerbaijan	51	-	105	90	-	1.1	14	-	-1.3	4.6	3.0	1.8	2.1	3.6
Bahamas	140	49	29	13	2.6	5.7	55	1.9	0.3x	3.6	2.6	2.3	1.6	0.9
Bahrain	148	82	19	11	7.3	3.9	42	-1.9x	1.9x	6.5	3.7	2.4	2.8	3.1
Bangladesh	58	239	149	77	2.4	4.7	48	0.5	3.1	6.4	4.4	3.2	1.9	2.3
Barbados	143	54	16	12	6.1	2.1	25	1.8	1.4x	3.1	1.7	1.5	3.0	0.9
Belarus	148	27	17	11	2.3	3.1	35	-	1.6	2.3	1.9	1.2	1.0	3.3
Belgium	172	29	10	5	5.3	5.0	50	2.2	1.8	2.1	1.6	1.7	1.4	-0.4
Belize	81	-	49	39	-	1.6	20	2.9	2.2	6.3	4.5	3.1	1.7	2.7
Benin	23	252	185	152	1.5	1.4	18	0.3	2.1	7.0	6.8	5.7	0.1	1.3
Bhutan	56	267	166	80	2.4	5.2	52	5.4x	3.6	5.9	5.7	4.2	0.2	2.2
Bolivia	62	243	125	69	3.3	4.2	45	-1.1	1.3	6.6	4.9	3.8	1.5	1.8
Bosnia and Herzegovina	131	82	22	15	6.6	2.7	32	-	11.7x	2.9	1.7	1.3	2.7	1.9
Botswana	41	142	58	116	4.5	-5.0	-100	8.1	2.9	6.9	4.5	3.1	2.1	2.7
Brazil	88	135	60	34	4.1	4.1	43	2.3	1.2	5.0	2.8	2.3	2.9	1.4
Brunei Darussalam	150	78	11	9	9.8	1.4	18	-	-	5.7	3.2	2.4	2.9	2.1
Bulgaria	131	32	18	15	2.9	1.3	17	3.4x	1.0	2.2	1.7	1.2	1.3	2.5
Burkina Faso	16	295	210	192	1.7	0.6	9	1.3	1.8	7.6	7.3	6.6	0.2	0.7
Burundi	17	233	190	190	1.0	0.0	0	1.4	-3.1	6.8	6.8	6.8	0.0	0.0
Cambodia	26	-	115	141	-	-1.5	-23	-	4.1x	5.9	5.6	4.0	0.3	2.4
Cameroon	25	215	139	149	2.2	-0.5	-7	3.4	0.4	6.2	5.9	4.5	0.2	1.9
Canada	162	23	8	6	5.3	2.1	25	2.0	2.3	2.2	1.7	1.5	1.3	0.9
Cape Verde	86	-	60	36	-	3.6	40	-	3.3	7.0	5.5	3.6	1.2	3.0
Central African Republic	15	238	168	193	1.7	-1.0	-15	-1.2	-0.5	5.7	5.7	4.9	0.0	1.1
Chad	12	-	203	200	-	0.1	1	-0.9	0.9	6.6	6.7	6.7	-0.1	0.0
Chile	152	98	21	8	7.7	6.9	62	1.5	3.9	4.0	2.6	2.0	2.2	1.9
China	93	120	49	31	4.5	3.3	37	6.6	8.4	5.6	2.2	1.7	4.7	1.8
Colombia	113	108	36	21	5.5	3.8	42	2.0	0.4	5.6	3.1	2.6	3.0	1.3
Comoros	61	215	120	70	2.9	3.8	42	0.2x	-0.9	7.1	6.1	4.7	0.8	1.9
Congo	44	160	110	108	1.9	0.1	2	3.0	-1.2	6.3	6.3	6.3	0.0	0.0
Congo, Democratic Republic of the	8	245	205	205	0.9	0.0	0	-2.3	-5.8	6.4	6.7	6.7	-0.2	0.0
Cook Islands	113	-	32	21	-	3.0	34	-	-	-	-	-	-	-
Costa Rica	140	83	18	13	7.6	2.3	28	0.5	2.6	5.0	3.2	2.2	2.2	2.7
Côte d'Ivoire	14	239	157	194	2.1	-1.5	-24	-1.3	-0.6	7.4	6.6	4.9	0.6	2.1
Croatia	159	42	12	7	6.3	3.8	42	-	2.3	2.0	1.7	1.3	0.8	1.9
Cuba	159	43	13	7	6.0	4.4	46	-	3.5x	4.0	1.7	1.6	4.3	0.4
Cyprus	172	33	12	5	5.1	6.3	58	6.2x	3.1	2.6	2.4	1.6	0.4	2.9
Czech Republic	185	24	13	4	3.1	8.4	69	-	1.7	2.0	1.8	1.2	0.5	2.9
Denmark	172	19	9	5	3.7	4.2	44	1.5	1.9	2.1	1.7	1.8	1.1	-0.4
Djibouti	31	-	163	126	-	1.8	23	-	-3.0	7.4	6.3	4.9	0.8	1.8
Dominica	135	-	17	14	-	1.4	18	4.7x	1.1	-	-	-	-	-
Dominican Republic	90	127	65	32	3.3	5.1	51	2.0	4.0	6.2	3.4	2.7	3.0	1.6
Ecuador	104	140	57	26	4.5	5.6	54	1.3	0.3	6.3	3.7	2.7	2.7	2.3
Egypt	86	235	104	36	4.1	7.6	65	4.2	2.4	6.1	4.3	3.2	1.7	2.1
El Salvador	98	162	60	28	5.0	5.4	53	-1.8	1.9	6.4	3.7	2.8	2.7	2.0
Equatorial Guinea	9	-	170	204	-	-1.3	-20	-	16.3	5.7	5.9	5.9	-0.2	0.0
Eritrea	54	237	147	82	2.4	4.2	44	-	0.8x	6.6	6.2	5.4	0.3	1.0
Estonia	152	26	16	8	2.4	5.0	50	1.5x	3.7	2.1	1.9	1.4	0.5	2.2
Ethiopia	20	239	204	166	0.8	1.5	19	-	2.0	6.8	6.8	5.7	0.0	1.3
Fiji	120	61	31	20	3.4	3.1	35	0.6	1.7	4.5	3.4	2.9	1.4	1.1

	Under-5 mortality rank	Under-5 mortality rate			Average annual rate of reduction (%)		Reduction since 1990 (%)	GDP per capita average annual growth rate (%)		Total fertility rate			Average annual rate of reduction (%)	
		1970	1990	2004	1970-90	1990-2004		1970-90	1990-2004	1970	1990	2004	1970-90	1990-2004
Finland	185	16	7	4	4.1	4.0	43	2.9	2.5	1.9	1.7	1.7	0.6	0.0
France	172	24	9	5	4.9	4.2	44	2.1	1.6	2.5	1.8	1.9	1.6	-0.4
Gabon	49	-	92	91	-	0.1	1	-0.1	-0.4	4.9	5.4	3.9	-0.5	2.3
Gambia	36	319	154	122	3.6	1.7	21	0.9	0.2	6.5	5.9	4.6	0.5	1.8
Georgia	75	-	47	45	-	0.3	4	3.2	-0.7	2.6	2.1	1.4	1.1	2.9
Germany	172	26	9	5	5.3	4.2	44	2.2x	1.2	2.0	1.4	1.3	1.8	0.5
Ghana	42	186	122	112	2.1	0.6	8	-2.2	1.9	6.7	5.8	4.2	0.7	2.3
Greece	172	54	11	5	8.0	5.6	55	1.3	2.2	2.4	1.4	1.2	2.7	1.1
Grenada	113	-	37	21	-	4.0	43	4.9x	2.3	-	-	-	-	-
Guatemala	75	168	82	45	3.6	4.3	45	0.2	1.0	6.2	5.6	4.5	0.5	1.6
Guinea	22	345	240	155	1.8	3.1	35	-	1.6	6.8	6.5	5.8	0.2	0.8
Guinea-Bissau	10	-	253	203	-	1.6	20	-0.2	-2.5	6.8	7.1	7.1	-0.2	0.0
Guyana	67	-	88	64	-	2.3	27	-1.5	3.3	5.6	2.6	2.2	3.8	1.2
Haiti	40	221	150	117	1.9	1.8	22	0.0	-2.8	5.8	5.4	3.9	0.4	2.3
Holy See	-	-	-	-	-	-	-	-	-	-	-	-	-	-
Honduras	78	170	59	41	5.3	2.6	31	0.6	0.3	7.3	5.1	3.6	1.8	2.5
Hungary	152	39	17	8	4.2	5.4	53	2.9	2.7	2.0	1.8	1.3	0.5	2.3
Iceland	192	14	7	3	3.5	6.1	57	3.2	2.2	3.0	2.2	2.0	1.6	0.7
India	52	202	123	85	2.5	2.6	31	2.2	4.1	5.6	4.0	3.0	1.7	2.1
Indonesia	83	172	91	38	3.2	6.2	58	4.7	2.1	5.4	3.1	2.3	2.8	2.1
Iran (Islamic Republic of)	83	191	72	38	4.9	4.6	47	-3.5x	2.3	6.6	5.0	2.1	1.4	6.2
Iraq	33	127	50	125	4.7	-6.5	-150	-4.3	-	7.2	5.9	4.7	1.0	1.6
Ireland	162	27	10	6	5.0	3.6	40	2.8	6.5	3.9	2.1	1.9	3.1	0.7
Israel	162	27	12	6	4.1	5.0	50	1.9	1.5	3.8	3.0	2.8	1.2	0.5
Italy	172	33	9	5	6.5	4.2	44	2.6	1.4	2.4	1.3	1.3	3.1	0.0
Jamaica	120	64	20	20	5.8	0.0	0	-1.3	0.0	5.5	2.9	2.4	3.2	1.4
Japan	185	21	6	4	6.3	2.9	33	3.0	1.0	2.1	1.6	1.3	1.4	1.5
Jordan	101	107	40	27	4.9	2.8	33	2.5x	1.1	7.9	5.5	3.4	1.8	3.4
Kazakhstan	60	-	63	73	-	-1.1	-16	-	1.3	3.5	2.8	1.9	1.1	2.8
Kenya	37	156	97	120	2.4	-1.5	-24	1.3	-0.6	8.1	5.9	5.0	1.6	1.2
Kiribati	66	-	88	65	-	2.2	26	-5.3	2.5	-	-	-	-	-
Korea, Democratic People's Republic of	71	70	55	55	1.2	0.0	0	-	-	4.3	2.4	2.0	2.9	1.3
Korea, Republic of	162	54	9	6	9.0	2.9	33	6.2	4.5	4.5	1.6	1.2	5.2	2.1
Kuwait	143	59	16	12	6.5	2.1	25	-6.8x	-2.3x	7.2	3.5	2.3	3.6	3.0
Kyrgyzstan	64	130	80	68	2.4	1.2	15	-	-1.7	4.9	3.9	2.6	1.1	2.9
Lao People's Democratic Republic	53	218	163	83	1.5	4.8	49	-	3.7	6.1	6.1	4.7	0.0	1.9
Latvia	143	26	18	12	1.8	2.9	33	3.3	2.9	1.9	1.9	1.3	0.0	2.7
Lebanon	93	54	37	31	1.9	1.3	16	-	2.9	5.1	3.1	2.3	2.5	2.1
Lesotho	54	190	120	82	2.3	2.7	32	4.2	2.3	5.7	4.9	3.5	0.8	2.4
Liberia	5	263	235	235	0.6	0.0	0	-4.6	3.7	6.9	6.9	6.8	0.0	0.1
Libyan Arab Jamahiriya	120	160	41	20	6.8	5.1	51	-4.8x	-	7.6	4.8	2.9	2.3	3.6
Liechtenstein	172	-	10	5	-	5.0	50	-	-	-	-	-	-	-
Lithuania	152	28	13	8	3.8	3.5	38	-	1.2	2.3	2.0	1.3	0.7	3.1
Luxembourg	162	26	10	6	4.8	3.6	40	2.7	3.5	2.1	1.6	1.7	1.4	-0.4
Madagascar	35	180	168	123	0.3	2.2	27	-2.2	-0.8	6.8	6.2	5.3	0.5	1.1
Malawi	19	330	241	175	1.6	2.3	27	0.3	0.9	7.3	7.0	6.0	0.2	1.1
Malaysia	143	70	22	12	5.8	4.3	45	4.0	3.3	5.6	3.8	2.8	1.9	2.2
Maldives	74	255	111	46	4.2	6.3	59	-	4.6x	7.0	6.4	4.1	0.4	3.2
Mali	7	400	250	219	2.4	0.9	12	-0.3	2.5	7.5	7.4	6.8	0.1	0.6
Malta	162	32	11	6	5.3	4.3	45	6.5	3.0	2.1	2.0	1.5	0.2	2.1
Marshall Islands	69	-	92	59	-	3.2	36	-	-	-	-	-	-	-
Mauritania	33	250	133	125	3.2	0.4	6	-0.6	1.7	6.5	6.2	5.7	0.2	0.6
Mauritius	131	86	23	15	6.6	3.1	35	5.1x	3.9	3.7	2.2	2.0	2.6	0.7
Mexico	98	110	46	28	4.4	3.5	39	1.7	1.4	6.8	3.4	2.3	3.5	2.8
Micronesia (Federated States of)	110	-	31	23	-	2.1	26	-	-1.4	6.9	5.0	4.3	1.6	1.1
Moldova, Republic of	98	61	40	28	2.1	2.5	30	1.9x	-4.6	2.6	2.4	1.2	0.4	5.0
Monaco	172	-	9	5	-	4.2	44	-	-	-	-	-	-	-

TABLE 10. THE RATE OF PROGRESS

	Under-5 mortality rank	Under-5 mortality rate			Average annual rate of reduction (%)		Reduction since 1990 (%)	GDP per capita average annual growth rate (%)		Total fertility rate			Average annual rate of reduction (%)	
		1970	1990	2004	1970-90	1990-2004		1970-90	1990-2004	1970	1990	2004	1970-90	1990-2004
Mongolia	72	-	108	52	-	5.2	52	-	-1.8	7.5	4.1	2.4	3.0	3.8
Morocco	77	184	89	43	3.6	5.2	52	2.1	1.1	7.1	4.0	2.7	2.9	2.8
Mozambique	23	278	235	152	0.8	3.1	35	-1.6x	4.8	6.6	6.3	5.4	0.2	1.1
Myanmar	45	179	130	106	1.6	1.5	18	1.6	5.7x	5.9	4.0	2.3	1.9	4.0
Namibia	68	135	86	63	2.3	2.2	27	-2.0x	0.9	6.5	6.0	3.8	0.4	3.3
Nauru	95	-	-	30	-	-	-	-	-	-	-	-	-	-
Nepal	59	250	145	76	2.7	4.6	48	1.3	2.0	5.9	5.2	3.6	0.6	2.6
Netherlands	162	15	9	6	2.6	2.9	33	1.5	2.0	2.4	1.6	1.7	2.0	-0.4
New Zealand	162	20	11	6	3.0	4.3	45	0.8	2.1	3.1	2.1	2.0	1.9	0.3
Nicaragua	83	165	68	38	4.4	4.2	44	-3.9	0.9	7.0	4.9	3.2	1.8	3.0
Niger	3	330	320	259	0.2	1.5	19	-2.2	-0.6	8.1	8.2	7.8	-0.1	0.4
Nigeria	13	265	230	197	0.7	1.1	14	-1.6	0.2	6.9	6.8	5.7	0.1	1.3
Niue	-	-	-	-	-	-	-	-	-	-	-	-	-	-
Norway	185	15	9	4	2.6	5.8	56	3.4	2.8	2.5	1.9	1.8	1.4	0.4
Occupied Palestinian Territory	107	-	40	24	-	3.6	40	-	-6.0x	7.9	6.4	5.4	1.1	1.2
Oman	140	200	32	13	9.2	6.4	59	3.6	0.9	7.2	6.6	3.6	0.4	4.3
Pakistan	47	181	130	101	1.7	1.8	22	3.0	1.1	6.6	6.1	4.1	0.4	2.8
Palau	101	-	34	27	-	1.6	21	-	0.0x	-	-	-	-	-
Panama	107	68	34	24	3.5	2.5	29	0.3	2.5	5.3	3.0	2.7	2.8	0.8
Papua New Guinea	48	147	101	93	1.9	0.6	8	-0.8	0.0	6.2	5.1	3.9	1.0	1.9
Paraguay	107	78	41	24	3.2	3.8	41	2.9	-0.7	6.0	4.7	3.8	1.2	1.5
Peru	97	178	80	29	4.0	7.2	64	-0.6	2.1	6.3	3.9	2.8	2.4	2.4
Philippines	88	90	62	34	1.9	4.3	45	0.8	1.3	6.3	4.4	3.1	1.8	2.5
Poland	152	36	18	8	3.5	5.8	56	-	4.2	2.2	2.0	1.2	0.5	3.6
Portugal	172	62	14	5	7.4	7.4	64	2.6	2.1	2.8	1.5	1.5	3.1	0.0
Qatar	113	65	26	21	4.6	1.5	19	-	-	6.9	4.4	2.9	2.2	3.0
Romania	120	57	31	20	3.0	3.1	35	0.9x	1.0	2.9	1.9	1.3	2.1	2.7
Russian Federation	113	36	29	21	1.1	2.3	28	-	-0.7	2.0	1.9	1.3	0.3	2.7
Rwanda	10	209	173	203	0.9	-1.1	-17	1.4	0.9	8.2	7.6	5.6	0.4	2.2
Saint Kitts and Nevis	113	-	36	21	-	3.8	42	6.3x	2.9	-	-	-	-	-
Saint Lucia	135	-	21	14	-	2.9	33	5.3x	0.3	6.1	3.5	2.2	2.8	3.3
Saint Vincent and the Grenadines	112	-	25	22	-	0.9	12	3.2	1.9	6.0	3.0	2.2	3.5	2.2
Samoa	95	101	50	30	3.5	3.6	40	0.0x	2.2	6.1	4.8	4.3	1.2	0.8
San Marino	185	-	14	4	-	8.9	71	-	-	-	-	-	-	-
Sao Tome and Principe	38	-	118	118	-	0.0	0	-	0.0	6.5	5.3	3.9	1.0	2.2
Saudi Arabia	101	185	44	27	7.2	3.5	39	-1.2	-0.5	7.3	6.0	3.9	1.0	3.1
Senegal	29	279	148	137	3.2	0.6	7	-0.4	1.4	7.0	6.5	4.9	0.4	2.0
Serbia and Montenegro	131	71	28	15	4.7	4.5	46	-	4.1x	2.4	2.1	1.6	0.7	1.9
Seychelles	135	59	19	14	5.7	2.2	26	2.9	1.7	-	-	-	-	-
Sierra Leone	1	363	302	283	0.9	0.5	6	-0.4	-2.5	6.5	6.5	6.5	0.0	0.0
Singapore	192	27	9	3	5.5	7.8	67	5.7	3.5	3.0	1.8	1.3	2.6	2.3
Slovakia	150	29	14	9	3.6	3.2	36	-	2.6	2.5	2.0	1.2	1.1	3.6
Slovenia	185	29	10	4	5.3	6.5	60	-	3.1	2.3	1.5	1.2	2.1	1.6
Solomon Islands	70	99	63	56	2.3	0.8	11	3.4	-2.6	6.9	5.5	4.2	1.1	1.9
Somalia	6	-	225	225	-	0.0	0	-1.0	-	7.3	6.8	6.3	0.4	0.5
South Africa	65	-	60	67	-	-0.8	-12	0.1	0.4	5.6	3.6	2.8	2.2	1.8
Spain	172	34	9	5	6.6	4.2	44	1.9	2.4	2.9	1.3	1.3	4.0	0.0
Sri Lanka	135	100	32	14	5.7	5.9	56	3.2	3.3	4.4	2.5	1.9	2.8	2.0
Sudan	49	172	120	91	1.8	2.0	24	0.3	3.3	6.7	5.6	4.3	0.9	1.9
Suriname	81	-	48	39	-	1.5	19	-2.2x	0.9	5.7	2.7	2.6	3.7	0.3
Swaziland	21	196	110	156	2.9	-2.5	-42	2.1	0.2	6.9	5.7	3.8	1.0	2.9
Sweden	185	15	7	4	3.8	4.0	43	1.8	2.1	2.0	2.0	1.7	0.0	1.2
Switzerland	172	18	9	5	3.5	4.2	44	1.1	0.6	2.0	1.5	1.4	1.4	0.5
Syrian Arab Republic	130	128	44	16	5.3	7.2	64	2.2	1.3	7.6	5.3	3.3	1.8	3.4
Tajikistan	38	-	128	118	-	0.6	8	-	-5.1	6.9	5.2	3.7	1.4	2.4
Tanzania, United Republic of	31	218	161	126	1.5	1.8	22	-	1.3	6.8	6.1	4.9	0.5	1.6
Thailand	113	102	37	21	5.1	4.0	43	4.7	2.9	5.5	2.2	1.9	4.6	1.0

	Under-5 mortality rank	Under-5 mortality rate			Average annual rate of reduction (%)		Reduction since 1990 (%)	GDP per capita average annual growth rate (%)		Total fertility rate			Average annual rate of reduction (%)	
		1970	1990	2004	1970-90	1990-2004		1970-90	1990-2004	1970	1990	2004	1970-90	1990-2004
The former Yugoslav Republic of Macedonia	135	119	38	14	5.7	7.1	63	-	-0.5	3.2	1.9	1.5	2.6	1.7
Timor-Leste	56	-	172	80	-	5.5	53	-	-	6.3	4.9	7.8	1.3	-3.3
Togo	27	216	152	140	1.8	0.6	8	-0.2	0.3	7.0	6.4	5.2	0.4	1.5
Tonga	105	50	32	25	2.2	1.8	22	-	2.0	5.9	4.6	3.4	1.2	2.2
Trinidad and Tobago	120	57	33	20	2.7	3.6	39	0.5	3.5	3.5	2.5	1.6	1.7	3.2
Tunisia	105	201	52	25	6.8	5.2	52	2.5	3.2	6.6	3.6	1.9	3.0	4.6
Turkey	90	201	82	32	4.5	6.7	61	1.9	1.4	5.5	3.0	2.4	3.0	1.6
Turkmenistan	46	-	97	103	-	-0.4	-6	-	0.2	6.3	4.3	2.7	1.9	3.3
Tuvalu	73	-	56	51	-	0.7	9	-	-	-	-	-	-	-
Uganda	28	170	160	138	0.3	1.1	14	-	3.8	7.1	7.1	7.1	0.0	0.0
Ukraine	127	27	26	18	0.2	2.6	31	-	-3.5	2.1	1.8	1.1	0.8	3.5
United Arab Emirates	152	83	14	8	8.9	4.0	43	-4.8x	-2.1x	6.6	4.4	2.5	2.0	4.0
United Kingdom	162	23	10	6	4.2	3.6	40	2.0	2.5	2.3	1.8	1.7	1.2	0.4
United States	152	26	12	8	3.9	2.9	33	2.2	2.1	2.2	2.0	2.0	0.5	0.0
Uruguay	129	57	25	17	4.1	2.8	32	0.9	0.8	2.9	2.5	2.3	0.7	0.6
Uzbekistan	62	101	79	69	1.2	1.0	13	-	-0.1	6.5	4.2	2.7	2.2	3.2
Vanuatu	79	155	62	40	4.6	3.1	35	-0.6x	-0.8	6.3	4.9	4.0	1.3	1.4
Venezuela	125	61	27	19	4.1	2.5	30	-1.6	-1.3	5.4	3.4	2.7	2.3	1.6
Viet Nam	110	87	53	23	2.5	6.0	57	-	5.8	7.0	3.7	2.3	3.2	3.4
Yemen	43	303	142	111	3.8	1.8	22	-	2.1	8.5	8.0	6.0	0.3	2.1
Zambia	18	181	180	182	0.0	-0.1	-1	-2.2	-0.6	7.7	6.5	5.5	0.8	1.2
Zimbabwe	30	138	80	129	2.7	-3.4	-61	-0.3	-0.8x	7.7	5.2	3.4	2.0	3.0

SUMMARY INDICATORS

		1970	1990	2004	1970-90	1990-2004		1970-90	1990-2004	1970	1990	2004	1970-90	1990-2004
Sub-Saharan Africa		244	188	171	1.3	0.7	9	0.0	0.6	6.8	6.3	5.4	0.4	1.1
Eastern and Southern Africa		219	167	149	1.4	0.8	11	-	0.7	6.8	6.0	5.1	0.6	1.2
Western and Central Africa		266	209	191	1.2	0.6	9	-0.5	0.2	6.8	6.7	5.8	0.1	1.0
Middle East and North Africa		195	81	56	4.4	2.6	31	0.4	1.2	6.8	5.0	3.2	1.5	3.2
South Asia		206	129	92	2.3	2.4	29	2.1	3.7	5.8	4.3	3.2	1.5	2.1
East Asia and Pacific		122	58	36	3.7	3.4	38	5.6	6.2	5.6	2.5	1.9	4.0	2.0
Latin America and Caribbean		123	54	31	4.1	4.0	43	1.4	1.3	5.3	3.2	2.5	2.5	1.8
CEE/CIS		86	54	38	2.3	2.5	30	-	0.1	2.8	2.3	1.7	1.0	2.2
Industrialized countries		27	10	6	5.0	3.6	40	2.3	1.9	2.3	1.7	1.6	1.5	0.4
Developing countries		167	105	87	2.3	1.3	17	2.6	3.5	5.8	3.6	2.9	2.4	1.5
Least developed countries		244	182	155	1.5	1.1	15	-0.1	1.8	6.7	5.9	4.9	0.6	1.3
World		147	95	79	2.2	1.3	17	2.4	2.1	4.7	3.2	2.6	1.9	1.5

Countries in each category are listed on page 132.

DEFINITIONS OF THE INDICATORS

Under-five mortality rate – Probability of dying between birth and exactly five years of age expressed per 1,000 live births.

Reduction since 1990 (%) – Percentage reduction in the under-five mortality rate (U5MR) from 1990 to 2004. The United Nations Millennium Declaration in 2000 established a goal of a two-thirds (67%) reduction in U5MR from 1990 to 2015. Hence this indicator provides a current assessment of progress towards this goal.

GDP per capita – Gross domestic product (GDP) is the sum of value added by all resident producers plus any product taxes (less subsidies) not included in the valuation of output. GDP per capita is gross domestic product divided by mid-year population. Growth is calculated from constant price GDP data in local currency.

Total fertility rate – The number of children that would be born per woman if she were to live to the end of her child-bearing years and bear children at each age in accordance with prevailing age-specific fertility rates.

MAIN DATA SOURCES

Under-five mortality – UNICEF, United Nations Population Division and United Nations Statistics Division.

GDP per capita – World Bank.

Fertility – United Nations Population Division.

NOTES   -   Data not available.

x   Indicates data that refer to years or periods other than those specified in the column heading, differ from the standard definition or refer to only part of a country.

INDEX

marginalization, understanding factors behind, 59

marriage (*see* early marriage)

    impact of early, on childhood, 44–46

    laws fixing minimum age for, 64

maternal health, improving, 2, 4, 53

media, 81

    role

        in addressing discrimination, 29, 31, 35

        in empowering people, 59, 60

        partnerships with, in enhancing campaign effectiveness, 77–78

        in raising awareness, 75, 77–78, 80–81

Mexico

    assessing the rights of children in, 70–71

    lack of health care for indigenous people in, 24

Mexico City, street children in, 42

Millennium agenda for children, 1–7, 8–9

    statistical tools for monitoring, 61

Millennium Declaration, 1–4, 7, 85–86

    vision of, 5, 86, 88

Millennium Development Goals (MDGs), 1–7, 8–9 16, 30, 32–33, 53, 86, 82–83, 88

Millennium Project, 6

Millennium Summit (September 2000), 2, 86

mines, child trafficking into, 50

mobile services, provision of, for remote or deprived locations, 69, 72

Moldova, life-skills education project for children, 55

Montenegro, Roma people in, 24

Moscow, filming world of homeless children in, 80

Multiple Indicator Cluster Surveys (MICS), 17, 61, 62

multivariate analysis, 62

Mutawinat Benevolent Company, accomplishment of, in Khartoum, 73

Namibia, budgeting for marginalized children in, 67

National Network of Native American Youth, 68

National Programme for the Eradication of Child Labour, 69

Nepal

    children in domestic service in, 51

    child trafficking in, 50, 51

Niger

    child marriage in, 45

    fistula prevention in, 47

    lack of vaccines in, 20

    polio in, 28

Nigeria

    children and young people in detention in, 44–45

    fistula prevention in, 47

polio in, 28

non-discrimination, principle of, 7, 59, 64

non-governmental organizations (NGOs), role of, 42, 45, 66

    influence on UNICEF policy decisions, 87

    role of, in bringing issues to forefront, 72–73, 78

nutrition (table), 102–105 (*also see* malnutrition)

    excluded children and, 13

    disability and, 25

Nwokocha, Uche, 44

Occupied Palestinian Territory, birth registration in, 37

Office of the United Nations High Commissioner for Refugees (UNHCR), 38–39

Open Society Institute, 24, 25

ordnance, unexploded, 14

orphans

    early marriage and, 45–46

    HIV/AIDS in creating, 16, 30, 39

    as invisible children, 39–40

    lack of education for, 39

    vulnerability of, 39–40

    supporting of, 68, 73

osteogenesis imperfecta, 26–27

Otunnu, Olara, 62

packaging services in increasing access, 69

paediatric treatment, providing, for HIV/AIDS, 30

Pakistan, polio in, 28

parents, loss of, 39–40

partnerships, 71, 85–88

    in combating HIV/AIDS, 30

    with the media, 77–78

Peru

    under-five mortality in, 18

    social expenditure in, 66

Philippines

    adoption of act against trafficking, 64

    budgeting for children, 67

    Coalition Against Trafficking in Women Asia Pacific in, 81

Plan International, role of, in birth registration, 72

plantations, child trafficking into, 50

Polak, Hanna, 80

polio, 28, 72

politics, 86

pornography, 51

poverty, 3

    early marriage and, 45, 47

    eradication of extreme, 2, 3, 11, 12, 60

    need for action in combatting, 6, 11

    reducing, 12, 29, 60, 65, 66, 73, 74

as root cause of exclusion, 7, 8–9, 11, 12, 28, 30, 35

    trafficking and, 50

    underweight and, 20, 29

    vaccinations and, 20, 21

pregnancy, 47

premature entry into adult roles, 43–48

prevention of mother-to-child transmission, 30

primary school enrolment, 8–9, 12, 86 (*also see* education)

    armed conflict and, 15

    barriers to, 19

    excluded children and, 14

    gender discrimination and, 19

private sector, role of, 59, 60, 78–79, 81

programmes

    need for strong research in developing effective, 59, 60–63

    role of, in inclusion, 59, 68–69, 72

protecting childhood, 82–83

protection rights, violations of, 11–12

protective environment

    creation of, in making children visible, 51–52

    key elements of, 35, 52

Protocol to Prevent, Suppress and Punish Trafficking in Persons, Especially Women and Children, 64

qualitative studies, compiling on excluded and invisible children, 61–63

quantitative data

    analysis of, 62

    lack of, as no excuse for inaction, 62–63

'quick impact initiatives', 1, 6

refugee children

    lack of visibility for, 38

    primary responsibility for, 38–39

religious leaders/organizations, participation by, as vital, 72–73, 81

remote locations, provision of satellite services for, 69, 72

research, 59, 60–63

Roma

    discrimination against, 22

    marginalization of, 24–25

    poverty among, 24

Roma Education Initiative (REI), 25

Romania, Roma people in, 24, 25

Romanian Federation of NGOs Active in Child Protection Issues, 25

root causes of exclusion, 11–31, 35, 59, 60

rural areas

    early marriage in, 46

    children out of school, 19

    child mortality in, 19

GLOSSARY

AIDS acquired immune deficiency syndrome

CEE/CIS Central and Eastern Europe/ Commonwealth of Independent States

CPIA Country Policy and Institutional Assessment

CRC Convention on the Rights of the Child

CSO civil society organization

DDR disarmament, demobilization and reintegration

DHS Demographic and Health Surveys

DISHA Developing Initiatives for Social and Human Action

DPT3 three doses of combined diphtheria/pertussis/tetanus vaccine

ECOWAS Economic Community of West African States

ECPAT End Child Prostitution, Child Pornography and Trafficking of Children for Sexual Purposes

EU European Union

FGM/C female genital mutilation/cutting

G-8 Group of Eight (Canada, France, Germany, Italy, Japan, Russia, UK and US)

HepB3 three doses of hepatitis B vaccine

HIV human immunodeficiency virus

ILO International Labour Organization

IPEC International Programme on the Elimination of Child Labour

MDGs Millennium Development Goals

MICS Multiple Indicator Cluster Surveys

NGO non-governmental organization

OHCHR Office of the United Nations High Commissioner for Human Rights

PMTCT prevention of mother-to-child transmission (of HIV)

U5MR under-five mortality rate

UNAIDS Joint United Nations Programme on HIV/AIDS

UNFPA United Nations Population Fund

UNGEI United Nations Girls' Education Initiative

UNHCR United Nations High Commissioner for Refugees

UNICEF United Nations Children's Fund

USAID United States Agency for International Development

WHO World Health Organization

unicef

UNICEF Offices

UNICEF Headquarters
UNICEF House
3 United Nations Plaza
New York, NY 10017, USA

UNICEF Regional Office for Europe
Palais des Nations
CH-1211 Geneva 10, Switzerland

**UNICEF Central and Eastern Europe,
Commonwealth of Independent States
and Baltic States Regional Office**
Palais des Nations
CH-1211 Geneva 10, Switzerland

**UNICEF Eastern and Southern Africa
Regional Office**
P.O. Box 44145
Nairobi, Kenya

**UNICEF West and Central Africa
Regional Office**
P.O. Box 29720 Yoff
Dakar, Senegal

**UNICEF The Americas and Caribbean
Regional Office**
Apartado 3667
Balboa Ancón
Panama City, Panama

**UNICEF East Asia and the Pacific
Regional Office**
P.O. Box 2-154
Bangkok 10200, Thailand

**UNICEF Middle East and North Africa
Regional Office**
P.O. Box 1551
Amman 11821, Jordan

UNICEF South Asia Regional Office
P.O. Box 5815
Lekhnath Marg
Kathmandu, Nepal

**Further information is available at
our website <www.unicef.org>**